Books Big Ben

HELL ON EARTH

The Rev. C. V. Burder MC. MA.

Big Ben Books

HELL ON EARTH

The Rev. C.V. Burder MC MA

A catalogue record for this book is available from the British Library
ISBN 978 0 9523890 7 1

Book design and layout by Georgina Pensri

Books Big Ben
Email: Booksbigben@aol.com

Big Ben Books

Printed in Great Britain

For Mary

Introduction

by John Burder
The author's only surviving son

This book might never have seen the light of day, which would surely have been a criminal offence as it contains graphic first hand descriptions of some of the most important events in recent history. The author, like many men of his generation, would never discuss the war. After reading this book I can understand why. He was my father.

When he died in 1968 at the age of 87 he took his secrets to the grave – or that was what we all believed. Forty years after his death I was delving through an old tin trunk, which had been moved from house to house and ended up in my garage. I was looking for pictures to illustrate my own autobiography when I came across my father's hand written notes for this book. Further exploration revealed a brown paper parcel containing several volumes of typescript, which he had apparently completed in 1942, when the world was heavily involved in another horrendous war, which was also to have devastating consequences for our family.

As the author's only surviving son, I have spent a year preparing his words for publication. I have changed very little. His extraordinary story speaks for itself. It is a plea for world peace and a lasting memorial to a very wonderful man. I only wish I had had been able to know him better.

Dad dedicated his book to my sister, who died before it was completed. That, too, I have left unchanged. What happened to her, and other things which have taken place since the events he describes, is outlined in a short postscript, which I have added, after his last words.

John Burder, *London 2010*

Part One

❖

from

Peace to War

The original manuscript

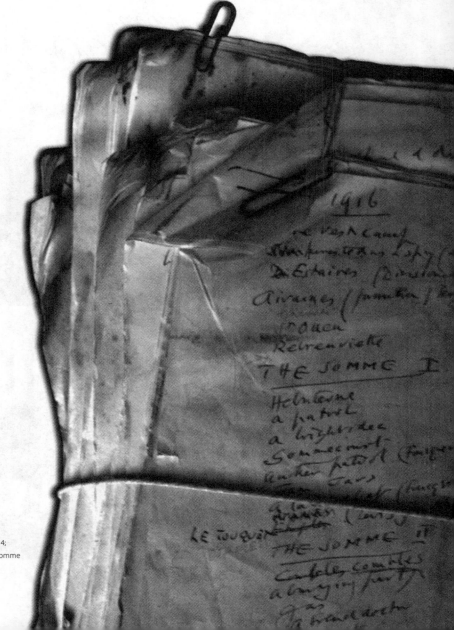

1914 – 1915

"Great Britain has declared war on Germany"

Events in London happen in Buenos Aires four hours and seventeen minutes earlier by the clock because of the difference in longitude, which made it seem that the news of the outbreak of war had reached us in good time. A contemporary account reported: *"Towards 11:00pm when the news reached Buenos Aires, a calm expectancy gradually spread over the multitude and a silence that indicated the intensity of anxiety pervading this agglomeration of different races and creeds."*

We had actually received a brief cable message. "Great Britain has declared war on Germany," was all it had said. The pent-up feelings of the crowd at once gave way to delirious manifestations of relief, that will long linger in the memory of all those who were present. Flags of Great Britain, France, Belgium and Russia appeared on the scene as if by magic, and were carried through the streets of the city by cheering crowds to the accompaniment of the National Anthems of each country in turn.

The following day life in Buenos Aires continued much as it always had. Apart from the commercial dislocation resulting from any war, there were only a handful of unusual incidents, which was perhaps surprising as about a third of the population was made up of nations that were now at war with one another. I did hear that a blow had been struck for the Fatherland by a German who refused to show his ticket on our local railway line, because it was owned and run by the British, but that is the sort of tale that gains in the telling.

On August 16th, seventy-five volunteers boarded the *S.S. Torakina* to sail to England from Montevideo. Newspapers reported that they had paid their own fares. I had

Parish Church, Buenos Aires

been employed as Chaplain to the English community in Buenos Aires since the beginning of 1914, after holding similar posts at Bassein and Mandalay in Burma. I was 33 years old and had been ordained at Bristol cathedral in 1904. After working as a curate in poor parishes in Bristol and Swindon, I had resolved to try to see something of the world. As I came from a long line of clerics and did not have any money, I had to find a way of paying my way. When I was offered work in places I would otherwise have been unable to visit, it did not take me long to set off on my travels.

Experiences in Burma had introduced me to a new way of life and my months in South America had been equally fulfilling. When the outbreak of war was announced, no one had any idea what would happen or how the news would affect us. Buenos Aires is a world away from London and, in those days communications of any kind always took time. After the official announcement that war had been declared, it took a while for the information to affect our daily lives. The first time I realised it was going to affect me was when a member of our church choir came to tell me that he had decided he ought to return to England and "do his bit." I remember wishing him good luck in the vestry after service and feeling a little shy that I was not going. I said I would meet him in Berlin, but as events turned out I never did. He was killed at Gallipoli[1].

I had been living and working in Buenos Aires for several months. I conducted church services for English residents and spent some time in the country, where I had worked part time as a Gaucho[2] on various ranches. My first experience of that kind of life was when I was invited to be a guest at a small estate run by a manager who could have stepped straight out of an English public school. He had little to say and probably thought it a nuisance to have me there at all, but he provided me with a horse and

1   Campaign which took place at Gallipoli peninsula in Turkey from 25 April 1915 to 9 January 1916, during the First World War.
2   Gaucho could be described as a loose equivalent to the North American cowboy. (vaquero, in Spanish).

some riding breeches so I could go about by myself. The estate covered a vast area and I was warned not to go too far in case I got lost. It was a warning that I soon realised was necessary because the land for miles around was completely flat. There were no trees, houses or any other landmarks as far as the eye could see. I quickly learned that it paid to note where the sun was and look back from time to time to see if the house we lived in was still in view. Over a boundless plain there roamed immense herds of horses, cattle and sheep in a wild state. There was so much space that they were only occasionally seen when, for instance, it was necessary to round some of them up. Then 'Gauchos' would speed after them driving them in the required direction. If one of them broke away they would ride at immense speed after it and, with an unerring lasso, bring it to a standstill.

One day I found myself in the middle of a rounding up of cattle when the day's

Working as a Gaucho, Buenos Aires

activities were drawing to a close. As I sat on my horse in the enclosure they plunged hither and thither in a last attempt to escape and I wondered at first if they would charge in my direction. I had seen bulls charge and rip open horses at a Spanish bullfight. But on this occasion they never showed any sign of it, and my well-trained horse remained quite motionless never blinking an eyelid. For that I was most grateful.

At one point, hearing a sheep bleating I asked why that was, thinking perhaps that it had not been noticed or that it was going to be rescued later on. The manager told me that never happened, because the expense of bringing in such an animal would be more than its value. It had probably broken its leg, and would die there, he said. That explained the carcasses one saw at intervals. A callous world it seemed and I felt depressed about it and understood more what it meant to be a lost sheep.

Just before I left, I found myself with nothing to do so I wandered forth towards the sunset on my quiet horse. We dawdled on and on until I was some way from home, looking round at times to make sure of my direction to return. The distant horizon lay round me in an unbroken ring. In every direction there was vast expanse of ripening maize. I felt as if I was at sea in the middle of an ocean. The immensity of it all was overpowering. Two years later, when I was under fire in the trenches I tried to recall the vastness of it all and the peace and quiet, which by then was impossible to find.

As an Englishman living in a neutral country I could have stayed in Buenos Aires and enjoyed the surrounding country there forever, without being concerned with any thoughts of war. That was what many of my contemporaries thought was the right course to adopt, and it was one they quickly chose to follow. It was an easy and attractive option. Others felt it was their duty to return to England and fight for King and country. I considered both options and decided to write to the man who had given me my job in Buenos Aires, and ask for his advice. He was based in London and held the impressive title of Chaplain General. I resolved that if he felt I should return to England and become a military chaplain I would follow his advice. I wrote a carefully composed letter and sat back to await his response but, as far as I am aware, no reply was ever sent.

Regular steamers were still running to England but the number of passengers was very small. This was partly because German raiders had recently captured several ships. The raiders seemed to have been principally interested in obtaining coal, and passengers were put to work transferring it from their ship to the German one. The British ships were then sunk and the passengers and crew were put ashore some time later, when our fleet was not in evidence. I met some of those who had been involved. They told me that they had not been badly treated and were even allowed to take their luggage when their ships were sunk, but of course that did not encourage people to book passages to England.

It did not take me long to decide what I would do. I felt it was probably my duty to return to England as soon as I could. It proved difficult to book a passage on a ship and it was of course years before civilian air travel was even envisaged. I eventually left Buenos Aires on December 7th 1914. It was a beautiful day in early summer. There were very few passengers on board. Most were volunteers going back to the war. We moved down the river with its mud-coloured water. It was so wide it felt as if we were already at sea. We expected to call at Montevideo but perhaps because of the war, we anchored outside, probably at the future grave of the *Graf Spey*[3]. From there we moved on to Santos. Wireless reports had told us about a battle, which had been fought off of the Falkland Islands. The news depressed us but we were glad to know that the German Fleet was not heading for us. We sailed on till we got to Rio.

It was at that point of the journey that we received a wireless message telling us that German warships had bombarded Scarborough. I remember thinking then it was rather cheek and a little more than that, but it made the war seem closer to me.

Our next stop was Pernambuco where there were some large German ships including the *Blucher* – one of the German navy's most powerful ships at that time. An armoured cruiser launched in 1908, she was eventually sunk at the Battle of Dogger Bank[4] on 24th January 1915. As we sailed past, the crew looked sulkily at us. One of our sailors stuck out his tongue a German shook his fist in reply. At night we sailed without lights and, on leaving Pernambuco, altered course because we had been told that a German cruiser was lying in wait for us not far away.

We reached the equator and crossed it without incident. It was dull, muggy and very hot and we were glad of the ices the ship provided. As we sailed on, stopping at Madeira and Lisbon, we gradually left the good weather behind us. Off the cost of Ireland we got lost in thick fog and were warned that there were German submarines in the area. Just one year later, on 17th May 1915, the Cunard liner *LUSITANIA* was to be torpedoed at much the same point with the loss of 1,200 lives. We continued unscathed and arrived in England at the end of December, disembarking under leaden skies in pouring rain. Having left a country bathed in sunshine and ablaze with flowers, I found myself wondering if I had perhaps made one of my less apt decisions.

We were told that there would be a special train for passengers wanting to go to London and bright red labels with "Special Train" in white letters were handed out. Minutes later the train was cancelled and we waited for ages for a very ordinary train. When it eventually arrived it was so full it was almost impossible to board. Then I knew I

---

3   German battleship the Graf Spey was sunk on 13th of December 1939 by the British Fleet.
4   Naval battle fought near the Dogger Bank in the North Sea, 24 January 1915, between the British and the German Fleet.

was home at last. When I eventually arrived in London I thought it might be a good idea to go and see Chaplain General, who had made no response to the carefully composed letter I had sent him from Buenos Aires. I thought that if I arrived in person, from a land six thousand miles away, and asked for an answer to my letter, it would at least show that I was keen. I made an appointment to call at his office and arrived to find him seated at a large table, while a lesser cleric moved about the room moving piles of papers from place to place. I explained what I had come about. Ignoring me, he spoke to his assistant who seemed to be unable to throw any light on the matter. He then told me that he had the names of two thousand men on his books, most of who had applied to be service chaplains. As he felt the war would soon be over, he did not think my services would be required.

As I had lived in different parts of the world for several years I decided to spend the rest of the day exploring the streets of London. In the evening I went to a theatre. It was as full as a theatre can be and I managed to squeeze into a seat and join the audience who were listening with rapt attention to a singer called Basil Hallam, who was singing a well-known song called *"Gilbert the Filbert."* I did not know then that, at a later date, (July 1st 1916) I would see Mr. Hallam again. On that occasion he would be trapped in a captive balloon which had broken loose and drifted towards the German lines. He jumped out with a parachute, but it failed to open and he died on the spot. Perhaps I should have listened to his song with greater interest than I did at the time.

As my visit to the Chaplain General had proved so unhelpful, I found myself wondering what I should do next. I eventually decided to visit the Inns of Court, where I was told I would find the headquarters of the Officers Training Corps (O.T.C.).

I walked straight in and asked an uniformed officer, who was sitting by the door, if they were interested in people who wanted to train for commissions. He explained that they were, but only wanted young men. I was 33 at the time, which did not seem to me excessively old, but at the Inns of Court it was obviously not going to open any doors.

I walked the streets of London for hours trying to decide what to do next. The obstacles I had encountered had discouraged me and I was beginning to wish I had stayed abroad. As a last resort I decided to visit the Artists' Rifles, which I had in fact been advised to go to first, and made an appointment to see their Adjutant the following morning. His name was Captain Bloomfield and he received me with open arms. I was assured that wanting to enlist was the most natural thing in the world and that the Artists' Rifles would be delighted to have me. I then descended into the subterranean box, which acted as the Adjutant's office, and there I became a soldier of the King. That unimpressive ceremony took place in the company of another man. His name was Woolley. I remember that because, far from being woolly, he was quite hairless on the chin, and only had a little soft down on his head. A printed card was thrust into our hands and we were instructed to read it together. Thus I gabbled my way into the army with as much ceremony as meat is put into a sausage machine.

Before we could be allowed to defend the realm we then had to be examined by a doctor. To accomplish this, we had to go upstairs to a large empty room. A debonair and carefree medic sat at a long table, piled high with rubbish. There were several other aspirants in various stages of undress that had been tapped on the chest and asked to say "99." With my experience of public speaking it I did not think it would take me long to say "99" to his satisfaction and away I went.

The Medical Officer made quite an impression on me. He was a good-looking man with an excellent figure, a well-cut uniform and a South African medal. The medal impressed me because in those days medals were rarely seen. I felt that it gave the necessary military touch to a well-fitting uniform, which might otherwise have adorned the form of a mere civilian without war experience. I later discovered that he attended to his military duties as well as his own practice and could be seen alighting at the doors of private houses resplendent in his uniform, which no doubt did not cause his practice to diminish.

As I was now a soldier it was necessary for me to make myself look like one. I rather clung to the hope that I might, like many others who could not get uniforms due to a shortage of supplies, still go about in my civilian apparel, but that was not to be. I was told to follow an N.C.O. to a dungeon below the drill hall which was known as the Armoury. The N.C.O. was sure he could provide everything that was required. In the prewar army, for which the uniforms he stocked must have been made, it seemed that people who had as large a chest measurement as mine (54) also had huge necks, short arms and a bulge where the waist might be expected to be. When I put on the coarse, thin garment the N.C.O. provided, the result as not very happy. Round the chest the measurement was not far out, but the huge neck made me feel as if I had put my head through a lifebelt. The sleeves were so short that inches of shirt protruded and the material of the jacket hung round my slim waist like a loose curtain. It was a short curtain too. It hardly reached the top of my trousers so that buttons were exposed showing their means of support. The curtain flapped too, as no belt was available. The worst thing about the trousers was their coarseness. I felt as if I was clothed in sack cloth, and the buttons were so loosely attached they came off at once. It was also news to me that puttees had to be wound round the outside of the trousers, making a shapeless bodge. The socks were even more remarkable. They were a light tawny colour, very thin and much longer than a foot. The hat was a surprise too. It was hard, coarse and far too small. I was also given a pair of boots which I was told I must take even if I didn't want them.

Before I was allowed to go anywhere I was initiated into the mysteries of forming fours and doing right and left turns, which I had not done since I was a small boy. An instructor, a Lance-Corporal, aged 15, was sarcastic when someone turned right instead of left and told us that formerly recruits had a white mark dabbed on one boot to save them from thinking. We were then marched to Cartwright Gardens, where we slithered about in a sea of mud.

The life I now began was not very severe. I think the idea was to break us in by degrees. We were allowed to find our own quarters and no questions were asked if we arrived daily at 9 am, Sundays exempt, unless we were on guard. We paraded on the cobblestones in Duke Street outside St. Pancras Church and were sometimes kept there for an hour before marching off, which gave us plenty of time to take in our surroundings. The chief object, which met our gaze, was a group of melancholy females in stone, which we were told was a reproduction of a Greek tomb. In contrast to that were the factory girls who worked in a butterscotch factory next to the drill hall and shouted out ribald remarks as we marched past.

We could only think or talk to the next man in the ranks. In my case that was a stockbroker on one side and on the other a young man with artistic leanings. His family presided over one of the Oxford Street drapery establishments. The usual thing was to march by devious routes to Hampstead Heath where we were expected to engage in drill and physical jerks. We also dug trenches in the Grand Duke Michael's garden. I found the quick rifle step irksome; being by nature inclined to do things deliberately. Sometimes it snowed but that did not prevent us having to flop down wherever we happened to be at the time. We were told that would prepare us for active service where conditions were much worse. It wasn't much fun after the hot sun of Buenos Aires a few weeks earlier. Boredom was my chief memory of these days of drill, and looking forward to the time when we marched back to freedom. Some people sang as we marched along but, by this time, soldiers were a common sight. I never remember anyone stopping to look at us unless we had a band marching alongside.

I was living at a boarding house in Guildford Street at this time. I had quite a good room and I saw next to nothing of the other boarders. One evening I ventured into the drawing room and found a Belgian refugee family there. One of them made me a pair of khaki mittens which I never wore but kept for years. I then moved to a hotel in Bloomsbury Square. It was quite smart and the food they provided was generally very good. Food was important in those days of unaccustomed fatigue for, after much marching, drill and physical jerks; I was so stiff and exhausted that I felt almost unable to move. A night in bed did not make me feel any better. One little triumph came my way at this point. I wanted to get a uniform which was not as ridiculous as my free gift one and went to a well known department store (Gamages in Holborn) to see if they could help. I was measured up and in due course received a suit which fitted me quite well and felt noticeably less coarse. It cost me eight pounds and it was worth every penny.

Hearing that a special inspection was going to take place I thought I would wear my new uniform for the first time and instructed the German-Swiss waiter in my hotel to be sure the buttons were well polished. With officers puttees wrapped round legs I felt slightly less awful. The parade was to take place in Russell Square, on a sunny Saturday morning, and I was curious to see what the inspecting officer would make of Gamages' efforts. The officer passed along in silence accompanied by an N.C.O., noticing little

New uniform

things here, until he came to me. Then he paused and took a longer look. Turning to the N.C.O. he remarked quietly "I think this the best." I laughed inwardly recalling the costume I had been issued with, which was usually regarded as a joke, and felt obliged to Gamages – and to my German waiter.

Not wishing to be thought peculiar in any way, for some time I managed to conceal the fact that I was had been ordained as a priest. That worked for a while until one day an official envelope was put in my letter rack. It was addressed to me by name as "The Rev. Private C.V. Burder," After that my secret was out. From time to time we were drilled by a Corporal from the real army. I knew the idea of my being a parson tickled him. One very wet day on Hampstead Heath, when I thought I would not be spotted, I took a big step over a puddle instead of marching through it. The Corporal was on watch, and his wrath was considerable. I was given extra guard duty, which was very annoying because it meant lying on the bare floor all night and then doing the full next day's duty as usual.

We were often told that as we were not real soldiers it was necessary to be stricter with us to make us useful. That was the theme of our Commanding Officer. He was a retired Indian army Colonel, whom we regarded with much awe as he lived on some Olympus top, to descend only with thunder to destroy. Whoever was on sentry duty in the morning when he first arrived, had to spot him and call out the guard. The C.O. was a very quick walker so that took some doing. One special occasion remains in my mind. We had paraded in the Drill Hall and the C.O. appeared on a balcony at one end of it to address us about something. I have forgotten what it was, but I remember vividly what happened to my stockbroker friend who was in the ranks next to me. During the Colonel's speech he was misguided enough to blow his nose. Having until recently been a civilian, he was no doubt accustomed to doing so when necessary. The C.O. saw him, stopped dead as if he had been shot and shouted torrents of abuse and oaths which made me giggle at the childishness of it all. At least I would have giggled if I had dared. The gist of it all was that he had to learn that he was a soldier now and could do no such things. He was told he must report daily at some unearthly hour instead of 9 a.m. That meant making the journey from his distant home before the buses started to run. The C.O. had a reputation for being tough but I must confess that once, when I was sent to him with a message, he seemed quite pleasant. I talked to him like an ordinary person, which perhaps disarmed him. He was a very good lecturer and once a week he addressed us on the war, producing statistics based on the researches of Hilaire Belloc, to show that it could not last longer than 1915.

Basic training, Richmond Park

We soon got bored with the road to Hampstead Heath and the interminable drill and physical jerks, and were delighted when one day we were told we would march to the Tower of London. That seemed to make us more a part of English history than Hampstead Heath. When we marched back through Piccadilly Circus I felt that we were part of London too. The actual purpose of our visit was to draw rifles, which we could use for drill purposes. A few - a very few - typists came to the upper office windows and waved, shouting inaudible greetings as we marched past.

It would soon be spring and we wondered how long our comparative freedom in London was likely to last. We heard there was a shortage of men in France and there were also rumours of a move to a camp in Richmond Park. Any doubts about our immediate future were set at rest by orders to report to the drill hall for a series of inoculations. Two days later we moved to Richmond. We travelled there by train and duly arrived a camp which, like all camps I have ever known, was incomplete. We slept – or rather lay down on the ground in tents, into each of which were crammed fifteen men. To add to the discomfort of my tent, we had the misfortune to be next to the one where the

Digging trenches, Richmond Park

band lived. They took no notice of "lights out" and went on jabbering for hours.

During the short time at Richmond we engaged in tactical exercises which involved rushing at top speed with rifles and full packs and flopping down at intervals. This was the only time I ever saw packs worn except on route marches. The effect on us of carrying a rifle and all our worldly belongings, and rushing about after a sleepless night and next to no food, was to make us unfit to do anything at all. The camp was so awful that we were almost relieved when we were suddenly told that we were going to France. We were warned not to mention our impending move, because it was thought that news of our movements might be of use to the enemy. We were also told (hush, hush!) we would be going in three days' time!

The first stage of our journey involved travelling by train via Waterloo to Southampton. It was uneventful and when we arrived we were told to march to a camp some miles outside the town. No food had been provided since we had first set out. The camp consisted of a few ancient tents and a water tap some distance away but there were no messing arrangements. Some fragments of greasy bacon found their way to us in the early morning, but for the rest we were left to buy our own food. We were not allowed to leave the camp because at any moment orders might be received for our departure to France. There we remained in idle boredom till the news we were awaiting finally came through. Close by there was a Y.M.C.A. hut where we were able to buy something to eat. Apart from that we spent our time getting a little dirtier each day and slightly more depressed. We were, however left in peace and no officer or N.C.O. made an appearance to worry us with drill. We might have been tramps.

After some days were ordered to go to the docks to draw some rifles. I had never held a service rifle in my hands up to this point let alone fired one. The rifles were heavily coated with Vaseline, which we were not given time to remove before dragging then back to camp. I managed to get away from my comrades for an hour on the pretext of trying to have a bath. There were some public baths near the station. After the time we had spent on route and in camps, I felt dirty and smelly and was glad to pay two pence for the luxury of a bath. I also tried to telephone a friend in London from a local hotel but the line was too indistinct to hear very much.

We knew that in a matter of hours we would embark and were pushed hurriedly through a medical inspection as a final effort. It was just a formality and nothing less than someone collapsing in front of the doctor would have stopped any of us from going to France. It was Saturday evening when we finally boarded the S.S. Invicta. A watery sunset was reflected in the harbour and gusts of wind suggested we could be in for a rough crossing. The way through Southampton water was pleasant enough, but previous experience reminded me that it might not be the same when we moved away from away from the shelter of the harbour. I was certainly not prepared for the tremendous tossing that was in store for us. There was, of course, no food, and we lay down where we were, on deck. There were around a thousand of us. Away from the protection of Southampton water, the sea became rough and the weather boisterous. Our ship plunged through the troubled waters at a great pace, rolling and pitching. I remember listening to the noise of the mens' boots as we rolled from one side of the iron deck to the other. To escape being drenched, some of us took refuge below, making a rush between bouts of seasickness. We felt our way in the darkness and held on to anything handy. It was difficult to get past men who were sprawling or sitting on the staircase, so far gone that they sat there in the darkness, calmly vomiting over each other. Fortunately even bad channel crossings come to an end and, as the skies got lighter, we found that we were nearing land.

By dawn we were sailing along a river between green fields, basking in the sunshine on our way to Rouen. We could almost have been on a pleasure steamer. After our experiences during the night it was a relief to proceed on an even keel, passing through the placid French countryside. Church bells rang and little groups of people passed us on their way to mass. Just before we reached Rouen an officer emerged from his cabin and told us to polish our buttons, shave, and to be sure that our appearance was everything that it should be when arriving in a foreign country. His comments were greeted with little enthusiasm but we did what was required. After putting on full packs and grasping our rifles, we shuffled down the gangway on to the French soil.

We fell in on the quayside, which I had last languidly surveyed from an adjacent cafe when I had been there on holiday. We remained in the sun, standing to attention with full packs on our backs, for over an hour. We were not allowed to break ranks for fear of spoiling the impression we were expected to make on the French people. In fact no one took any notice of us at all. At last we moved off, hoping the march would not be long and that some food might be provided for us at the end. We had had nothing to eat since breakfast on the previous day.

I think we all felt the ghost of a thrill landing in France as a soldier, and treading in the footsteps of other generations and. Perhaps that was why some sang loud, boisterous songs as we marched along. The people we passed could not have cared less. No one stopped to look at us, on the pavement or from the windows of the houses we passed. They had seen it all before. English soldiers were now taken for granted as much as a gendarmes or dustmen. After emerging from the meaner streets, we marched up a hill towards our camp, which was we were told was three miles away. It seemed much further and it was named, not inappropriately, Sotteville.

When we arrived we found that our presence had not been expected. No preparations had been made and we were told that we should have to go and get some tents and put them up. We were directed to a patch of arid, gravelly land on the edge of the site. We had not been given any food since we sailed from Southampton and were hungry and exhausted. I decided to explore the surrounding area and managed to find a Y.M.C.A. where I was able to buy some snacks - the first solid food I had seen for 24 hours.

We were forbidden to leave the camp, as it was thought that orders to send us to the fronts could arrive at any moment. To give us something to do we had a kit inspection. The next morning I was summoned to the orderly room. I wondered why and found out it was because the kit inspection had revealed the absence of a body belt which had been presented to me at Waterloo-Station. I asked what a body belt was for and explained that I had no use for one, but a fine was deducted in my pay book and my pay was reduced by two pennies to grand total of two shillings a day.

The camp itself was slightly less hateful than the one we had endured in Richmond, perhaps because it was in France and one expected to be uncomfortable in a land where the war was really going on. Besides the tents we lived in there was also a hospital with a notice outside painted in large red letters, about "smiling miles of smiles". That was no doubt intended to improve our morale but it only called attention to the fact that it was a hospital.

We did not have much to do during our first week and could have been allowed to go into the town, which I knew from earlier visits and would have enjoyed seeing again under different circumstances. Instead some of us were sent on a fatigue to the docks to unload a cargo of grain. In spite of our strenuous training I found the sacks so heavy that I could only just stagger along with one on my back. I spent another day cleaning the flues of the camp kitchen. The N.C.O. who was in charge, seemed to be permanently entrenched in the job. He was an old army man who believed in upholding established traditions. As an item of news one of the other Privates detailed for kitchen work told him that I was a parson. He asked me if it was true and said that, if was, he did not like me working in a kitchen. My only concern was the devastating effect that damp soot was having on my Gamages' uniform. It was still better than going on a route march, which was the only other diversion we suffered.

In due course we moved on and were told to report to the station to board a train. It consisted on a few dilapidated passenger coaches but we were able to sit on seats, which was a welcome change. We waited for an hour or so before we set off and then slid out of the darkened station without being able to see the attractive old town. I did not know then that I would not to be able to see it on my next visit either. In two and a half years time I would return here by road at 3 a.m., travelling in an ambulance with my head covered in bandages, en route for a hospital and eventually home.

The train moved so slowly that at times it seemed as if had stopped, and the journey took twelve hours. At eight o'clock the following day we found ourselves in a siding with a number of trains on both sides of us. I shouted to the driver of a neighbouring train to find out where we were.

"Abbeville," he replied.

As we had not had any food since the middle of the previous day we were not too concerned. We stayed on that train for eight more hours and then arrived at Grouck where we moved to another train. It did not have seats. On opposite ends of the carriage we were in there were two signs – *"Chevaux"* (Horses) and *"Hommes"* (Men). We spent seven more hours on that train and eventually reached Bailleul, where our battalion H.Q. had apparently been based for several months. It did not take long to find out that it was not there now and we were huddled back to our train and sent on to St. Omer. It was on this leg of the trip that we first heard the dull grumbling of distant guns. When the train eventually stopped we were glad to hear we would not be going to be going any further. It was well past midnight on a Saturday night when we arrived at St. Omer. It was, of course, in complete darkness and the rousing songs of my comrades must have been a nuisance to the inhabitants as we marched through the cobbled streets.

For a time our battalion was quartered in an ancient French barracks – The Caserne De La Barre. It was built round a cobbled courtyard and we were not sorry to march through its whitewashed gateway after more than thirty hours slow travel without any food. Once again we found that we were not expected and a drowsy N.C.O. explained that neither food nor accommodation had been prepared. It was the usual army muddle. After a while we were taken to a large room where there were a number of iron bedsteads and mattresses, which might have been made of concrete. As it was warm we did not miss blankets much. We were just glad to have a roof over our heads as we tried to go to sleep for what was left of the night. The man in the bed next to mine was very young and inclined to take things rather too seriously. I think all our recent sudden moves had got on his mind because he talked in his sleep. In his dreams he thought he heard the order to move off. As I was unable to sleep, I decided to try and talk to him. As a joke I pretended that we really had to go. He immediately got up and started to put on his equipment, which I never thought he would do. I had to quiet him down by telling him it was only a joke. When he got up in the morning he remembered nothing at all.

The little town of St. Omer had outlived the prosperity it had enjoyed some centuries before. Then it had been an important trading centre. It was like a much duller Bruges in that respect, but it lacked the charms, which attract tourists to that Belgian town. In 1914 it owed its importance to presence of the British military H.Q., though the Commander In Chief – General French - lived in a country house not far away.

Here the Artists' Rifles[5], to which I now belonged, were stationed and we provided guards for G.M.Q. and at all the entrances to the town. From time to time we lost a few men who found they had been selected to be trained as officers. There was a great shortage of officers because so many had been killed early in the war and now replacements were being sought from our unit. In October 1914 our Colonel interviewed fifty private soldiers who were on their way to Ypres and promoted them to the rank of second Lieutenant. They were sent straight into the trenches, their private's uniform being distinguished by a single star on the shoulder strap. They were not expected to last long. A list of all who had become 2nd Lieutenants was kept and the length of time before they were killed worked out at an average of a few days and sometime just hours. Naturally "Suicide Club" was the name given by these hopeful by the mathematicians in our battalion. So although we did drill and guards and fatigues and nothing that was of any special use to future officers, we were still regarded as an O.T.C.

Every morning at 9 a.m. guards were mounted in the Grand Place outside the Town Hall. To make the occasion look impressive the band, which shared our sleeping quarters, played appropriate music of the usual whistly variety with lots of the beating of drums. By the time they had to report on parade they had usually managed to recover from the night before. The Guard then marched off to General French's office where it was inspected with due ceremony but was practically unnoticed by the civilian population.

Much of our time was spent doing fatigues. The most popular one was known as the "Convent". It entailed arriving at the Quartermasters stores at 6 a.m. but the cleaning duties it involved were very light so we often got away by 6.30. For some reason, which I never discovered, we were then free for the rest of the day. We also escaped drill. It was generally assumed that this was a mistake. To ensure it was not corrected every new man who was put on that fatigue was told that it was a point of honour to lie low for the rest of the day lest

---

5   A volunteer regiment of the British Army. Raised in London in 1859 as a volunteer light infantry unit, the regiment saw active service during the Boer War and World War I, earning a number of battle honours.

awkward questions should be asked.

The Convent had a swept and garnished look. It was sparsely furnished and adorned with numerous trite sayings painted on framed boards, which hung on the walls. One of them read: "Today everything happens quickly. Tomorrow is eternity." With our casualty lists increasing daily, we felt that was a point which required very little emphasis. I was made cook for a day but evidently did not give satisfaction. When I reported to the cookhouse after seeing my name in orders I discovered that my duties were more strictly those of a scullion. I was given a large frying pan to clean. It had been used to cook bacon and fat had stuck to the sides like glue. Cold water and sand were provided for cleaning purposes but I found that after much rubbing the chief result was to ingrain my hands with a mixture of sand and grease, which refused to come off for days. The pan emerged looking virtually untouched. As my washing up skills was not appreciated I was put on preparing vegetables. I began cutting up beans quite early in the morning and was still doing it at 5 p.m. when I spotted a girl who worked in a shop where I had eaten some of my meals. She was carrying a basket of provisions and, when she saw my clumsy efforts, she sliced a few beans herself to show me that French people cut them differently. She worked so fast that I was immediately aware that my efforts could never be any use at all.

The peak of my military career as a private was reached a few days later when I was put on sanitary fatigue. I was relieved to find that this did not entail emptying latrine buckets but only inspecting them, after they had been emptied by civilian experts. My job was chiefly concerned with bringing boxes of evil smelling refuse down from barrack rooms and dumping them in a lorry. It was scavenger work but it had had its advantages. We were only answerable to a lance corporal who we were told was a Scottish Laird in private life. His chief aim was to remain permanently in the post he had got and he gave us no trouble. There was an absence of drill too, with its jerky and disturbing movements. Indeed, it was possible to think of something else all the time we were on duty and by 11 a.m. we were free for the day.

One day a special fatigue took us to the neighbouring village of Blandenques, where there was a chateau, which we were to whitewash inside. The house itself had been gutted, and all the walls were closely covered with scribblings of names and crude drawings made by soldiers of the old army who had been billeted there in the earlier days of the war. One of them ran –

"Send him victorious
Happy and glorious
Half a loaf between four of us
Thank God there's no more of us,
God Save the King."

Having spent a very short time in the chateau – hardly long enough for anything but reading the wall inscriptions, we were ordered out into the garden and began to do various drill formations. We had been doing our drill very badly and had got into a hopeless tangle over a right form at the double, when I looked up and saw a figure in civilian clothes approaching. We were speedily halted, sorted out, called to attention and told to try and look like soldiers, so I guessed that the civilian was someone important and wondered who he was. At first I could only catch a glimpse of him out of the corner of my eye, having by this time learnt not to look at interesting things when standing at attention in the ranks. At first I thought he might be the owner of the chateau. When he came in front of us I could see he was dressed in a quite bright blue suit with blue stripes on his stiff double collar. When I noticed that he had a red face and quite white hair I changed my views and thought he might be a retired actor or singer. That seemed even more likely when he spoke very slowly in a deep and mellow voice. He was led past us walking slowly with his hands behind his back and looking all the time on the ground. As he passed me I heard him say, as if talking to himself, "These respirators, I am told, are found to be very useful." It was about a month after the first gas attack at Ypres. I later discovered that our visitor was Mr. Asquith[6] who at that time was England's Prime Minister.

St. Omer, being British G.H.Q, was of course an important place from a war point of view. Many notable people came there, some of whom I happened to see. I remember seeing the Prince of Wales, looking very boyish one day as he passed me in the street with a Staff Officer. He evidently was not trying to have the ultra polished

6   Herbert Henry Asquith, 1st Earl of Oxford and Asquith, Liberal Prime Minister from 1908 to 1916.

look which youthful Staff officers sometimes had, which showed that he was wise and understanding. Another celebrity we saw as General Kitchener – then Secretary of State of War. He arrived one day with Asquith in a car. I stood on the pavement in an empty street and gave the jerkiest salute I had ever produced, which Kitchener noticed and returned. He looked more red-faced and bloated than I expected from the pictures I had seen. I also saw "Papa Joffre", who looked exactly like his name. *(General Joseph, Jacques Cesaire Joffre – born in 1852. Commander in Chief of French army on the western front 1914–1916).* He arrived at General French's office while I was loitering about one day and, though I got no nearer than talking with his chauffeur, it was I felt, interesting to have seen him at all. Twenty-two years later I was to sleep in the bedroom he used in Amiens, at the Hotel du Rhin.

Apart from distant gunfire there was little evidence of war at St. Omer at that time, but one day a few bus loads of troops arrived in the Grande Place. They were very merry, which we soon discovered survivors often are after a fight. Some of them were wearing captured German spiked helmets. The open topped London buses they came in looked pleasantly familiar but from then on we realised that the war was not far away. It came a step nearer to a few days later when a German aeroplane was seen flying high in the sky at about 9 a.m. Soon afterwards another German plane came in at night. It flew low over G.H.Q. and dropped two bombs. One landed on the left of the G.H.Q. buildings and the other on their right, which was probably just as well because if they had fallen in between they would have landed on our barracks.

Another kind of diversion, but one which also involved life and death, was a murder trial that took place in the Town Hall around this time. I decided to attend to see what it was like. The place was so packed that it was hard to find anywhere to sit. The case was a rather unusual one in which the prisoner was accused of murdering his wife. His defence was that he had been forced into the marriage by his mother-in-law and was therefore not to blame. The Public Prosecutor gave a theatrical performance full of arm waving, tears in voice and so on. It was probably effective, but the proceedings, as a whole, seemed to be casual and lacking the dignity of an English court. When the Judge returned to the court to pass sentence, he had to push his way in. There was such a hubbub of talking that it was some time before his words could be heard. He seemed to be more like the Chairman of a meeting of shareholders where something had gone wrong than a State Official representing the majesty of the law. I thought afterwards that if the culprit was found guilty and given a long sentence he would at any rate be safer than many of us were likely to be in the weeks ahead.

One day we were told that some of us would be required to go to an unnamed place to do a job, the nature of which was not disclosed. We would be travelling to our unnamed destination on London buses. That would at least be better than marching. We set off on a beautiful morning and enjoyed a ride through pleasant countryside in summer sunshine. It would have been nice to know where we were going and what we should have to do when we arrived. In due course we drove into Norville, which was then a pleasant little town. We were turned out of the buses in the Grande Place and told to form up, while an N.C.O. walked down the line ticking us off in sixes.

We then learned that there was a battle going on nearby and that G.H.Q. had been moved here to direct operations. Our unit had been chosen to guard roads entering the town and to do other various other duties connected with G.H.Q., as we had done at St. Omer. Most of the men were detailed for guard duties. As hardly anyone ever came their way, they were taken off after the first day. The "powers that be" had by then been told that the French people objected to being stopped whenever they entered or left their own town. That meant that most of the men now had nothing to do. My job was to share the duties of errand boy at the Operations office with another man. Working six hours on and six off so that we did the job between us, working night and day. Whenever a telegram came saying that a trench had been captured, copies of it were sent off to the heads of departments and the French Mission, where a few French officers for liaison purposes were kicking their heels doing nothing. The messages did not come often, and we found it very boring sitting still in a passage leading to the office. To while away the time I borrowed a typewriter and tried to learn how to use it. The first thing I typed was a post card to an old school friend saying that I was working in General French's office, no doubt having been chosen for the job on account of my good looks! Many years later, after the war I was staying with the man who received it and I was amused to see that the censor had blotted out the part about General French and my good looks.

Being restless I decided to explore the rooms of G.H.Q. and went into an empty sitting room where I saw a copy of *La Vie Parisienne* lying on a table. I was idly turning the pages when a stentorian voice roused me with the question "What the devil are you doing here?" I replied meekly that I was an orderly and had got tired of sitting on the same chair for six hours doing nothing. He cleared me out "at the toot," as they used to say.

Night duty was even more tedious than working during the day. It was so dull that no one ever thought it was necessary to stay up for it, even though there was a battle going on nearby. The whole G.H.Q. of the British Army slept, with the exception of one orderly, who in this case happened to be me – a mere private and in civilian life, a parson! When I came on duty the staff sergeant in charge of the office told me that all I had to do was to listen for the telephone. If anything urgent came along he would be sleeping in the room next door. He then told me that he had been in the retreat from Mons and felt he had had about enough of it all for the time being. Thus briefed, he left me sitting at the table covered with documents with a telephone nearby. To while away the time I began to read the sheaves of telegrams I found carefully filed on the table in front of me. They didn't seem very important and were chiefly reports of progress, or the lack of it on the front. One was a very cordial message from General French to the Commanding Officer whose battalion had grabbed a few yards of trench at goodness knows what cost.

The main drawback to life at this time was the absence of food. Orderlies were provided with nothing at all. We had to buy it in town at our own expense. There was nowhere to wash either, so I made friends with some people who ran a tiny café. They gave me permission to wash in a scullery sink. They were very polite about it, perhaps because I could speak to them in their own language. It was a kind gesture but washing in a scullery sink has its limitations!

At night we watched flashes of gunfire in the sky like a distant display of fireworks. The sound of the bombardment heightened the impression I had, being at advanced G.H.Q. that something of special interest was going on. It seemed tame at the time to be confined to a miserable office doing errand boy's work, so I decided to make an expedition to the front line, or as near to it as I could get to it.

I had six hours at my disposal between turns of duty. Without, of course, saying anything to anybody I hurried off early one afternoon in the direction of the firing and walked briskly, hoping to get to the front. The first object of interest I encountered, before I had gone very far, was an Indian camp. Their brown faces and way of living seemed familiar to me having lived in their country only three years before. I stopped and talked to some of them in scanty Hindustani, trying to explain that I knew their country and wondered what they made of this damp and cold European war. They looked lost and miserable and I thought they would appreciate friendliness. After that effort I thought I deserved a little refreshment, so when I espied a cafe which went by the name of "L'Alouette" I went in and asked for grenadine. There, too as one does on a holiday, I chatted with the owner, asking questions about one thing and another, as one does on these occasions.

It was proving to be quite an interesting day. As I left the cafe I had noticed a French Interpreter who did not respond as politely as usual to my efforts in French. I put that down to the fact that he wanted to show off his English at least as much as I did my French and moved on. I soon reached another village which turned out to be La Fosse. The narrow streets were crammed with English soldiers and many of the houses had been damaged by shell-fire. The clattering of machine guns was so incessant and loud that they seemed to be coming from in the next street. "This is more like it," I thought as I ambled along chatting to some of the men. At felt that last I had got to the war I had heard so much about. I felt rather like a tourist and almost forgot I was wearing the uniform of a private soldier. My reflections were interrupted when I came face to face with a large gendarme. He asked as where I came from and what I was doing. That seemed a cheek at first, but I realised that he had a right to ask. I walked along with him and tried to give the impression that I was pleased to see him, appreciating that that situation required some tact. I asked where he himself came from and when he said "The Midi." I told him how much I had enjoyed staying there one winter and wondered why anybody wanted to live anywhere else. We were getting on so well that I thought the time had come when I might try to bid him a cheery adieu and see if I could shake him off, but I had my doubts. He stuck to me quite definitely and said he must hand me over to the British authorities. The surly interpreter I had seen at the cafe proved to be the cause of all this. A private, who had been seen talking to native troops and then asked questions in French, was no person to be allowed to go free.

The "British authorities" in this case turned out to be a sergeant in the Leicesters, who had evidently been making up for the wear and tear of warfare by imbibing liberal potions of anything to hand. He was not drunk, but he was certainly un-sober, quarrelsome and ready to vent his ill-feeling on anyone he could find. He immediately consigned me to a subterranean cellar and posted a sentry with a fixed bayonet over me, instructing him to shoot if I tried to get away. It was now beginning to be more than a joke and I asked the sergeant what he was up to. He refused to answer any questions and told me that I would shortly be shot. I told him not to talk rubbish and demanded to see an officer, but nothing happened for a long time and I did not relish stopping where I was under the orders of an ignorant and rather squiffy sergeant. The six-hour interval between my turns of duty would soon be up and I realised that I would be late going on duty at G.H.Q., which would lead to more inquiries and cause a hullabaloo.

When I was beginning to be really anxious I was ordered out of my dungeon and put in a car. I was then taken to a house where I was confronted by an officer who turned out to be in charge of the whole district. He was seated at a table in his office, probably not too pleased at being brought back when he thought he had finished for the day. He put some questions to me very curtly. I ignored his manner and hoped he would see the absurdity of the situation as soon as I began to talk but he remained obdurate and seemed to have made up his mind that I was an impostor and a spy. I wondered whether it would be any good telling him that I knew someone in his regiment - for I had noticed the initials "B.L." on his shoulder straps, which I knew meant Bengal Lancers. By now, however, I was afraid to say anything for fear of appearing to know too much. A private who talked a bit of French and Hindustani and knew the gendarme's home in the South of France, had already made them so suspicious but as there seemed no other course I decided to tell him. My comment made no impression at all, so I added that I knew a certain Bishop in India too, which I thought would sound highly respectable. I did not say that I had been a chaplain there as I thought that would be too much. This further evidence again failed in its purpose and I was sent back to my dungeon.

By now it was nearly dark and past the time at which I was supposed to go on duty. The dark form of the sentry with fixed bayonet continued to block the door. When I asked him what was happening next, he had nothing better to offer than to tell me what happened to spies. By now I was getting seriously worried and then at last another visitor arrived. This time it was a chaplain. I couldn't think what a chaplain had been brought in for and thought that perhaps I was going to be shot? I was told to get into a car with the chaplain and an escort. I did as I was told and we drove off. I had no idea where we were going but as we rolled along the chaplain casually referred to the bishop I had mentioned to the officer in charge. I told him enough to show that I knew him but he did not respond so I decided to say no more. The car rattled on and then I realised that we were going back to Merville, which seemed like good news to me, but not another word was said. When we eventually reached the town I was asked where my battalion was quartered. By then it was late and no one was about. I led my gaolers into the hall, which served as my billet. Rows of mounds in blankets, like so many churchyard graves hardly visible in the gloom, showed where my fellow privates were asleep. The chaplain approached a mound and flashed a torch at me.

"Do you know who this is?" he asked.

"Yes," mumbled the mound as he turned over and went back to sleep. I was then told I was free and my escort and the chaplain faded into the night.

It was with regret that I heard a few days later that we were to return to St. Omer.

The battle we had been expecting had fizzled out. Life had been more interesting recently and, if it had not been for the absence of any kind of food or sleeping place, it would have been better still.

Back in St. Omer it seemed as if someone had suddenly woken up to the fact that we were soldiers and we were put through a course of musketry. Although I had been four months in the army and done endless guards requiring a rifle and ammunition, I had never yet fired a service rifle. The standard of shooting at the range was not very good and I was surprised to find that, without my ever having fired anything other than a shotgun, my performance was better than most.

When that was over I went back to the usual round of fatigues which made me feel that I would soon have had enough of the St. Omer life. With my future in mind I decided to send a reminder to an uncle with whom I had once discussed the possibility of applying for a commission. He was retired Indian Colonel who had been dug up for the war and had an office at the Horse Guards, where I think he sometimes went to doze. It was there that I had called on him one day attired as a private. He was talking to an old army friend at the time and introduced me as his parson nephew. Such a monstrosity was no doubt beyond the ken of an old time army man and he looked at me as if he had had a bad dream. Ought I to have sprung to attention? Another time, when I met my uncle in the street, and we were both in uniform I gave him a friendly wave. There again I felt I might be wrong, but it takes time to forget old habits. He had subsequently arranged for me to see Lord Claylesmore who at that time was Chairman of the Territorial Association. Several months had passed since that meeting took place and I thought that perhaps it was time to find out if my visit had triggered any response. My uncle replied telling me he was surprised that I had heard no more. He promised to see what he could do while I continued to wait and hope and got on with my military chores.

The news I had hoped for eventually came through but it took some time. While I was waiting and getting very bored more with sanitary fatigues there was little I could do. Eventually I felt I must act. I timidly mounted the steps of the battalion orderly room and put my head round the door to ask the sergeant major if he had heard anything about my getting a commission. The idea seemed to shock him slightly and he responded with a definite "'No" but as events turned out I did not have long to wait. Soon after that I was told to report to the Orderly Room again. The same sergeant major was still there but he was noticeably less curt. He picked up some files and told me that I was now a second lieutenant and must report without delay to a battalion in France, to which I apparently now belonged. As my commission dated from some six weeks earlier, the probability was that it had been overlooked in the orderly room and that had accounted for the haste in sending me away on my first visit. It was actually dated June 24th and, as it was now August, I had been doing sanitary fatigues as an officer for several weeks.

Having been a 2nd Lieutenant so long I thought that there would be no great hurry about finding my battalion and that a spot of leave might be vouchsafed for the purpose of acquiring the necessary outfit. I was speedily disillusioned when the same official, who probably did not want me to complain of the delay in telling me of my appointment,

The town of Armentieres, 1914

said I must set off that afternoon to visit the G.H.Q. ordnance store and to pick up the officer's equipment I needed. I bought a Sam Browne, an officer's valise and two gilt stars, which I proceeded to put on the shoulder straps of my private's uniform. And that was that! With my new kit, and a pink signal form, on which someone had jotted down a

map reference, I was told to find my way to my new unit as best I could. Before leaving I had to hand over the rest of my private's equipment. I was heartily glad to give up my rifle but would have liked to have kept my overcoat and haversack, which had been useful and had shared my discomforts long enough to be old friends.

The first part of my journey was by bus and very pleasant it was to be driving somewhere instead of walking, but as the light began to fade I realised that there was no chance of reaching my destination that day. That did not worry me and, when my bus arrived at a little town I decided to stop there for the night. The town was Armentieres. In 1915 it was for the most part intact. Apart from a few demolished houses and splashes of shell fragments it was much as it had always been. The area near the station bore most traces of war. A hotel next to the level crossing had its entire front pock marked with the results of frequent bombardment, but it had not been destroyed. Rumours suggested that it was being kept intact because it had been the German G.H.Q. whilst they were in the town and they had hopes of coming back again before long. It was there that I found a room for the night. It was poor sort of place but after six months sleeping on dirty boards in the midst of all kinds of filth it seemed to me quite luxurious. I looked forward to sleeping in a bed. A rather slovenly girl appeared and to show me upstairs. We went up two flights of steps and into a little room, which she explained looked out over the railway towards the trenches. The furniture consisted of the meanest type of single iron bedstead with a mattress that might have been made of concrete. There were some rough bedclothes, a torn cotton counterpane and a cheap basin and jug. As I was looking at them with the aid of a torch, the girl hastened to tell me that I must not show a light, because the trenches were so close. As if to illustrate her remarks, a rattle of machine gun and rifle fire broke out, which showed me she was right. But it was a real bed and that was enough for me and I decided to make the best of it.

Before retiring I decided to go downstairs and try to get something to eat. I was hoping for peace and quiet but I found there was someone else there, which meant I would have to talk. He was an interpreter. My last encounter with a French interpreter had not been very pleasant. As the memory of it still lingered in my mind I said as little as I could and addressed most of my comments to the owner of the establishment, who came to sit at the table with us. I asked the interpreter how long he had been involved in the war and what his general impression of it was. He said he had been in it from the start and was fed up. "War," he said somewhat crudely, "is blood, mud and shit."

I finished my food and escaped upstairs to my longed-for bed. It was very dark when I got there and began to undress. I heard shots in the not distant trenches and when a Very light went up there was a momentary glare and shadows passed swiftly up the wall. Then from the doorway I heard a voice coming from the doorway. I looked up and could just distinguish the girl who had seen me to my room. She was partly undressed, and explained that they had sent her to tell her to come down into the cellar as they were expecting a bombardment. I had noticed the interpreter going up to the floor above, so that must have been the information he imparted during the minutes he was there. I pictured the cellar with the owner, servants and the interpreter, who would probably talk incessantly, but it was the thought of losing a night in a real bed that finally decided me. I looked toward the shadow in the doorway, which was waiting for my answer.

I said, "I think I will stay here." And that was that was what I did.

The next morning, after my first night in bed for several months I descended in a leisurely way to the ground floor. I was relieved to find that the interpreter had gone. I decided to look round the town, find whoever was in charge, show him my map reference and see if he could tell me where I needed to go. I discovered an office in what had been a good-sized private house. I went in and I explained that I was really an officer in spite-of my appearance. The officer in charge looked at my unusual uniform in silence, stretched out his hand for the map reference and then turned to some maps.

After an interval he said, "I've found where it is but it's inside the German lines. Things have moved on, but I think I can tell you where your battalion is now or where it was when we last heard from them." He scribbled down a new map reference and told me where lorries that were going in that direction were likely to be found. I was advised to collect my bags, sit down by the side of the road and hope.

I went back to the hotel, picked up my officer's valise, which was very heavy with things I had bought at St. Omer, and went back on the road once more.

After I had gone a little way I heard someone running after me. Looking back over my shoulder I recognized the girl who had showed me to my room the night before. She ran towards to me and asked me where I was going and if I wanted any help.

"Thanks for the offer but I am used to carrying things," I replied but she insisted on coming and grabbed one of the valise straps while I held the other. Together we moved on. One or two whizz-bangs came over, with their sudden disconcerting burst like an amplified squib. The echo reverberated through the streets, making it sound as if there had been more than one. I looked at my companion who took no notice of them at all. We began to talk a little. I asked where she came from and where she had been since the war began. She said she came from Lille and had been there when the Germans arrived. She told me how bullets had spattered the pavements and, after that, nothing had mattered much. We carried on to the accompaniment of shells bursting nearby. Several lorries drove past and then quite suddenly, she stopped, dumped her end of the luggage and said she must get back. I offered her a tip, which she firmly refused and watched her frail little figure as she walked away. She reached the end of the road, turned and waved. Then Celeste - for that was her name - was gone. Ten years later, when I was re-visiting Armentieres after the war, I asked a hard-faced female behind the bar of the same hotel if she had heard of Celeste or knew what had become of her. She said she did know her but would not add anything else, only shaking her head and pursing her lips.

I moved on alone. Eventually, just as it was getting dark, a lorry stopped and the driver agreed to take me as far as Estaires. I stayed there for a night and then moved on to Sailly Sur la Lys, where the headquarters of my battalion was now supposed to be. It had taken me two days to travel fifty miles and I was still looking for the soldiers I had set out to join. I eventually found them in the village of Doullieu, which consisted of a few scattered cottages and barns and the ruins of a church which the villagers told us been filled with bodies and then set alight by the Germans. It had been burned to the ground.

I found my battalion H.Q, complete with Adjutant and orderly room, in one of the cottages. It stood near a refuse heap, which stank to the heavens and rebuked the stars. It was now afternoon and the battalion, which was supposed to be resting, had finished its work for the day. It took some time to locate the Adjutant. He was a vigorous and cheerful person who greeted me with surprise and interest. He had, of course, heard nothing about my coming and seemed to think it was all mildly amusing. He was also entertained by my unusual costume and looked at me, as he would have observed an unusual specimen in the Botanical Gardens at Kew, where before the war he had been Assistant Director. Even botanical specimens have to be kept alive so he arranged for me to have some food. I was then sent me to a farmhouse where I found a bedroom, which was almost completely filled with a huge feather bed. It was so large that if anyone sleeping in it had wanted to stretch, he would have to put his head out of the window and his feet through the door. There were some scribbled names on the whitewashed walls and, as I lay on the bed, I deciphered the nearest one which was that of a German officer who had been there earlier in the war.

The Adjutant's interest in my private's uniform had not escaped me and when I suggested that it would be more suitable if I were dressed as an officer I saw that he had come to the same conclusion. It only remained for me to point out that uniforms could only be satisfactorily bought in England with which, being a sensible person, he immediately agreed. It did not take long to get the necessary leave voucher and a few days later I was on a train to London. It took me three days to get there and I stayed for one day and one night. It was just long enough to get my officer's uniform and to spend a delightful night in the Queens Hotel. When a neat chambermaid brought me a late breakfast in bed it seemed hardly right to have someone in cap and apron to pull up the blind and ask me if I had all I wanted but the dream did not last and I was soon back in France.

My battalion, which had suffered severely at the 2nd battle of Ypres, had been amalgamated with another battalion and new officers and men had recently arrived. We embarked on a further period of training and reorganisation. Some of us were sent to learn about bombs from a sergeant who had been awarded a Victoria Cross for his talents in throwing them. We sat on the ground while he gave his lesson and displayed various bombs. There was a German stick bomb for which you pulled a string to light the fuse. It was almost foolproof. And there were our own type, made out of old jam tins. They had a fuse, which had to be lighted with a match. A bomber had to wear a piece of emery paper round his left wrist and use it to light the fuse (if it was not raining too hard). When it began to smoulder it had to be thrown at the enemy, who seemed to be expected to wait until it arrived.

Bombs were very much in the air just then, in more senses than one, because of static warfare and the difficulty of getting at people in trenches. It was curious how various things came into fashion. Then it was bombs. Later it was rifles and then Lewis guns[7]. After that gas and even bayonets became the craze. Many of our senior officers were rifle enthusiasts because good shooting had played its part in the Boer War which most of them recalled. During the years I spent in the front line I can only remember bayonets being used for toasting bread.

One day I was sent up to a reserve trench with a working party. It was the first time I had been in a trench. We were quite unmolested on the way up. The ground was dead flat and it was not until we had nearly reached our destination that the whining of tired bullets warned us that we were getting near. Once we were in the trench they dropped harmlessly over us but one man, who asked permission to get out of the trench for a

7   Light machine gun of American design widely used by the British.

certain purpose, paid a high price. He was shot in the behind! He was my first experience of a war casualty. We put him on a stretcher for the return journey and then went back. I felt that little by little I was getting into the atmosphere of things.

At that time our C.O. was an old Territorial and consequently as little a professional soldier as any of us. One afternoon, when we were doing some sort of exercise, he summoned us in a fatherly way and invited us to confide in him. Had we any "difficulties"? That was all right but I was getting too old to be asked questions like that. I had been warned in advance that at the end of each interview he was apt to ask what the soldier concerned did in everyday life. In the few minutes at my disposal I wondered what I should say when my turn came. I had found it pleasant so far not immediately being identified as a parson, but I guessed that sooner or later I would be found out. Hoping he would keep the information to himself I outlined the facts. Suppressing the shudder which my answer caused him, he replied politely but I knew that henceforth I would be regarded as a curiosity. As it turned out I could have held out longer because that particular C.O. soon left. He was replaced by a regular soldier who came to us from by another regiment. I met him first at Fleuraix, which at that time was heavily fortified with rows of barbed wire in front of every house in the main street. I was amongst the last of the last officers to be introduced, but he had evidently heard about me because he advanced with a twinkle in his eye, though he was too tactful to make the inevitable remark. That twinkle stood him in good stead during the two years of trench life that he spent with us. Everyone got to know him well and value his care for us, and his complete disregard of his own interests. He always put our interests first.

One of his principles was to see to the comfort of the men. However long a march had been and however done up he was, before he found his own billet we had to check and report that the men of his company or platoon had been housed as well as possible. I can remember times when at the end of a long march I felt I could not drag one foot after the other. Having to walk all over the place to find the barn where our quartermaster had fixed our company billets was a responsibility I could have done without but that would never have been acceptable under his command.

At first, I think his ideas of discipline, learnt in the regular army, were a little stricter than they afterwards became. When he first arrived there was nearly a big bust-up over my platoon sergeant. He was an old army man who could hardly read or write, but he was much more effective than any other N.C.O. I ever had. He was fond of beer and coming back to billets from a tour in the trenches we had fallen out on the side of the road for a rest. My platoon had halted exactly outside a nice little cafe. After days of mud and rain in a waterlogged trench, the temptation was too much. My sergeant slipped inside for a quick drink. I did not see him go but unfortunately the C.O., who happened to be riding past at the time, did. The Sergeant was going to be severely punished but I told the adjutant that he was easily the best N.C.O. I had. It was true and nothing much happened after that, which seemed to me to be a sensible result.

On another occasion, in billets a long way from the line, a senior sergeant of another company got drunk. He was reduced to the ranks. All the officers were summoned to a meeting with the men of his company to hear the sentence. I remember at the time thinking that was severe, but with so much ahead, I daresay it was right to make an example. He had his preferences, which it must be admitted were pretty obvious and not always based on very good grounds. It was a joke to me and one or two others that one of our most inept officers - whose courage was only equalled by his inefficiency in performing the simplest task - was made a captain before lots of others, because he was a good on a horse. When he was rode on ahead as billeting officer, he always made sure that there was a good omelette ready for the C.O as soon as he arrived. At least that is what people said! We laughed about it but my chief memory of him is of a good man who never sacrificed us for nothing. There were times when senior officers had plans for us which, owing to previous casualties, we were quite unfit to carry out. Our C.O. never hesitated to say so, when another man more intent on his own promotion would probably have acquiesced. He had no thirst for decorations and was never a popularity hunter. I have a vivid recollection of a big gathering of officers and other ranks held in London three years after the end of the war. He we not a particularly good public speaker but when he stood up and started to talk he was cut short by a tremendous burst of applause which went on for five minutes. I think that must have been some little reward to him and I hope it was. It was never equalled by any of the spontaneous greetings I witnessed in subsequent years.

My first experience of living in the trenches was not with my own battalion but with a battalion of the Lincolns to which I was attached for instruction.

As we went in at night we passed over some very exposed land just behind the front line, where there was no communication trench. We were ordered to be absolutely silent, because it was swept at times with machine gun fire. Once in, we were given dug-outs or what were really above-ground shelters, with a few sandbags on the top. I thought myself lucky because mine was not in the trench but just behind, and I had it to myself. I soon discovered how wrong I was. When shelling began I found the parapet of the main trench did not protect it, and I had to move out fast. One shell burst just outside the opening. Bits of earth fell on the coat of my new uniform, which I had taken off as I lay down to rest. That made me decide to buy one locally and save my good uniform for when we were out of the trenches. When we got back to billets I found to a little local tailor who produced a garment which was a recognizable attempt to be khaki uniform, but in the course of time it faded to a curious hue.

The Company headquarters in the front line was no better-protected overhead but, being built up against the parapet; it was shielded from direct fire to some extent. This flimsy kind of shelter was the only kind I had any experience of till 1917, except when we inhabited a deep German dug-out which had been captured. It had been built to a much higher standard. The growing intensity of bombardments made real dug-outs necessary. In the earlier days, the guns being fired against us were mostly field guns. Crouching under a parapet could sometimes protect us from them.

On the night of my arrival I was sent, with an N.C.O, into No Man's land[8] to see what it was like. The company commander lent me his revolver to make me feel safe. We were told to go out by a sally port - a term quite new to me, which I found out, had more to do with sallying forth to meet the foe than having things thrown at us. Word was passed along that we were going out, and I hoped it had been duly noted.

I it was dead quiet outside and we wandered about amongst impenetrable weeds which, in the darkness, to take on human forms. The German trenches were very close so

---

8   Describes the area of land between two enemy trenches that neither side wishes to openly move on or take control of due to fear of being attacked by the enemy in the process.

we had to be quiet. We went as far as a listening post, which had been established in a gap, which was being dug by night for some purpose. I found my first visit to No-man's land a little trying to the nerves and I never, even in subsequent years, developed a love for lingering there. The N.C.O., who accompanied me, told me that an officer of the Rifle Brigade used to roam about No Man's Land for pleasure. Sometimes, when he wanted to examine something, he used a flashlight. He was evidently quite different to me. He subsequently won a V.C. so perhaps appropriate legends are to be expected with that in mind.

At about this time we began to hear rumours of an impending attack. The various officers of the battalion were assigned to do different jobs when the attack took place. One of those jobs was to lead bombers along the trench, while the main attack went over the top. The officer chosen for the bombing, from which it seemed to me there was little hope of a return, said he thought it was an honour to be selected. Another officer I remember, who was chosen to lead the attack, did not take it so calmly. It was one of those cases of a presentiment, which amounted to certainty. When he knew what he had to do, he came into the company dug-out and talked freely to the officer who was going to do the bombing. That was quite natural, as they had been together in the regiment long before the war.

"Old man," he said, to his friend, "I know I am going to be killed in this show." His friend treated it lightly and told him he was mistaken; though he was evidently surprised. There was silence after that as we all sat in the semi-darkness. It was a very quiet night, as it could be in the trenches and often was when both sides knew that an attack was imminent. As we listened an owl hooted dismally. The officer who had just come in got up abruptly and went out.

The actual day of the "show", as we called battles in those days, was not made known but we knew it would be soon and I wondered where I would come in. My doubts were set at rest by an order to rejoin my battalion, so I departed alone in the September sunshine, feeling that I was rather leaving them to it though I knew that I would not have long to wait, as my battalion was likely to be equally involved.

It was shortly after this that one of our officers was killed - the first since I had joined the battalion. A German mine had gone up a short way down the line and he had jumped on to the fire step to see how it looked. A sniper, who had no doubt expected something like that to happen, shot him in the head.

We had still not been told when the battle would be, but things were evidently things coming to a climax. A couple of days later our battalion went to dig a communication trench to lessen the distance re-enforcements would have to travel over open ground. It was then that I had an experience which afterwards made me suspect that I might have figured in another spy episode, though this time I was not cast in the title role.

We were just behind our front line trenches and relied on the flatness of the ground to be unobserved while we were digging. A few tired bullets whined over us as they came down to earth. I was walking about on top, whilst the men dug the trench, when I suddenly saw two officers coming towards me. They had very new uniforms and no badges and asked me, with unusual politeness, if I could tell them where the artillery observation post was. They seemed rather flustered and in a great hurry which, of course may have been due to exposed position and being new to the job. I told them it was in an old barn just behind the front line and they went off to find it. I offered them an N.C.O. to act as their guide, but this they firmly refused my offer. I think it was that refusal, and the determined way it was made, which put doubts in my head. As I had already been the victim of one spy-mania, I was the last person to imagine anyone else to be one. It is of course so easy to be wise after the event. On the day of the battle the observation post was demolished by German guns. It went on merrily burning well into the night.

Around this time I was detailed to attend the funeral of a man who had been killed. The burial ground was just behind the reserve trenches and it was under rifle fire, which at accounted for the fact that the chaplain, who was a sensible man, began the service as soon as he could with the men who had brought the body. When I arrived at the appointed time with a few of the man's friends, we found he had nearly finished. He obligingly said some of the prayers again and then the men presented arms by way of farewell. We looked down on the figure in khaki, wrapped in a brown army blanket at the bottom of a shallow grave, as a few spent bullets whined over our heads. In the gathering darkness it started to drizzle.

The Chaplain who conducted that funeral was the first one we had seen and he did his difficult job very well. He was a large man with gray hair who was active but no longer young. His parish was the trenches and billets. I remember seeing him in the fading autumn twilight, sitting on a packing case in a barn full of men, preparing them for confirmation. Just before the attack, a confirmation service had been arranged in a village just behind the line. As I was near at the time I went along. It was remarkable to see a large room full of men who were shortly to go into battle waiting for the Bishop to come and confirm them. Bishop Gwynne, who was the Assistant Chaplain General, was expected to arrive but had been held up. The Chaplain had the difficult task of occupying the men for an hour or so of their precious time until he appeared. I think what struck us about him was that he was natural, genuine and so certain that what he was doing was important. The story was that he had been turned down by the Chaplain General and had travelled to France at his own expense. He proved so popular that he was then he was taken on as a chaplain.

During the last few days before the attack the Germans started shelling the area between our billets and the front line. That was known as "registering," and the Germans did it so that, when the battle started, they would have the range of their targets precisely worked out. Further along the line a heavy bombardment went on all day, but we still did not know if we were going to be involved.

While this preliminary bombardment was proceeding the C.O. summoned us to a conference. He then told us that September 25th was going to be the day when the fun would begin and that we would be in close support of the attacking battalions, so we would definitely be involved in the show. The conference, which was attended by Officers and the N.C.O.s, took place in a local school. We sat at the children's desks while the C.O. talked to us from the platform where a schoolmaster usually sat. Before the meeting ended he told us that the morning we moved off there would be a celebration of Holy Communion in the same place. I went to that, as nearly all the officers did and a number of other ranks so that the room seemed quite full.

On the afternoon of September 24th we moved on, planning to arrive at a place where we were intending to spend the night, while it was still light. We moved along roads which had been shelled during the last few days, but no shells came over while we were moving up. We just heard a continuous bombardment going on away to our right, where the main battle of Loos was to begin next day. It brought vividly to life what for most of us was to be our first battle. Nobody said much as we trudged along on a gloomy autumn afternoon. We moved slowly because we had plenty of time in hand and were carrying extra things like spades. Packs were left behind, and instead haversacks were put in their place for officers and men alike. I had an extra shirt and pair of socks in mine because we had been told that it might be some days before we saw billets again.

The aim of the battle was to get as far as Lille but that it turned out was being too hopeful and Lille was to remain in enemy hands for another three years. Our action was principally a retaining exercise. It was meant to mislead the Germans into thinking that they had another big battle to deal with in our part of the line, and pin down re-enforcements, which might otherwise have been thrown into the main battle.

It was nearly dark when we reached a small cafe near the end of our side of the trenches. My Company Commander, who had remembered it from earlier visits, suggested we should pause and have some coffee. He was a quiet man, who might have passed for a country squire. Not at all military by nature, but like many others prepared to do what was required. In private life he was an auctioneer and sold very gentlemanly cows and things belonging to the King at Windsor. He was easy to get on with, being good-tempered and reasonable and I was sorry when he was wounded next day and never re-appeared. We talked for some time and then moved on.

Two hours later we got the men on to the road again and made our position in support. It was in the dry bed of a small stream, which made a convenient ready-made trench. Here we began to scrape out little niches in the side nearest the front with our spades and sat down to await events. At 3.30 a.m. an ear-splitting din suddenly burst forth. It came from batteries of our own field guns, which we discovered were only a few yards away from us and shooting just came over our heads. There are fewer disturbing noises than the short sharp burst of a field gun if you are just in front of it, and there were a great number of them. Their fire drew a certain amount of German shells in reply

– so we stayed put. Soon it began to get light and, having else nothing to do, I produced a copy of Punch magazine which I had been carrying with me, and tried to think of pleasanter times.

It was soon clear that the offensive had begun and I thought of the officer in the Lincolns who was leading the attack with bombs of the jam tin kind. The fuse of each bomb had to be lit separately with a match. As it was now raining that feat, which was difficult at any time in battle, must have become almost impossible.

After a while I got out of my niche and looked over the top to see what I could see. It was getting lighter, but dark clouds and spitting rain held back the daybreak. A few hundred yards away on lower ground, there seemed to be a tremendous scrimmage taking place. It gave the impression of a huge slag heap of a coal mine and volumes of smoke, some black, some yellow, were lazily rolling over it, lit up from time to time by especially large explosions. The din was terrific.

It was an inferno seemed awesome to any one going into battle for the first time and I felt sorry for those in the middle of it. My sympathetic thoughts were cut short by the order to advance. We were going to follow up the attack. At first, that was only going to be a matter of following like sheep and leaving the job of finding the direction to those who were in front. After wandering down an interminable length of trench we found ourselves at last in the old front line. The attack had by now reached the end of its first stage. The attacking battalions had taken the section of German trench opposite us, but had failed to keep the reserve trench beyond and had been bombed out. It was now a question of when a German counter attack would begin, so there was nothing to do but wait.

While we were there, our second in command came along and spoke to me. He was a nice man, dreamy and preoccupied in manner. In a quiet voice, as if he were asking for a match he said to me:

"I hear they've run out of bombs over there." (He was talking about our men who were now in the German trench). "Do you think you could take them some - you and your platoon?" I immediately realised that this would mean going over No Man's Land in the daylight, dodging shells and rifle fire, which did not seem very inviting. I told the platoon to help themselves to the bombs, which were in some boxes farther along the trench, and off we went.

We went through a sally port and ran, doubled up as much as possible, hoping we would not be too conspicuous. In that way we carried over 200 bombs wasting no time on the way. Just outside the German trench there were some dead English soldiers who had been killed in the morning attack. Passing them we went into the captured German trench and deposited our bombs. As it was my first visit to a German trench I was naturally interested to note that it was much better made than our own, with good duck boards and well drained. The sandbags were remarkable too, being made of bits of all sorts of coloured flannel. It was as if patriotic German housewives had handed over their petticoats for the defence of the Fatherland. There was an English officer sitting down inside. He told me he was the Medical Officer of the 2nd Rifle Brigade and explained that the trench was held by bombers who had made blocks at either end. Persistent and accurate rifle fire from positions, which had not been captured, made it impossible look above the top even for a second. The M.O. asked me if we had come to stay and I told him that we had orders to deliver the bombs and then go back. After a brief rest I collected the men and we retraced our steps. In the general turmoil our few men must have escaped notice for there was only some shelling and rifle fire both coming and going. No one was injured, though the man next to me had a bullet through his haversack. As we were in battle order it was on his back in place of a pack.

When we returned to our trench I was surprised to find our platoon sergeant, who was a man who always had a lot to say, sitting calmly on the fire-step. I asked him what he was doing and his reply was that he thought someone ought to look after the trench. We sat down again glad to be alive. Before long a heavy bombardment of our trench began, but as it was all by field guns the shells mostly burst on the parapet or went over. There was no reply from our own guns because they were no longer there. They had been taken away and sent to the main attack at Loos. The bombardment was intended to make us keep our heads down while the Germans were counter attacking to win back their trench.

As darkness fell it became comparatively quiet and rain started to fall again. My first little battle was over. I was wondering what would happen next when news came that we were to be relieved. The Worcesters, of whom we had not heard before, were going to take our place and we were to move out. They had in fact already arrived but we had not seen them as that they were out in the darkness of No Man's Land between us and the Germans. It was fortunate that we had had no patrols out and had not done any shooting.

It was midnight when we eventually moved off. By then the weather had cleared and a full moon was shining. It shone on a sea of liquid mud, which we had to wade through for a mile in order to get out. At least now we felt we were going in the right direction. I passed the C.O., who was waiting to see us depart, and remarked that it was good news to be going out so soon. He said he had not been told that the Worcesters were already between us and the German line and added – "We don't get much money but we do see life!" Hours later we arrived at a place which we called Elbow Farm. The exhausted men threw themselves down and slept, wet as they were and caked with mud from head to foot. I lay down too on some hay in a stable, but I was too tired to sleep much.

The following day, when two other officers and I were strolling along, the General who had directed operations stopped us. He spoke very politely to us and thanked us for what we had done. He said that aeroplanes had seen lots of Germans hurrying up to our front in buses which, was just what they had wanted, as our action had been designed to divert the German's attention from the main front at Loos. Later that day we moved further up the line and I met the men from company of Lincolns, to which I had been attached earlier on. I was glad to see that the officer who had led the bombers was at their head. He was already wearing the bright red ribbon of the Legion of Honour, which presumably a grateful nation had bestowed upon him for his exploits. Another

The town of Armentieres, 1916

Lincolns officer I knew and liked had not been so fortunate. He wore spectacles, which must have been a handicap in an attack on a morning with a driving rain and mist. He had been killed. The officer, who had told us that that he felt he was not going to survive the attack, had also died.

Some years after the war, I re-visited this part of the line and tried to identity the trenches. By that time the French inhabitants were back in their homes, but none of them could tell me where the front line had been. I hired an antiquated fiacre in Armentiers and went to what had once been Bois Grenier. That part of the line had remained quiet for two and a half years but the tide of the war had once more swept over it in 1918 completing the destruction. If there had ever been a village of Bois Grenier it was no longer to be found. The only traces were at a cross roads where a few gaping walls and sagging roofs were all that remained of what once had been a group of houses. Over a broken doorway which must have belonged to a cafe there was still a signboard hanging on one wall. It read: "A La Tranquilite" (To Peace)"

After our baptism of fire the battalion entered a quieter period in which prolonged turns in water-logged trenches alternated with night working parties, often under fire.

At one point we were in the trenches or in close support for forty days, the last half of which we spent in the trenches all the time. That had a dispiriting effect after a time and an officer from headquarters, who I met hurrying back from the front line, remarked as a bullet just missed his head "I've had about enough of this." He must have been cleverer than the rest of us who felt much the same as he disappeared after that for quite a time. One of our Company officers also disappeared about this time with what was described as "a collapse of nerves". After the September 25th affair, when he went back to the front line he had become excited and said that he couldn't stand it anymore. The C.O, feeling that he would be more bother than he was worth, had him transferred. I liked him personally and regretted his departure. When we met a year later in Boulogne, I found he had settled down happily to some peacetime occupation and was as smart as could be in highly polished riding boots with spurs. He survived the war and after it had ended offered me a job as a commercial traveller in a business he was then running.

When we were in the line our part of the battalion used to occupy an old trench.

It was waterlogged and the only overhead protection was a few sheets of corrugated iron and some decaying sandbags. It was very near a German trench so we had to keep a sharp lookout for raiders. In the day time small mirrors were held up on the end of bayonets, because it was impossible to look over. They were always shot to pieces at once though they were only about three by two inches in size. The very accurate short range rifle fire meant that if you were moving around you had to be bent double. The bullets made a deafening sound like the crack of a whip. Between spells of duty, officers were put to it to find somewhere to lie down, and I remember creeping under a bit of corrugated iron to lie on one of two stretchers which raised us a few inches above the surrounding water. An officer I never got on with occupied the other stretcher. My dislike of him grew after seeing him using his revolver to shoot at a mole that he had caught and tied by the leg with a piece of string to a nail on the parapet. I felt that my own life was so like the mole's that I couldn't understand anyone trying to inflict pain and death on a small defenceless creature.

Presently it froze and on moonlight nights it was quite a sight to see the rats scurrying about as if they were having a skating party. The discomfort and wet made washing and shaving impossible and my very black bristles became quite a joke. When one November afternoon a sergeant started a spy scare and said he had seen a disreputable person in a faded officer's uniform wandering about the trench the general conclusion was that it was only me.

The messing arrangements were very bad. We only had only a little burrow into which we had to crawl on our hands and knees. Heavy rifle fire made standing upright impossible, which in itself can be tiring day after day. The water we used to make tea came from a handy shell hole, but it was not made any more pleasant by the fact that a body was lying at its side. Of course no smoke could be allowed which restricted our ability to cook. Going out and coming in were difficult because there was so little cover. The few communication trenches that existed were impassable because they were filled with mud, which was at least a yard deep in places. We had the choice of ploughing through that or getting out on the top, where we were likely to be swept by machine gun fire. We generally did as much wading as we could and finished the journey on the top when it seemed a bit quieter.

We were always pretty exhausted when at last we reached the front line. I remember lying down under a bit of corrugated iron to recover and being too tired to move when a mouse came and sat on my forehead for warmth. It was always a great relief to escape to billets after a turn of duty, though the billets were very near the line and did not add up to much. By way of showing that we had arrived in our trench the custom was for everyone to get on the fire step and fire 5 rounds, rapid. Where this idiotic practice originated I could not discover but I suppose it was meant to be an exhibition of high morale. In practice of course it was simply a waste of ammunition and it gave the Germans the latest information about our movements. During one relief a very efficient sergeant, who had hurried out to a listening post in front of the line and taken it over, was shot dead by his own men.

We were reminded how close the front line was to our billets by a new officer who had just joined us. He was taking afternoon tea in an upstairs room when a long distance shot from a rifle came through the wall and wounded him. He never got as far as the trenches and was on his way home a couple of hours after he arrived. It was strange how sometimes, people lasted months and even years, going through innumerable dangers without a scratch and others became casualties almost before they had begun.

Although the trenches were quiet, as trenches go, the time we put in between Bois Grenier and Christmas was anything but a rest cure. When we were not in the line all the time we returned to it nightly, over ground often briskly peppered with rifle fire.

By way of helping and to occupy our minds we used to dig as well as the men. I was digging one night with an officer from South Africa when our trained ears detected a betraying flutter. We leaned on our spades and waited. Flutter, flutter it went and then there was thud just by us. Fortunately it failed to explode. At the time it struck us as funny. The contrast between the inoffensive thud and what we had been expecting. Another officer who was quite a friend of mine had hysterics. He couldn't stop laughing and he was never got tired of describing that scene.

The brighter moments of the war did not make up for the long drawn out weariness of life in waterlogged trenches. My latent malaria was also giving me problems and

I was feeling more and more played out. Having spent the last seven winters in the tropics and two years just before the war recovering from very bad dose of malaria, I thought that if I survived to the end of the year that might be as far as I could go. With that in mind I decided to write once again to the Chaplain General and ask if, in the event of my being unable to go on as I was, I might be able to move into the Chaplains' department. That may not sound heroic but few of us made any pretence of that kind. His reply may be worth referring to in view of the unfavourable opinions sometimes expressed about parsons being combatants and the fact that having been one was not at that time generally considered to be a recommendation by the church authorities. The reply came from the Deputy Chaplain General at GHQ It explained that whilst Chaplains were plentiful there was a shortage of officers so that such a transfer could not be contemplated.

One of the towns we were billeted in was Fleurbaix. When we arrived there first I walked around looking for somewhere to stay and found a house which was set apart from others and only appeared to be inhabited by an old man and his wife. It had a shell hole in the roof but seemed so much better than any other I had seen and I wondered why it was vacant. The old people pointed out the hole in the roof and said it was a dangerous place to be but I thought that if it was safe enough for them it was safe enough for me. They were right and when shelling occurred in our part of the line it did not last long.

One afternoon we were filling up time by playing cricket with a stick and a tennis ball in an enclosed yard belonging to a house near Battalion H.Q. It was quiet until a salvo of H.E. shells suddenly burst all round. I happened to hit a full pitch to leg at that moment. It went straight through the window of a room where the C.O. was sitting. He jumped up thinking it was a shell. I felt I had made rather a fool of myself and hastened to apologise.

Fleurbaix was quite near Armentieres, where I had briefly paused on my way to join my battalion. The road to the town was frequently shelled but at that time in Armentiers itself it was still possible to enjoy quite a civilized life. It gave an added feeling of attainment to get there in one piece. The hotel in which I had stayed was still said to be in tact so I began to feel almost at home. In the first street I came to there was a shop where you could be photographed. Alongside there was a barber who did a roaring trade. To have my hair cut, followed by a friction in good Coty or Houbigant, was almost sacramental, standing as it did for a life to which I had so long been a stranger. Farther along the street there was a house which had been hit by a shell that had gone through two walls of a bedroom without exploding. I was curious enough to go up the stairs, and found that a crucifix was still hanging on the wall and some ornaments on the mantelpiece remained untouched with just a little powdered dust around them. The large church was still intact except for a shell hole in the roof of the nave. In the late afternoon of an autumn day the interior seemed a huge cavern of quiet blackness with only one thing to focus the eye upon - a sanctuary lamp which burnt steadily like a great ruby in the darkness before the High Altar.

Near the church there was a brewery which was also used as a washing place where troops went for bathing parades. A large number of tubs, which were really wine casks sawn in half, were dotted about one of the buildings. To see them at night filled with naked men with clouds of steam ascending in the dim light from a few oil lamps was reminiscent of some of the attempts of mediaeval artists to depict souls in hell.

I got a bath here myself once and lingered in it. You have to have lived in the same clothes for a few weeks in the dreary mud of waterlogged trenches and in dirty billets to understand the transfigured feeling a bath can give. To take off dirty clothes and feel warm water against your skin and then to put on a clean shirt (in my case a white one) amounted to a ceremony! It seemed possible to go on again after such a baptismal break with the past.

Washing was always a problem when living in billets near the line followed long spells of trench life. Judging from the arrangements made for the de-lousing of shirts, private soldiers also suffered much from lice. Our divisional concert party was put on this job when there was a battle and concerts were suspended. I am glad to be able to report that I only found lice once, and that was after being in a spell spent in a captured German dug-out. Then I had I begun to itch at once and the immense discomfort of it made me decide to keep free from them at all costs, which I succeeded in doing by changing my underclothes when a wash was impossible for any length of time.

It is amazing what you can get used to. Being without a bath every day was a calamity we quickly learned to cope with. This was the routine. First I shaved in the little mug of water, being careful to dip only the tip of my brush into it, and squeeze it out again into the mug. The tip of the sponge would then be made damp and the soap removed. Hands were then washed in it and the soap cleaned off with the sponge. If a little privacy were possible the water was not done with yet. Indeed one day late in 1917, after one such ceremonial ablution, I found myself gazing thoughtfully at the little mug filled now with much-used water. I was in a deep dugout 20 feet down in a captured bit of the Hindenburg line. No light penetrated the depths and there was only a spluttering candle on the rough packing case table to light our eight days' sojourn there, and as I gazed, I felt a little proud. I had learnt to adapt myself.

"I have been at this for two years and a half years," I meditated. "One can do a lot in that time. Many people may have been more usefully employed in England it, but I have learned to shave, wash, and have a bath – all in a teacup!"

Another problem we learned to cope with was dressing and undressing in the dark.

Boots, puttees and uniform had to be removed and I then slept in my underclothes. Collar studs and tie went into a pocket. My collar and the puttees were then neatly rolled up and put into the boots. My Sam Browne hung on the uniform. The most difficult items to put on, using touch only were the puttees. It took lots and lots of practice but in a remarkably short time I found I could appear without anything out of place.

As this dreary round of trench life continued we heard rumours of a move and one day they proved to be correct. We were told we were to be in Corps in Reserve, which had a pleasant sound and suggested it might mean being away from gunfire. When we heard it was also called a rest camp we knew it would not be good as there would be no billets and we would be living in tents.

In the fading light of a December day we marched out of Doulieu. To pay us a compliment the fifes and drums of our C.0.s former regiment, which was also in the neighbourhood, came with us and played us on the first mile or two of our way. As I trudged along a sense of great peace settled on me and I wished the shrill piping far away, as it turned a peaceful country walk into something much more martial. There were plenty of images I wanted to forget. The long drawn-out weeks spent in the mud. The incessant crack of bullets, the thudding of guns and the bursting of shells. Night working parties sleeping on the floor, or no sleep at all, and being unable to wash. Badly cooked scraps on rancid tin plates and all the other images I had stored in my mind and wanted to forget could all perhaps fade as we passed through the flat landscape in the gathering gloom of a winter's day. We were on our way to a rest camp and Christmas was coming.

Three days later we were still marching. By this time steady drizzle had set in and it looked like lasting for days. We were hungry too and were glad when the word came to halt. We had visions of food, rest and safety. It seemed odd to stop in such a spot, with rain falling steadily. We could surely have pushed on and got to the camp. And that is where I was wrong. We were already there. There was nothing to see because it consisted of nothing. It was just a reference point on an army map.

Eventually we were told there would be a special tent for the officers, who would be all together. That turned out to be a rough wooden hut. The sides were about four feet high. There was then a gap of two feet, to let air in, and above that there was a canvas roof. Being mid-winter we soon saw the disadvantages. The weather turned colder and a severe frost set in which froze anything liquid inside as well as us. For the first week or so it was often very wet and the men suffered great discomfort. They were living in waterlogged tents. Even when floorboards were provided they had to wade through mud to get to their tents. To cheer everyone us up we paraded at 6.30a.m for physical jerks. After a night in sub zero temperatures in a tent with no sides, to turn out, shaved and washed at that hour, on frozen ground, made us feel that we might as well be back in the trenches. The rest of the day was spent doing company drill to smarten us up.

While we were marooned at this idyllic spot, a certain amount of leave was granted but it was apt to be cancelled at the last moment. That was especially disappointing for the other ranks. More than once I saw them being told to go back to their tents after they had paraded with pack and rifle full of hope, because there was no room for them on the leave train. I hoped my own chance would come around Christmas time, so I would not have to spend Christmas in the dreary mud, but it actually came sooner that I had hoped.

We were several miles from the small station where the leave train picked people up. When my turn came, I was lent the company Commander's horse and accompanied by an orderly to who was instructed to bring it back. It was much better than the last time I had gone on leave in a private's uniform, carrying my own kit. We set out on a wild night with gale force winds and rain. It was also very dark and we could easily have lost our way. Eventually we reached the station where I had to wait for my train to arrive. The orderly set off for home with the horse and I moved into a temporary wooden shed. There were about 30 officers inside, in varying stages of fatigue. Some had been there for hours, lolling on benches in the dim light of an oil lamp. No one spoke. Our thoughts were already on the other side of the water. Having seen enough khaki of late I went out and wandered about but the train was so long coming that at last I went in and sat down too. Hours passed in silence but there was still no train. From time to time a rumbling was heard and drowsy officers would gather up their bundles and make for the station, but it always turned out to be a goods train of interminable length which clattered slowly through in complete darkness without stopping.

At about 4 a.m. we heard another rumble and saw a train emerging from the rain not far away. We scrambled along the line in pitch darkness and when the train came to a halt I managed to climb aboard. I threw myself into a carriage and collapsed in a heap. When the dawn of a December day began to appear in the sky I looked around. All the windows had been broken and a door, which I had found impossible to shut, had been partly wrenched off its hinges. It was all rather grim but, after the camp I had been in, it was luxury. It was also going in the right direction and that made up for everything.

It was a Sunday afternoon when I eventually arrived in London at Victoria Station. It always seemed to be a Sunday when anything special happened to me. As I was driving past Buckingham Palace, a military funeral came along, complete with a gun carriage and a Union Jack. How different from the unceremonious burials on the other side, with a few stray shots passing overhead. It seemed wonderful that anyone had time to do it this way but I knew that in a few days I would have to return.

I got back to my Battalion was just in time for Christmas Day. Fortunately it was mild and the sea of mud everywhere was less distressing than the cold. By now I had got used to getting up, washing and shaving in the crowded tent in which the officers slept. We had a lot to do before we could attend the Christmas communion service, complete with polished buttons and belt. The C.O. was there and a handful of officers and we knelt together on the earth in the gloom of a muggy December morning.

We slid from 1915 to 1916 imperceptibly. As the days gradually lengthened, our hope was that we should perhaps forgotten and left to our uneventful life. At least it was safe. Soon after the New Year had begun, a very young soldier turned up at the camp saying he had orders report. His equipment was complete and, everything seemed normal but we had not been advised of his arrival and no one knew anything about him. After due inquiry it turned out that he wasn't a soldier at all but, wanting to see the battle had somehow got hold of the necessary outfit and come to us on his own. As he was under 18 and was sent back to England.

One bright Sunday morning I was strolling along a street in a nearby town thinking that life was more peaceful than usual, when I noticed a sergeant who seemed to be following me. I stopped after a bit to let him go by. To my surprise he stopped as well and then very politely asked me if I would accompany him and tell his officer who I was. I wondered if I was about to be involved in another spy scare. As we moved off together I wondered how it would end. It transpired that a sharp lookout was being kept for someone who had simply been described as "looking suspicious." It appeared that the sergeant had felt the description fitted me. It was perhaps because the uniform I was wearing had turned an unusual shade of green after being liberally soaked on numerous occasions. Inquiries were made. My innocence was re-established and I was allowed to return to my unit, where I arrived just as orders came through to return to the trenches.

Ten days after returning to the slime and weariness of trench life I was told to attend a course at the divisional school at Estaires. The course itself was of the usual useless kind but it was not very exhausting and we regarded it as a welcome rest from a more strenuous life. Time passed quickly. For our mess we had a large comfortable room in an old farmhouse. At first selected soldiers did their worst with the food. To change that situation I was asked to become Mess President. I accepted the post and found I only needed to make one decision. I got the soldiers out of the kitchen and persuaded a French girl, who normally cooked for the farmhouse, to cook for us. The standard of cuisine improved dramatically!

One of our mornings was spent watching a display of trench mortars, which at that time were considered something of a novelty. There were some distinguished officers present. They watched the show from behind a haystack because the projectiles, after exploding, had a habit of boomeranging back to the place from which they had been fired. We were less wise and stood out in the open. After the explosion we all advanced solemnly to inspect a crater, which would have swallowed up a fair sized cottage. On the way back I helped a one-armed staff officer to climb out of a ditch. He was wearing an immaculate, well cut uniform which looked strangely out of place. Several weeks later I met a tailor who told me he had made it but that was the nearest I ever got to being on the staff.

It was shortly after this that we were issued with tin hats for the first time. The ones we were given seemed very inferior to the French ones we had seen already. They did not fit closely to the head and they wobbled about, unless the chin–straps were pulled very tight. We were sent on a route march to get used to them. It was a sunny morning and quite hot for the time of year, with the trees already showing signs of new shoots. Life seemed hopeful but the ill-fitting hats were rather a setback with their constant reminder of war. When we arrived back in the billet I took my hat off and flung it as hard as I could into a wall. My show of brute force merely produced a tiny dent. If I had then been able to look forward eighteen months, I would have seen myself wearing the same hat when a heavy piece of shell landed on top, severely denting the helmet and my skull. That incident ended my career in the front line. Without the hat, it might have ended my life.

We knew that we would soon be returning to the trenches. While we waited for our orders to arrive we enjoyed the area we were in as much as we could. There was much not much to see but I managed to find a large and rather seedy hotel, where it was still possible to order dinner. The dining room had large floor to ceiling mirrors spotted with fly marks all round the room. The floor was bare and there were artificial flowers on the tables and a strong smell of drains. The food was poor but going there made a change and one could be pretty sure of being alone. In the hotel bar there was a dilapidated sofa in a window and a barmaid who looked rather dilapidated too. I went in to look round and remember being struck by her appearance, which I thought, was unusually repulsive. When I sat on the sofa she joined me there and started to make conversation. I explained that I was going to get a battery for my electric torch. She disappeared and returned with one of her own, which she gave to me. I offered to pay but she refused to consider it, which made me feel I had been rather harsh in the judgment I had made.

Opposite the hotel there was a little shop where such things as scent and handkerchiefs were still being sold. The two ladies who presided were well connected and one of our Company Commanders was known to be a friend. On the strength of that, I was once allowed into the back parlour. It proved to be so distressingly refined that I was glad to escape.

As spring turned to summer we prepared to leave the quiet countryside where the trees were bursting into leaf, we returned to the trenches where we knew we would face a very different scene. We would once more be surrounded by dirt and destruction and have to deal with injuries and death. Perhaps that was why the picture of a beautiful little wood we had passed through remained in my mind. I could not forget the dark brown trees with their delicate green leaves, standing against a warm blue sky.

We moved on and, after a long march, went into the trenches at Hebuterne – a ruined village we were to know a good deal better before we had done with it. It was quiet when we arrived. We were told that was because the French, who had held the trenches before us, did not believe in rousing the enemy unless it was for a battle. We were told that it was quite the done thing to sit on the parapet and read a newspaper. I always thought that, if that was really the French method, it was a far better than perpetually nagging the people on the other side, who sooner or later retaliated inflicting casualties for which there would be nothing to show. That was the British method. We were continually being told, especially in Comic Cuts - the name we gave to the official magazine on trench warfare, to cultivate the offensive spirit and never to leave the enemy alone. That was no doubt all right for those who gave the advice. They lived in comparative comfort miles behind the line.

Life was so quiet when we first arrived that we had time to look around. We found a little cottage, with its roof still intact on the edge of the trenches. The trenches in this sector were very different from those in Flanders, where they had been close together and waterlogged in flat low-lying country. Here in Artois – an area full of pleasant undulations - they were as far apart as seven hundred yards and you could almost have picnicked in No Man's Land. The trenches were deep and protected by many rows of barbed wire. If a trench could be pretty, you would expect to find it here. Near the safe end there were some which had been in existence long enough to grow ferns. When we saw them first, the young tendrils of plants were covering the sides with their fresh spring green. But this policy of live and let live was soon to end and our (56th) Divisional Artillery pounded away pretty regularly waking up the Germans. Air raids and counter-raids began to be the fashion. Indeed we were warming up for the second great effort after Loos, when the new British Armies would be thrown into the fray. We were actually nearer to it than the usual rumours of a push, which had already reached us, had led us to believe.

We were now preparing for the battle of the Somme. During our first weeks in our new trenches we had to get to know the ground and make preparations for it. Numerous patrols took place by day and night and we had to take part in them and roam about in No Man's Land. On one occasion I was sent out to examine the German wire to see if our bombardment had broken it up enough for an attack to get through. I was told I must take a man with me. Half way across No Man's Land I decided it would be safer to go on alone, because a second person makes quite twice as much noise. After my companion and I had travelled quite a long way on our hands and knees, I told him to stop and went on alone.

As I got nearer the German wire I lay down and squirmed forward through the grass, stopping at intervals to listen. It was not pitch dark. There was as much light as a midsummer night gives when the stars are all out. Long grass under those conditions, moving in the breeze, is apt to take on other forms and I stopped more than once thinking I saw someone stalking me but in the dead silence. After a while I concluded it was only imagination and moved on again. By the time I got across, the moon was up and I could see where the ground fell away for a few yards in front of the German wire. There was no grass there. It had been cleared away to give no cover at all to anyone approaching. The earth was bare and flat. I felt that it would be stupid to venture into this cleared space and, as I could see the wire quite clearly from where I was in the bright light of the moon, I thought I had done enough. The wire had not been damaged at all. I wormed my way back, and eventually found the man I had left behind when I was half way across. Together we made our way back to our trench.

After the strategic retreat of the Germans in the following year, which left a zone of devastated land in our possession including Gommecourt, I was curious enough to go back and explore the part of the line I had set out to examine that night. Just behind the wire I found some deep dug outs where many men could have remained in security under a heavy bombardment. That was interesting because the bombardment, which generally preceded a raid, would have left them unharmed and ready to deal with any raiders who arrived when it stopped. I found that particularly interesting as I had been put down for that raid if it had come off. We continued to hear rumours that a big push was coming and wondered what part we would be expected to play. We were told that before it took place we would be involved in a preparatory exploit. The distance between our trenches and those opposite had evidently seized the imagination of those in command. They apparently thought that, when the attack was made, too many casualties might be suffered by troops as they advanced for them to achieve their objectives. To reduce the risks, they had devised a plan. One night when it was dark our whole brigade would file out of the trenches we were in. We would then to be held temporarily by other units while we dug a new trench in No Man's Land, as close as possible to the German lines. To me the plan seemed so silly that I found it hard to believe it was even being proposed. Any doubts I had on that score were quickly dispelled when I was told that I would be in charge of the company in place of the usual Company Commander who was to be left out. The part our battalion would be responsible for would be a mile long and it would be dug in the short mid-summer night, 300 yards in advance of our old front line - under the very nose of the Germans.

We practiced in daylight far behind the line. All we then had to do was to repeat everything in the dark, where even a little sound would give us away and perhaps result in the loss of many lives. Strict instructions about not making any noise had been drilled into everyone and even smoking was stopped for some days in case anyone should cough. That was crucial, as any alarm would have been fatal to us all.

First there was a check by our patrols to give warning of any German patrols which might be prowling about. If any were met they were to be attacked with bayonets and killed. No one was to be allowed to escape. No shots must be fired. Once the patrols were in position a party armed with a tape went out and marked the site of the new trench. Then the whole brigade, moving by battalion and by companies, marched out through the old trench at various points in single file. They proceeded as far as the tape where they turned left and stopped each man at arm's length from the next. He had to touch him on the shoulder when he stopped. The interval between him and his neighbour represented his job of work, which he had to do with all speed and without making any noise. For that he had to carry a pick and shovel as well as his rifle, and they must not to be allowed to joggle against each other.

The first night I expected to hear the rattle of machine-guns at any moment, as we often did in that part of the line, but there was hardly a sound. Things were unnaturally quiet. Perhaps we had been spotted and the Germans were waiting for us to get a little nearer. We worked on with the utmost speed in the fleeting darkness of a summer night. After an hour or two a trench had been dug. The earth we had dug out was enough to give us cover from rifle fire and that was something. As it started to get light at around 2 a.m. we prepared to move off. The men who had come in first, and were therefore farthest along the trench, moved first and then turned right to get back to the our trench. They had to return before our patrols were withdrawn. Only then could our first night's work be considered to be done.

The task we had to complete the following day was not so simple. None of us thought it would be. The Germans were now aware of our plan, though they probably did not think we would be stupid enough to go on with for a second night. We repeated the operation and it was when we had got into position that the fun began. A heavy, accurate and continuous bombardment with field guns was kept up and there was a quite incessant and very accurate machine gun fire aimed exactly at the site of the new trench. The machine-gun fire was just a little too late. By the time it started we could crouch down in our partly dug trench. Each spade full we dug up made our position it safer, but it was very exhausting working in such conditions and there were some casualties. Quite early on, one of the men on patrol was killed because he knelt up to look around and caught a burst of machine-gun fire. I went along the line to see how things were going and found myself next to one of my platoon. He was sheltering as well as he could behind a little bank of earth he had thrown up, which was being sprayed by continuous machine-gun fire at short range. The loud and threatening splutter was interspersed with the ear-splitting bursts of salvoes of whizz-bangs overhead, which lit up clouds of acrid smoke with a red glare. The outlook was not promising, as he was well aware. He was weeping and saying his prayers. He was a nice lad with a fresh complexion and a very pleasant manner. He seemed to be rather young for his age. He survived the night but I was sorry when he was killed later on.

Getting out was the difficult thing this second night. The front men filed into the communication trench, which lead to the old front line. They moved very slowly and seemed to have forgotten those who were following them were still out in the open; and it was getting lighter every minute.

As I had to be the last man out I foresaw the moment when I would be left in No Man's Land in daylight, so I got out on the top and ran along, cursing the men who were being so slow. It was not a pleasant place. Because our departure had been spotted, whizz-bangs continually burst overhead and their acrid fumes filled my mouth with a sulphurous taste. We did get out at last, and by then it was quite light. I made sure everyone had got back and then. reported to our C.O., who had been watching from the old trench. He was waiting there with the Adjutant who gave a little start when he saw me. He said he was greatly relieved because, from what he had heard, he thought we might not get back. It could so easily have been otherwise.

We trickled back individually and in little groups to our billets at Sovastre, glad to be alive. It was still before sunrise. I passed little parties without being able to see more than shadowy forms. One group I overtook were talking loudly and seemed to be in especially good spirits. As I was overtaking them I heard my name being mentioned.

"Poor old Burder. 'E got killed," they said and then added. "E was on the top when the shellin' was awful. E never did care nowt wot E did!" I was not quite sure what they meant by that! A little later, when I hobbled past them with a blistered foot, they suddenly became silent.

Perhaps the fatigue of that exploit accounted for my spending the next four days in bed with fever. The periodical recurrence of malaria, which reminded me that it was still latent. During the next month, raids took place to find out what German units were opposite. Meanwhile we had to live in the trench we had dug. It was, of course, very rough. A mere ditch when compared with an old established trench, with its fire step, traverses and plenty of barbed wire. Being so near the German line they never left us alone and we heard the almost constant noise of machine-gun fire. That was trying enough when the weather was fine. Towards the end of June it started to deteriorate as we had noticed it often did before a proposed attack. By the end of the month we had to put up with almost continuous rain and the area we are in was becoming a swamp.

To give us a distraction, one afternoon we received a message telling us that a very heavy gun (with a shell said to be 15 inches) was going to be fired on the German trenches. We were instructed to keep our heads down The announcement caused us great concern because we felt that, as likely as not, the shell would fall in our own trench and not where it was intended to go. We also wanted to be impressed by the great explosion if it didn't. At that point the elements decided to take a hand. While we were waiting a terrific thunderstorm burst upon us, with the loudest kind of thunderclaps and rain, which flooded us up to the knees. That rather eclipsed efforts made be any earthly artillery. We were not quite sure whether we noticed the big shell's arrival, though there was a discreet 'phut' at one time, which we all declared must have been it.

After some days of existence in this new trench a few of us were told that we would be sent back to a village to await the return of the battalion and get some rest. On the last night before I left, things seemed to get very mixed up. There had been a lot of casualties from rifle fire, especially at one end of the trench where it had been beaten down by gunfire. The Company H.Q, which consisted of a sheet of corrugated iron and a few sandbags, had been buried. Amongst the ruins was a box of provisions that I had brought back from leave. They were from Fortnum and Mason[9] and included a tinned duck in aspic! We were all feeling very much the worse for wear in our waterlogged and exposed position. As it was impossible to bring up food by day, it had been decided to make a special effort to send up supplies of hot soup by night. It was supplied in large metal pots (which were known as known as Dixie's). The Dixie's were slung on poles and the bearers had to make their way in the darkness through the morass of liquid mud which filled the trench. When they found it impossible to move at all, they got out on the top. There they ran into a wiring party which I was with. In the pitch darkness and pouring rain we were attempting to put up barbed wire between our new trench and the Germans. So there we all were, in a hopeless tangle! It would be hard to imagine greater confusion. I wondered what would happen if the Germans suddenly decided to turn their machine-guns on us, as they often did throughout the night.

Suddenly a Verey light[10] went up. As it slowly descended our inmost thoughts seemed to be lighted up but we were well trained. We remained motionless and much to my surprise, nothing happened. Silence still reigned. Our luck was in.

When we first took up our position in this new trench, on June 21st, it had been arranged that our battalion would hold it until the night before the attack. Before that time arrived, half of the men had become casualties. The rest were so helpless from exhaustion that it was thought best to relieve them earlier, so I did not have long to wait until they joined me. It was on the night of June 24th that I left the front line, after the mix up of the wiring party and the soup carriers. It was very dark indeed as at last I got on to the road and set off to trudge the few miles to St. Amand, where I intended to try to get a billet and sleep for the rest of the night. It was quiet, apart from occasional shelling. Flashes of gunfire lit up the lowering clouds and skewed the jagged outline of ruined buildings, as I made my way from the city of destruction in a tempest of wind and rain.

9   Then and now a fashionable London Department store.
10   A coloured flare fired by a special pistol named after Edward Verey (1852-1910).

After an hour or two's blissful walk, I reached St. Amand, where there was no sign of life whatever. The chance of finding a billet seemed remote. I was, however, determined not to throw away my chance of a night's sleep and eventually got into a house where I had been billeted before. I lay down on a stone floor of an empty room and, in the quiet solitude, gratefully fell asleep. The next morning I got up in my own time and enjoyed the luxury of loitering down the Village Street. No one was about and it was hard to believe it was the same place where, a few days before, every barn and billet had been crammed to overflowing. Constant relays of tired and anxious infantry battalions had trudged their way through on their way to the great Somme battle. I wandered into the village church and sat down. It was empty and quiet and I felt very much alone. I had nothing to do so I went outside and started to look around. I met a soldier who told me that there was a battery of heavy howitzers in the village, but they had stopped firing because they had run out of ammunition. I was beginning to get bored when I remembered that the company mess box had been mislaid. It had last been seen at battalion HQ at Hebuterne. I knew that if it was lost we would have no tin plates or knives and forks, and that would mean trouble for the Mess President. As I held that post, I decided to fill in time by looking for it - but 1 wasn't going to walk. I managed to find a bicycle and off I went. It was pretty quiet going up to Hebuterne, even in daylight, but I wasted no time in finding what had once been our battalion H.Q. It was in ruins and empty, but under a pile of broken slates there was our mess box! I picked it up and cycled back without mishap.

It was about now that a captive balloon was shot down near my village. Its occupant was killed. I later discovered that the man who had died was the singer I had seen on stage singing "Gilbert the Filbert", when I arrived in London to sign up in 1914. Shortly after that incident the company returned to billets, having been reduced by casualties and fatigue to a more or less helpless condition. I visited the officers when I thought they would have recovered a little. I found them at mid-day, still lying in rows on the floor of a hut, totally exhausted. In the afternoon there was a roll call. Roll calls, when there had been a number of casualties, were not very bright. The names were read out and when there was no response a name was repeated. After a. pause someone would say in a low voice "wounded" or "blown up" or perhaps nothing would be said.

Our period of rest did not to last for long and on July 1st, soon after the great push had begun, they were back on their way to Sovastre, with the idea of following up the advance. Unfortunately no advance wad made. At zero hour on July 1st the two divisions opposite Gommecourt were supposed to attack. We moved forwards but something went wrong with the division on our left. They did not advance at all and remained in their trenches. The result of that was that, having no support on one side, our division was quickly dislodged after suffering casualties, which practically wiped out some battalions. By nightfall the same day the position was "As you were". Rows of men had been mown down by machine gun fire in No Man's Land. So this continuing action, which was subsidiary to the main Somme battle, had come to nothing so far as any gain of ground was concerned. There was nothing to show for it but desperately heavy casualties.

That same night we were ordered to take over our old trench - the one that we had dug in the dark - but we found it no longer existed. It had been bombarded until it was flat. We moved into some other trenches, which we found nearby. When the battle died down there was a truce for collecting the wounded and burying the dead. Germans mingled with our men in No Man's Land trying to identify their own casualties. One of our chaplains was foremost in this work and distinguished himself by wearing a white surplice, which left no one in any doubt as to what he was. This went on for some time, by mutual consent. It was brought to an abrupt end by a shell from one of our guns. It had probably been fired by someone who did not know of (or had forgotten) about the truce.

On July 8th we went back to some trenches near our old ones at Hebuterne. They had about two feet of liquid mud in them. At our first stand-to I found myself next to one of our officers who had been educated at Winchester and Oxford, where he was a classics scholar. There was a pretty sunrise that morning, with fleecy clouds and a pale blue sky. It seemed a pleasant contrast to the squalor of the last few weeks and the mud we were standing in. I thought it might be was a good time to trot out a line of Homer about the "rosy fingered dawn", which he seemed to appreciate. Not many of our officers suffered from the handicap of a classical education and I think he felt a little refreshed to hear a few Greek words in such unexpected surroundings.

Later In the day the sun grew hotter and things dried up a bit but then flies became a nuisance. They were much worse than usual. I wondered why until I found the roof of our Company H.Q. was reinforced with old sandbags and earth, in which someone had buried remains. As we ate our food in the presence of thriving bluebottles; I thought the situation needed to be explored a little more and I decided to have a look round as soon as it was dark. I discovered that there were some bodies directly on top of the trench in which we had been sitting. Just out of sight there was a stretcher on which the kilted body of an officer from a Scottish regiment was lying. He seemed to be asleep, but no doubt the stretcher bearers had been forced to dump him on finding he was dead and gone on to do something more pressing.

The routine in these trenches was now fairly normal again. It consisted of the usual turns of duty and patrols, but we could see and hear frequent flares-up farther along the front, especially at night. That told us that the main Somme battle was still going on. The bit of No Man's Land outside our trench had in it what was known as a "sugar factory". It consisted of a few broken walls, some rusty ironwork and a few water tanks. It did not amount to much but at night it was quite a nervy business creeping up to it, and wondering whether it was empty or not. I went there one night with my Company Commander. He was a rather dashing sort, who had come from Australia with a mounted unit. Dismounted, amphibious life in Flanders mud did not appeal to him at all. Just as we arrived at the sugar factory, after much cautious crawling, some misguided person sent up a rocket, which was the signal for every gun in France and Belgium to go off. My Company Commander flopped down, but when a Verey light[11] went up he found he was almost on the top of someone else, who seemed to be resting on his side.

"Who's that?" he whispered hoarsely.

"A dead man," I replied. "I saw him here the other night."

The spasm of shelling eventually died down and we managed to get back without mishap.

When we were in billets, working parties were rather a nuisance because they took

11   Flares from a Verey pistol should ignite and rise to an altitude of 300 feet without breaking up and burn brightly for about 9 seconds..

us back to the trenches, which we were trying to forget and they were often conducted under fire. There was one working party that I particularly recall. We were sent to dig a trench so near the German lines that I was almost sure our presence would be noticed. In their wisdom, those responsible for this farce had detailed men who had never been in a trench before. They had just arrived from England. When we arrived at our place of work, it occurred to me that perhaps they had not loaded their rifles, as they were so new to it all. I had to halt them in the communication trench to allow them to do so. After reminding them of the importance of working as quietly as possible, we crept up to the appointed spot. Having put them on the job with a sergeant and an officer, I stood at one end of the line and hoped for the best. Unfortunately we were heard and a shower of rifle grenades came over. For people with no experience that was a bit scary in the dark, and off they went. Some were hard to remark with bated breath as they fled, "The Germans are coming!" I went back to the place where they had been digging and only found one man - a sergeant - still there. He was sitting on a little mound of earth as if nothing had happened and he asked me where they had gone.

"Boulogne" I said.

That particular sergeant, who probably had more chances of being killed than anyone else in the battalion, went right through the war without a scratch. He was a very quiet man with a red, rather boyish face and a smile when it was wanted. I was told he had taught a bible class in a local chapel when he was at home. He deserved the decorations he eventually got. When they found that nothing happened the working party came to a halt. They were collected and sent home with an officer and the sergeant.

I knew it would soon be daylight and felt I had done enough of them for the time being, so I moved on alone in my own time. As I passed through the ruined village of Foncqvilliers, a flare-up took place a little farther down the line. For some reason it seemed to wake up the people in the trenches opposite, and they began to sweep the road I was on with distant machine-gun fire. As I was passing a small shelter I looked in, intending to wait until things had quieted down. There I found a solitary officer from the Cheshire Regiment. I have always remembered him because of he looked so young. He had fair hair and astonishingly blue eyes. He was very quiet and we talked about

The ruined village of Foncqvilliers

things in general for a bit. By then it was nearly daybreak, so I went on to my billet a few miles away. A few days later I asked someone about my acquaintance with the blue eyes. I was told that he had been killed earlier that day.

Going up to those trenches on the other side of Foncqvilliers (which was usually known as Funk villas) wasn't an easy job. More than once we were either spotted or came in for a chance salvo or two. My horse-riding Company Commander rode on ahead as usual, dashing back at intervals to see if we were still there. He went into the village and waved to me to bring on the company after him. I thought I knew a better way and turned to the right, under cover of a wood, which gave some protection. It was as well I did because in a few minutes he came cantering back, in a great stew saying, he had run into a lot of shelling at the point where we would have been if I had not acted on my own judgment.

On another occasion we ran into shelling when we were two or three miles from the trenches. It was totally unexpected as we were passing through a village, which had never been shelled before. Without any warning, out of the blue, came a shower of heavy shells, which fell on the road and the buildings we were passing. In less than a minute, the bright summer sun was lost in a fog of smoke from bursting shells and dust from collapsing buildings. I was crouching under a wall, hoping it wouldn't fall on me, when a wounded horse, of the heavy kind that did not generally run, shot past me into the fog of dust and smoke. We were being shelled from a captive balloon - a tiny speck so far away we had not thought it was worth noting.

Perhaps that shelling had something to do with a change of plans. For a time we were billeted in Foncqvilliers itself, when we were not in the trenches in front of it. It was a change no one welcomed. Foncqvilliers had long ago been destroyed and nothing was left but jagged walls, including those of the church at one end of the street. All that remained was a pile of stones and a few remnants of walls. On one, which was pockmarked with the fragments of shells, a life-sized crucifix still remained. It had not been touched.

After life in the trenches it was a relief to be billeted in the cellar of what had once been a stone house. It stood on the corner of a road which was often shelled. At night there were no turns of duty, but even that ointment was not without its fly for we had just acquired a new officer whose capacity for snoring rivalled the bombardments. His throat and nose must have been made of brass and no sooner were we all asleep than the cellar began to tremble with his trumpetings. Being generally the first to awake I threw my boots at him, but like other snorers he refused to believe he had made any noise and was rather angry so that it generally took a little time to soothe him down. He then fell asleep quickly and it all began again.

Sometimes in the afternoon I went across the road to lie down in what had once been the garden of a rather nice house and enjoy the luxury of being alone. It was pleasant to lie in the sunshine amongst the tall weeds but I could not quite banish the thought of the shellings we often got, one of which might come while I was here. One night, to our surprise we found the village alive with silent forms, dark-skinned and bare of foot. They were a party of Bengal Lancers (29th) who were carrying gas cylinders up to the trenches to be let off when the wind was be favourable. It seemed odd to see them flitting about silently in the darkness. It was about this time that a comic device was being issued for dispersing gas in trenches. It was known as the Ayrton fan. It consisted of a cane or stick with a flap about one foot square at the end. The idea was that soldiers (presumably wearing gas masks) would go down on their hands and knees and flap the bottom of their trench where the gas being heavier than air would tend to collect. The current fable was that some old lady had invented them and sold the idea to the war office for four thousand pounds. The troops got a laugh out of them but they were soon forgotten and put aside. The gas attack was supposed to be very secret and some weeks earlier, when we had been digging holes in the trenches for the cylinders we had been told that they were for drainage.

We had gone to the trenches at Fonequevilliers on July 22nd. The following day, which was Sunday, I was instructed to take out a patrol with another officer. We were to start as soon as the light began to fail. The idea was that we would get out and back before any patrols from the opposite side had thought it worthwhile to start. As the other officer had only just arrived I thought he would not be much use and I left him behind and started off with a small party of men.

In front of our trenches there was an immense amount of barbed wire and it took a while to get through as we had to make as little noise as possible. We had got through about ten yards and full moon was shining nicely when I thought I heard move. I told the men to lie down with their rifles, aimed in the appropriate direction, and waited. I had not been mistaken for a band of shadowy figures soon appeared and I heard an excited order being given, in which I recognized the word "Hier." The officer had no doubt had seen us and was telling them where to throw their bombs or shoot. I kept quiet until I thought they were a bit nearer and then said "Fire". At the same time I fired my revolver. That was followed by complete silence and I was beginning to wonder what had happened. There was not much we could do because we had several yards of barbed wire in front and behind us. If we moved forward, lit up by the brilliant moon, we would be a helpless target for any of the German patrols that might be waiting for us.

The C.O. told me later that he thought we were right to come back. It was a feeble affair but it would have been a lot feebler if they had shot at us first.

Whilst doing duty in the Foncqvilliers trenches my front line company headquarters was at the side of the road, just where it joined the trenches at right angles. Its exact position was clear to anyone who wanted to bombard it. It was also above ground and, as usual, it consisted of nothing more than a little corrugated iron on a few wooden supports with some earth and sandbags on top. A few yards away, in the trench itself, three Corporals lived. Their overhead cover consisted of some heavy beams, which must have come out of a ruined house and I remarked on the strength of them as I went by. They were great friends and fed together. One of them had been a professional cyclist. At that time it was fashionable for the Germans to bombard us with their big trench mortars, after lengthy quiet intervals. We called them "Jam Jars" because that was what they looked like. If by any chance your trained ear had detected their discharge, you could watch them in the air. They were insidious things because the noise they made when they were fired was so slight it was rather like a suppressed cough. Often the first thing you knew was a shattering explosion when they arrived. Towards the end of their journey a fluttering sound could be heard, like the beating of a bird's wings. If you heard that you knew it would explode, very near and very soon.

On a very quiet morning, when the three corporals and another man were just finishing breakfast in their shelter with the heavy beams overhead, a "Jam Jar" landed directly on top. It broke the heavy beams as if they had been matches. Hearing the noise I hurried along the trench to see what had happened. I found there was nothing left apart from a few fragments of limbs and a smell like a butcher's shop. On the top of the trench was a bare chocolate-coloured foot, standing by itself. I was told it had belonged to a young boy who had been having breakfast with the corporals.

It was about this time that one of our officers was killed. He was sitting, with several others, miles behind the line in his billet, eating a meal. A shell arrived and killed him on the spot without touching any of the others. We thought him rather well off to get away from the usual round of trench life.

One afternoon we were congratulating ourselves on having completed another tour and were all dressed up and waiting for our relief. The relief was behind time and we began to grumble about it, when I heard an ominous fluttering. I looked up in the brilliant afternoon sunshine to see if I could detect anything. Almost at once, a rending crash told me that a "jam jar" had fallen on part of our trench. The Germans had no doubt spotted our relief. Word was passed along that a man was missing and a search was made. Everyone in the trench seemed to be all right, but just behind it a flimsy shelter, made of the usual corrugated iron and a few sandbags, had been completely destroyed. Some hurried digging brought to light the missing man who had been buried alive. He was dragged into the sunlight but his face purple and he had clearly been suffocated. It cast a gloom over our departure on that bright sunny day. If we had been quicker in discovering the place where he was buried and if the relief had not been late...

Boredom with our particular part of the line was becoming a problem, as it always did after a time. We seemed to be so often under fire. The area where we were billeted was also very dreary, though we realised that the main Somme area to the south, where so many thousands were being killed in fruitless attacks, was far worse. During the day we heard the tremendous bombardments and at night they lit up the sky. We expected that the day would come when we would join in. On August 4th rumours of a move came to an end with a definite order to go by stages to this "blood bath" as the Germans called it. We marched for twelve miles and then stopped at Bouquemacson. My latent malaria once more reared its head and I found myself sweating with a high fever. The only thing I could do was to lie down in the billet and take quinine.

While I was resting I was told I had been detailed to go to Le Touquet, where there was a Lewis Gun school. There I would learn all about that weapon and qualify to be the battalion Lewis gun officer. I thought I might regret it if I let the opportunity go by, and as I had been careful not to go sick officially, I was able to get up and go. It was an interminable journey by trains that crawled along single lines with lengthy waits. After a long time I got as far as St. Pol. By then I felt far from well. I had to wait several hours for a connection so I went into a field and lay down under a hedge. It was about all I could do. Eventually I arrived in the late evening at Etaples and was driven out to the camp at Le Touquet. We passed through some very pretty woods, which I should have liked better if I had not felt so ill.

When I arrived I was not, of course, expected. There was nowhere to sleep until eventually they found a tent, which meant I would be sleeping under cover but lying on the ground. As I knew the only hope of getting rid of my temperature was to lie down and sweat with lots of quinine, I was not overjoyed with that arrangement. The next morning a hoped for improvement had not come so there was nothing for it but to go sick. That annoyed me, because hitherto I had not gone sick officially once since the war began and had always managed to recover after taking quinine and resting in billets. I was sent to the Liverpool Merchants' Hospital at Etaples. It seemed to me to be a well-managed place. Everyone was so efficient and anxious to help that I felt quite ashamed to be there with so little the matter with me. My fever vanished at once and I felt I could not decently stay any longer. They politely told me not to hurry away but stay and rest but I think the sight of seriously wounded people settled it for me. I felt they had a right to be there. After witnessing a rather painful dressing being applied to a patient in the bed opposite mine, I decided it would be rather humbug to remain.

The hours I spent learning about the Lewis Gun were not very long. After trench life, it was a pleasant change to sit round a table, in the summer sunshine and fresh air, while someone told us about what he thought we needed to know. I have no aptitude for machinery and always prefer to see other people fiddling about with it, but I learnt to strip the gun fairly quickly and what the various parts were for. I assumed an earnest look as often as possible, so that my report at the end of the course was really quite good. When we were not at work I strolled round in Etaples and Le Touquet. At that time Le Touquet was an interesting contrast to English seaside places, not only because it lacked a pier, automatic machines and a military band playing Gilbert and Sullivan, but because it was completely empty. Without exception the smart villas on the sea front were closed or had their windows boarded up. Although it was August, when normally the sea front and shore would be full of children and people on holiday people they were both deserted. There was no one on the shore at all and, on the mile or two of spacious front, only one person to be seen - a British soldier in hospital blue. I compared this scene of desolation with that of a seaside place in England, where greater crowds than ever thronged the promenades, with more money to spend than they had ever had before. I wondered what that all meant but I suppose it is one thing to have a war in someone else's country and quite another to have one in your own.

At the end of my course, I expected to be sent back to my battalion, but to my surprise, I was told I must report at number 41 Infantry Base Depot at the big camp at Etaples. The reason given was that as I had been in hospital so I could not return directly to my unit. A little more respite was welcome enough, but I rather felt that I was getting something I was not entitled to. All camps are dreary but there was a special dreariness about the camp at Etaples. The officer in charge of the part I was in seemed very sad, and I wondered why he didn't try to find a more active job. To give me something to do, one day he told me to censor some letters - a task I had been asked to do for quite a long time. Drafts of new troops had come to Etaples and the letters I checked had been written to fill up time. I didn't read any as a rule, because I knew there could be nothing in them that mattered, but I opened one out of idleness and read a most blood-curdling account of shells bursting overhead. It had been written by someone who wanted to impress his friends at home. He had arrived in France a few hours before. At that time no shells had fallen within miles of Etaples and we were out of earshot of bombardments of any kind. Those who censored our company letters at the front used to tell me of the passionate letters one platoon sergeant wrote to a lady friend. She was not his wife. He was a prim and pretentious elementary schoolmaster and quite useless as a soldier. We felt he was probably trying to make us think he was a bit of a devil in normal life.

The camp at Etaples was generally unpopular because life there was boring and there was too much drill. On one occasion I had to march a thousand men down to the area where drills took place. I had been told there was a feeling of discontent amongst the men but I saw nothing of it. I also marched a large party of Australians to a train on their way to the front. They seemed specially good-humoured and swung down the hill singing "Pack up your troubles in your old kit bag" in a way that cheered everybody up.

I was never very good at being bored and the little jobs I was given to do seemed to become more futile as the days went by. I had a brighter moment when one of our officers turned up at the camp unexpectedly and told me what had been happening elsewhere. They had had rather a bad time at Leuze Wood (known of course as lousy wood). There had been many casualties, with the usual lack of result, and some of the officers I had known well had been killed. That made me feel even more unhappy with the work I was doing and I decided to write to the Adjutant and explain that I was now quite well but very bored and wanted to rejoin the battalion.

I eventually left Etaples on September 24th. By mid-day on the 25th my journey by train and lorry had landed me at the village of Meaulte, which was on the edge of the Somme battlefield. Meaulte bore the usual traces of a place near the line when a battle was going on. It was ankle deep in dust and the few shabby buildings left looked tired with the unusual activity thrust upon the place.

This was my first view of the main Somme battlefield, by now nearly three months in the making, which meant that there were several miles of black shell-pitted waste to traverse before finding the place where our battalion was. The whole area was devoid of vegetation apart from a few blasted tree trunks. The bleak landscape seemed to swallow up battalions as if they were nothing. Shell holes, still acrid and discoloured with fumes, and parties of men marching either to or from the front, were all there was to see. I was surprised how quickly I managed to find my battalion in such a wilderness. I reported to the C.O. who gave me a pleasant welcome as he always did and almost in the same breath added:

"We are attacking Combles at midnight and I want you to take command of "D" company. You will go down the main street and you will have two ranks to work with. The French are cooperating. They will attack on our right."

I thought it was all rather sudden and began to wonder if I had not been in rather a hurry to quit the camp at Etaples. By then it was early in the afternoon, so I had a little time to pick up the threads of what had been happening. A fortnight earlier the battalion had lost heavily in an attack near Leuze Wood. The attack had been a muddle. The order had come to take a German trench within bombing distance. A scramble across the intervening space under machine gun fire produced many casualties. While it was going on, another message came in counter ordering the attack, because it was thought to be impossible. It was on that day that tanks were used for the first time. One was put out of action quite near us, at a trench known as the "quadrilateral." We were to pass it quite often in the next few days. Although there was nothing to show for it, the casualties for those five days had not been light. Four hundred and thirty eight people had died, including seventeen officers. As a result of that debacle, the battalion I was about to go into battle with consisted largely of drafts of men who had been hurriedly sent up to replace those who had been lost.

We were getting ready for a start on our Combles jaunt when news came that the French were not ready. A little later another message arrived telling us that the Germans had evacuated the town so that we only had to occupy it next morning. That was good news for me. When I inspected the sunken road down which I would have had to lead the troops at midnight, I realised just how good it was. On top of high banks on both sides of the road, there were rows of bombs methodically laid out ready for use. The road itself, which was already strewn with dead bodies, had been made more impassable with barbed wire entanglements.

About mid-day we arrived at a dip in the ground known as "Happy Valley" where we ate what we had with us. While we were halted our C.O. sent me a message telling me to try and find the bodies of some of the men who had been killed on the 15th and to bury them if possible. He mentioned one by name, who had been an officer in my own company. I took a sergeant and another man with spades and went off. After a while we managed to find them. They lay together as they had fallen and I had no difficulty in recognizing the officer of my company who had been mentioned by the C.O. Ten days had passed since they had been killed and the hot sun had accelerated normal decomposition. His hat was partly off and his head was full of white maggots.

 We did what needed to be done and completed our labours by saying the Lord's Prayer.

When we moved up to our position in Combles we passed Leuze Wood, the scene of so much desperate fighting, and then turned sharply to the right where the sunken road led down to the little town. We passed many dead men, one of whom I remember, partly because he was dressed in a kilt and partly because he was kneeling on one knee with his rifle still in his two hands as if he had been killed in the act of advancing. Only the bayonet was lowered to the ground.

We eventually turned to the right and entered the sunken road, which would have been the scene of our midnight attack if the Germans had not retired. There the number of dead bodies increased and for some reason their faces were almost black so that we had to look twice to see if they were English. We moved cautiously forward and descended a hill. Just before we reached the bottom, we climbed up the steep side of the road to reach the trenches, which we were told were to be our next abode. They were new and appeared to have been completed in a hurry but they gave some shelter. They also commanded a very good view of the country in front, so that we felt we knew where we were to some extent and were not so liable to a surprise attack.

When we arrived the trench was not quite empty. A party of signallers still remained. They had made the trench as comfortable as possible by covering the top with a rough kind of roof which to some extent kept out the rain. Having taken trouble to make themselves as comfortable as possible in the circumstances, they were not overjoyed to see us and seemed reluctant to go. My sergeant major – who was a London policeman in normal life – was all for moving them on at speed, which was right enough. I sometimes felt that he was a little fussy and told him to let them take their time. I watched them from a few yards up the trench as they were got ready. They seemed a pleasant little party, laughing and talking because they realised they were going back. Just as they were about to leave, a shell came over and landed on the top of their shelter, completely wrecking it and killing one of them. They quickly buried his mutilated body and put up an improvised cross; made of two sticks tied together with string with his name written on it in indelible pencil. The purple scrawl was still shiny because they had spat on the pencil to make it write better. And then they were gone. I watched it all happen from a few yards further along the trench, where I had been waiting in silence until they were ready. I stood for a few moments, and once again pondered on the uncertainties of life.

Before darkness fell a message came telling me to detail an officer and some men for a burying party. Our C.O. was always keen on this, partly no doubt, for reasons of health. I sent off a very young officer who had been with me earlier when a working party had stampeded. He didn't relish the job and came back from it rather depressed. He showed me a small crucifix, which he had taken from a man who had hung it round his neck by a string. When I said nothing he looked at me and said he did not like taking it.

"I would not have done" I replied without further comment.

He looked a little doubtful but said nothing. A day or two later, when we were in some reserve trenches which were supposed be safe, a stray long-distance shell came over and wounded him. Bad septic poisoning set in and we were told he was not likely to live. He was, like many of the very youthful ones, fresh from school. I found him rather a bore at times because he couldn't open his mouth without using some dirty word and one was inclined to put him down as a baby but, when danger was about, he suddenly grew up and became a very useful person. I never heard of him again.

One night, while we were trying to settle down as comfortably as possible on the bare ground, a tremendous din began in the valley below. Looking out I saw the biggest display of fireworks I had ever seen. For miles it seemed every kind of coloured rocket was going up with hundreds of Verey lights. It was, as we used to say, "A real Brock's[12] benefit." The cause of it was a night attack by the French and the rockets were the alarm given by the front line German trenches, asking for artillery support. That came quickly enough, but we were just out of the worst of it and only got a shelling with gas shells mixed with a little H.E. It was the mixture which we found trying. It is one thing to be gassed and quite another to be wounded at the same time. After a few sniffs I passed down the word to put on respirators. They were the old-fashioned ones, which fitted over the head like a hood with eyepieces. We lay there gasping in them and the situation was not improved by drizzle of rain, which began at that point, perhaps, as a result of the bombardment.

Next day there was a daylight attack, which broke out with great ferocity and suddenness about a mile below us. It was an affair of countless puffs of smoke from bursting shells and incessant bursts of machine gunfire rattling away. It died down as suddenly as it had begun. Our trench, its elevated position, gave us such a view that it almost seemed as if the attacks were being staged for us. We could have been in the Royal box in a theatre. As time passed I began to believe that this was a French battle into which we had strayed. That impression was confirmed the following day, when I set out to explore the sunken road beneath our trench, and met a French artillery officer. The sunken road, which had many shelters and dug outs along the sides, had evidently been the scene of a battle for there was a lot of debris lying about and several dead bodies, including a young fair-haired German officer, who was still wearing his green overcoat.

I retraced my steps moving along the sunken road to find a point where I hoped I would be able to get another view of the battle. To my surprise I came face to face with a French officer in the familiar horizon blue uniform. He seemed very animated. In his hand was the mouthpiece of a telephone into which speaking hurried directions. I could not imagine what he was up to. He explained that a French battery of '75s had been moved up to support the French attack. He was observing for them and sending back orders by field telephone along a line which had been laid out in a very short

<hr />

12   A well known firework manufacturer, founded in the early 18th century in Islington by John Brock, thought to be the oldest British firework manufacturer.

time. Perhaps he saw my look of enquiry, because he said "Regardez!" and pointed to the valley about 300 yards below us. At that moment the battery of '75s opened fire, spraying the ground he was pointing to with hundreds of shells. He stood there quite unmoved, as if he was a gardener watering some plants.

"I love killing the Bosches," he said with relish, and then he stopped his animated talk and looked at me intently for a moment in silence and then he went on:

"I am a doctor in private life, not a soldier. What about you? Are you a doctor too?" he enquired, as if he wished we had that in common. I wondered if something unmilitary about me had struck this quick–witted Frenchman. A thought flashed through my mind. Should I tell him what I really did in private life? I considered the possibility for a moment and then replied.

"No. I am not a doctor." He seemed disappointed.

"Ah well, I must be going", he said as he moved away and we parted with a mutual "Au Revoir."

Life seemed to be getting rather aimless at this point and I was beginning to wonder what would happen next when a message arrived telling us to leave the trenches and return to our billets. The idea of moving away from the battle of the Somme raised our spirits and we got ready to move on. French troops arrived to take over from us and, just before we were due to go; a party of officers took up their position on the sunken road below. I handed over to them. I had never been relieved by French troops before and it made me realise that we really were in France, in a land, which did not belong to us at all. I found a small group of Frenchmen sitting on a few planks in a little shelter, which had a sheet of corrugated iron over the top. They accepted me as a matter of course, saying very little. They handed me some wine and a very good sandwich while I made myself as pleasant as I could. They were going to attack shortly and it was easier for me to be cheerful going in the other direction. They had a chaplain with them who was not dressed as a soldier, which I thought was a better arrangement than our own. It seemed an odd position for me - an Englishman – to be with these French officers in their own country, engaged in the same occupation, trying to drive a hated enemy out of their land. I think it was their unusual silence, as well as their evident goodwill, which made me feel that the barrier of race, for once, was down. I told them how we had found life in that part the line - a point relief generally wanted to know about, and then we were silent. A man came in to report that the troops were ready and I got up to leave.

"Goodbye and good luck" I said, waving to them as I left. It was getting dark as I made my way along the sunken road and I knew that in a few hours time they could all have been killed.

Our way back took us past Leuze Wood, where the shell-pitted ground had been made so greasy by rain that it was almost impossible to stay upright. Every few yards we fell downs especially men carrying Lewis guns, which were top heavy. I fell down so often and so suddenly that I had the impression that someone was taking me by the shoulders and deliberately throwing me on the ground. There was something sinister about that corner of Leuze wood, where such desperate fighting had taken place and I felt sure poltergeists would feel at home.

My burying party had started to clear things up. Fifteen years later, long after the land had been returned to cultivation, I read in a newspaper that a deep dug out had been discovered at this point. It was full of men whose bodies had been passed over and forgotten. For many years I kept a clip of German cartridges which I picked up in Leuze wood. The bullets had been reversed to make them spread and produce a lacerated wound.

After much weary marching we at last reached some reserve trenches which were supposed to be out of the battle. Just before I arrived a few shells had came over; one of which had badly wounded the youthful officer who had taken out the burying party. The news that greeted us when we arrived was even worse. We were told that we were not going to leave the Somme area at all. We were to be moved back again at once, to some other reserve trenches nearer the line. Apparently the trenches we were in were now wanted for other troops moving up, so we had to leave and make way for them. We were directed to a point, which was nearer our objective. It proved to be a bare open site with no trench at all.

On our way there I decided to take a short cut, in the pitch darkness. It led me just in front of a huge gun, which went off with an ear-rending explosion just above my head. The sudden flash in the quiet and enveloping darkness, and the tremendous concussion, shook me to pieces and I had literally to pull myself together before I went on.

It was now October, which made sleeping on the bare ground impossible. The picturesque bivouacs and campfires of days gone by were now impossible because, of course, no lights were allowed. The only light ever seen was a small red one carefully screened, which was sometimes put up to guide troops through the vast area of the Somme desolation. On the following day, as we continued to trudge back to the front line, a battalion of guards who were going out to rest passed us. Their slow, measured step and greater stature made our own cockneys seem rather unimpressive. As we trudged on we met another party of very tired men who seemed to be more like us. They were using one of the little carts, which at that time were sometimes used for carrying Lewis guns. They had become hopelessly bogged down and their progress had come to a halt.

The Scots Guards had inhabited the trenches we took over. They were really no more than a ditch, flattened out by gunfire and surrounded on all sides by the debris of war. Broken rifles and equipment were scattered everywhere; as were a number of bodies including one, which had been hastily, buried with only a covering of earth so the toes of his boots poked up above the surface. There was a strong smell of excrement, which was unpleasant but excusable under the circumstances. I did not mention it when I spoke to the outgoing company commander. He was a man with charming manners who handed over to me as if we had just met by chance in the smartest part of Bond Street.

Battalion headquarters was in a little shelter surrounded by a trench which had been made so slippery by rain that one had to slide down to get in and be pushed from behind to get out. Our company headquarters was even worse. It was a very deep trench, exactly like a grave. I lowered myself into it hoping for a few hours peace to recover from the last few days. Before long however, in the pitch darkness I heard a voice calling me from above:

"Are you down there sir?"

I knew I had to say "Yes," and wondered what new and gruesome message my visitor had for me.

It proved to be a new officer who had come to report. He had just arrived from England and, in the dead of night by some miracle, had reached the right place. A charming place and hour to choose I thought as I put my head down again and tried to shelter from the cold and rain in a scooped out hole about eight feet below the surface.

Just before daybreak I extricated myself and took a stroll to inspect my immediate surroundings, which I not yet seen as we had arrived in the dark. It was a gray morning with heavy drizzle and it felt more like December than October. As I started to look around a great tumult suddenly broke out on our left where a big attack was being launched. A number of shells began to drop round us too, but they were not large ones and fell with a tired whine and a puff, exploding harmlessly.

A few yards away I could distinguish in the dim light three wooden crosses on new graves. I went to see what names, if any, were written on them. They were all captains from a Guards' regiment who had no doubt been killed in the recent attack. One I remember was called "Herschell." I said a silent prayer for them and thought how glad their relatives (who might not yet have heard of their deaths) would have been to be there instead of a stranger like myself.

Daylight was just breaking and the black threatening clouds were continually lit up by the flashes of a terrific bombardment. It was as if hell was opening its doors.

I strolled back towards my trench, stopping to inspect another, which ran parallel to it a few yards away. It was now light enough for me to see what was inside. At the bottom, lying and sitting at various points, there were a number of men. They were all in German uniforms and they were all dead. So far it had not been an encouraging day.

I made my way back to my grave-like headquarters and moved into the trench. It was now quite light and the shelling had got brisker. At one point a shell plumped hard into the back of our trench falling between me and a man called Tomlins. He was an older man than most and was generally thought to be a bit of a wrangler but I rather liked him. He had a sense of humour which showed itself in a rather disdainful smile, and that appealed to me. On this occasion we had both watched the shell after its arrival and no doubt wondered when it would burst. It didn't. Then our eyes met and I remember his smile and his unexpected remark – "That was Faith!"

Soon after my narrow escape a message came summoning Company Commanders to a conference. We went to the hole in the ground which was battalion headquarters and were told that we would be moving up to the front line that night and must reconnoitre the position while it was still light. That was unusual, but as the position was located on a ridge, it may have been thought that it would protect us and that the trip would be uneventful. I do not know who chose the route we took. It was certainly direct, but evidently one which the Germans did not like people using. We crossed a sunken road and then had to climb up a slope. The slope had, of course, been the field of fire for the trenches we were to occupy when they were in German hand. It was there that the German artillery put down and kept going with Teutonic persistence, a heavy barrage of shells which we had to get through. We decided to run for it. We scattered and did short rushes, flopping down for breath, while shells fell all round us with clouds of black smoke like coal dust where each one landed. It was indeed a surprise that none of us was hit.

We arrived at the trench and found that it was an old German one which, as it was now being occupied by our own troops was back to front, with the openings of the dug outs facing the enemy. In other words, their shells could drop down openings, which could not be shut. The bombardment showed no signs of stopping. We were told that it never did, so we decided to get back at speed. The faster the better as we knew we had to bring back our troops that very night. We set off through the barrage again and arrived breathless at a sunken road where we fell sprawling at the bottom of the bank glad of a little shelter. At that moment a shell, which I thought would pass me, hit a point just above my head covering me with a shower of earth. It was one of those very near misses, which made you feel that some huge beast had got hold of you and was trying to shake the life out of you. It took me a moment or two to recover from the concussion. When I looked up I saw that the others, who were now some way off, were actually laughing. I think we said something about being sent up on such an errand from which we had learned absolutely nothing.

That night, when we set off to take up our position, it was very dark and inclined to rain. We had a job keeping in touch, picking our way over the trackless waste of this devastated Somme area, though we did have guides with us this time. They led us by quite a different route and we were glad to find a safer way, which was perhaps the way we ought to have gone earlier in the day. We were advancing in single file; in parties of five or six when someone came back to tell us that there was a wounded man lying on the ground where we were passing. I went up to him and found him lying quietly on his side, as if resting. His head was propped up on his hand with his elbow on the ground. He had died like that and been left there some time before.

The position we were going to take over was actually a series of posts which had been established just the other side of a ridge. They were linked by a hurriedly made trench protected by a few strands of wire put up during the night. One of these posts, which generally consisted on one officer and about twenty men, had taken the wrong turning in the dark when they were going to be relieved. Instead of marching back, they had walked into the German lines and had been killed or taken prisoner. That rather puzzled our men who could not find anyone to relieve. They also reported that there were a good many wounded lying about. It was an unpleasant time.

We eventually discovered that our H.Q had been established in a captured German dugout. It was a very deep one. The first really deep one I had inhabited, with at least twenty steps leading down into it. It was thus well protected so far as head cover was concerned and quite heavy shells exploded on it harmlessly with a monotonous thudding sound. Being in a captured German trench its exact position was known and its opening faced the German guns, so it was perpetually under fire and coming in and going out were therefore hazardous tasks. It was quite an adventure to get as far as the adjacent latrine.

Descending the many steps I eventually found myself in a small square chamber lighted by one candle. On the floor there was a certain amount of straw, on which lay a major in a dazed condition. After exchanging a word or two I left him alone. The shelling continued without stopping all day and all night while I was there. It was quite remarkable in its clockwork regularity and made me realise once more what a methodical race the Germans are. It was a nuisance even when we were inside, because every now and again a heavier shell would blow out our candle and it would then have to be lit all over again. I wondered how long the heavy cover would stand such a bombardment. From time to time wounded men would be brought back and stretcher-bearers, not knowing the danger, would dump them in the doorway. One man was wounded a second time in this way before I could put a stop to it. We had one very good stretcher-bearer who worked very hard looking for wounded men and bringing them in. He only had one eye only in working order. The other was partly closed. Which made him look like a prize fighter, but he was one of those who were at their best when conditions were unpleasant. I recommended him up for an award.

It was monotonous sitting so far underground with shelling that never stopped, and we had time to wonder if a shell might come down the steps, as we were facing the German artillery. We also wondered if we might be caught in a trap in there was an attack. There was nothing to do but stay there until we were relieved, which we hoped would be soon as we were all getting very fed up.

At last the news we had been hoping for arrived and we were told we were to go out. The officer I handed over to was an old army major. He seemed to be rather dazed and said he had been told absolutely nothing about the position he was now to be responsible for. He did not know where he was or which way we faced. All I could tell him was that the positions we had held were very indefinite and were simply the result of a recent push. The bombardment had not stopped since we arrived. He did not look very reassured and must have come in for the attack which followed. My sergeant major reported that the last of our men were clear of the trench and we started on our way. It was a great to get out and into the air above.

We set off for Trones where we had been told our battalion would be. In pitch darkness, with no landmarks, it was a matter of instinct more than anything else to find the way. Eventually we stumbled on what seemed like the remains of an elaborate trench system and found some shelters, which had evidently been repaired, for use by troops who needed to break their journeys to and from the front. It was uncannily quiet after the noise of the fierce fighting that had taken place and was rather like spending a night in a cemetery.

We moved off early next morning and made our way through the remaining part of the black desolation which was the Somme battlefield. We passed some horse lines on which bombs had been dropped the night before leaving many horses dead. At that moment I heard a voice calling and looked up to see someone on horseback whose face I thought I knew. It took me a while to recall who he was. I had not seen him for a several years and in that time he had become a parson. I remembered him in his youth, and even when he was so small he had to be wheeled as a little white bundle sleeping in a pram. I recalled that as a boy he had been a very heavy sleeper. One day I had taken him out of bed and carried him into another room. He did not wake up which his brother had assured me was perfectly normal. Now, many years later and in an entirely different world, this was the person who was hailing me. He explained that he was now Chaplain to a Guards' battalion. We exchanged a few words and moved on our way.

Emerging from the devastated area we found our battalion at a place called the 'Citadel' - a name given to a patch of ground without any landmarks. We felt we had done rather well to find them without taking any wrong turnings. We were then moved away from the battle area to billets near Amiens. My first aim when we arrived as usual to get a little civilized food and at a small cafe I found the never failing French omelette and some palatable bread. For the rest, we were supposed to be recuperating and were little bothered by work. One day, however, a visiting General paraded us for inspection and I marched along with him past the ranks of my depleted Company. A good deal of equipment had been lost, which the General soon noticed as he passed along.

"There is a man here without his entrenching tool," he said, stopping and pointing. Never having seen an entrenching tool used for anything, except perhaps to prop up a mess tin for cooking purposes, I returned a slightly dreamy "No, sir," which I felt was adequate. I quickly realised that my response was not good enough. I could feel the General's displeasure, so a few minutes later, when he pointed out the next deficiency, I pinched myself metaphorically and said with becoming briskness, "He was blown up sir," meaning it as a gentle reminder that we had been all been under fire for many days. I don't think the General was convinced and when he had finished with me, he looked at me as if he thought I wasn't quite the right sort.

"Damned old fool! What does he think we've been doing?" I murmured, as he withdrew.

The fact was, that the deficiencies, numerous as they were, seemed a small matter to me in comparison with the losses of men which we had struggled to cope with. I felt that it would have been more to the point if the General had congratulated them on managing to stay alive. But Generals for the most part were strangers to us in those days of front-line stress. When they re-appeared, after the storm was over, I had little use for them. It was always trying if someone came along who thought he ought to smarten us up and make us look like real soldiers when all we wanted was to be left alone.

In Amiens we were able to lead a more civilized life that we had been able to experience for some time. Its streets of undamaged buildings rested the eye after being used to nothing but destruction. The civilians and the busy shops were a real joy. Amiens was then the headquarters of a French Army and a convenient place for conferences between important politicians. French Generals and people who looked important gave it a metropolitan look and there was the Cathedral, which seemed a particularly welcome reservoir of calm, its ancient beauty healing our war-scarred spirits. I sat there for some and then went to dinner at the Hotel du Rhin. It was full of people who were obviously used to good food and the staff had done their best to produce something better than the average. It was at this Hotel that Marshal Joffre – Commander in Chief of the French army - had a permanent bedroom, in which I was able to sleep, when I returned to the town several years later.

Our stay in Amiens was far too short. From there we were sent north to Estaires, where we had been a year earlier. To get there we passed through a number of quiet villages. As we marched along we heard that Sir Douglas Haig - the Commander-in-Chief, would be at a certain point to see us go by. We were told to be sure we were marching well and to give an "eyes left", smartly at the appropriate point. After marching for some time word was passed down that the big moment was drawing near. We were told we would know it was the C. in C. because he would be flanked by a mounted orderly, with a pennant on his lance. I wanted to have a good look at him but that would have been unmilitary so I did not see much.

We had heard that we were going to some very quiet trenches and, when we got to our destination, it was so quiet that one would hardly have known there was a war going on. We approached the waterlogged area in the gloom of a late autumn afternoon. Soon after we arrived (on Oct. 28th) I was instructed to report to the Orderly Room where I was informed that I was to go on a course which was to take place at the 1st Army School at Hardelot Castle near Boulogne. I was told to consider myself lucky. As a Company Commander I think the authorities wanted to smarten me up and provide me with the requisite knowledge and that was fine with me. So I never went into those very quiet trenches and I had reason to be glad of that. On the afternoon when my company took over, the first shelling for many weeks took place and the particular spot where the casualties occurred was amongst my own company where, presumably, I would have been.

I discovered that the school for Officers that I was attending was taking place in the grounds of what had once been a Norman Castle. A gateway with rounded towers on either side was about the only part that remained. The rest of the structure was an ugly modern house, which had first been a hospital and then a school. The army had added a few huts dotted around the grounds. My dreams of enjoying a quiet time in this establishment began to fade when, on my first day there, I found myself with a row of other war-weary officers parading for squad drill, just after daybreak. There was a bitterly cold wind and the ground was white with frost. My hopes then reached very low ebb indeed. We were evidently going to be "smartened up". We did squad drill and what was called musketry, which consisted in lying down on the frozen ground and letting off our beastly rifles at various targets. My hands were so numb with cold that I once fired mine by accident. I felt rather annoyed at being treated like a recruit, after a year and a half as an officer at the Front. I wasn't trying very much and my slack behaviour incurred the displeasure of the N.C.O. in charge of us, as I suppose I should have expected. Fortunately I proved to be a better shot than most.

The Adjutant was an old army officer who might have done well at Sandhurst, but our motley tribe of war worn officers, from all parts of the world and all walks in life, were not what he was used to. He was brisk and bright and seemed to think we were just boys.

The sergeant major was a man whose mind had long ago atrophied, if he had ever had one. I think they had been both sent there as a reward for being soldiers by profession and felt they had earned a cushy job which they could stay in for the duration. The lectures were laughably bad and parades so long and frequent that we were tired out, and there was no time left to escape to the nearest civilization at Boulogne. The food, which we ate in the repellent atmosphere of an army hut, was of the worst thing of all. It consisted largely of bully beef. We were told this was because the school had only recently started and catering arrangements had not been worked out yet. On my first day in this awful place I sat next to a very young French Canadian officer. We commented on the fact that we rarely descended to bully beef, even in the front line, where the men used unopened tins to prop up their mess tins while they were cooking something else.

Perhaps the most trying thing about the training course was the sleeping accommodation. We were all herded together in a large room and it was my lot to have next to me a hefty Canadian who was often completely drunk. He was all right when sober, but drink made him mad. He had a habit of coming in late when we were all asleep and making a great row while he stumbled to his bed. We remonstrated, but he threatened to smash up the room, which he could well have done, as he was immensely strong. He was one of those people whose conversation seemed to be exclusively about certain organs and their functions, and it was rather monotonous to listen to it first thing in the morning.

We discussed what might be done about him, but an old army private, who had just got a commission, said that he was nearing his pension and did not want to risk losing it, so we let him go on. I did my best to humour him, as wise men humour those much stronger than themselves who are under the influence of drink especially if they happen to be sleeping within arm's length!

On a more positive note, the area school was set in was quite beautiful with sand dunes and dark pine trees against a blue sky. The sea was not far away but all we wanted to do was rest and not do the sort of training that would normally be given to private soldiers. On one day, which I can still vividly remember, the Chaplain attached to the school, whose name was Pym, was given an hour given to talk to all the officers on any subject he liked. To our surprise he chose to talk about purity and self-control. I must say I rather admired him for presenting his arguments to an audience made up of people who were accustomed to so much strain and, as a result, were more put to it than most, to find an outlet which would balance them. They listened courteously and with interest to a well stated case. I think, he felt he was doing his job, though his audience may not have been greatly influenced by what he said and probably felt he was asking too much.

The only Sunday I was there I thought I must put in an appearance at the early service, which this chaplain had said would take place in a room not far away which had been fitted up as a chapel. I made the effort and got there and waited. Presently the Chaplain came but no one else did so after a bit I agreed with him that no service would take place.

One day my C.O. arrived at our school when we were running a relay race. He greeted me as cheerily as, he always did, addressing me as "captain", to which rank I had recently been promoted and wanting to know why I hadn't put up the three stars of my new rank instead of the solitary one of a second lieutenant. He took me in his car to Boulogne where we had tea. He said was getting tired of war having been involved in from the autumn of 1914. As we drove back he remarked:

"How I long to get away from khaki," which I thought was remarkable coming from a regular soldier who had been in the army for twenty years. I had only done two but his comments summed up how I also felt.

My training course ended on December 2nd. I can't say I was sorry, though I was not very keen to return to the dreary round of discomfort and danger which was trench life. My battalion was now in the region of La Gorgue where I had joined it first.

La Gorgue at that time could best be described as a country slum. In the dark December days its dreary streets were covered with mud and crowded with soldiers passing by. I made one tour of the trenches and was then told I would soon be going on leave. I rather hoped it would be put off for a little so I could find be in England in time for Christmas. Christmas in the trenches was something I wanted to avoid but that was not to be, and a few days later I found myself of my way. I knew that my break was going to be brief and I would be back well before Christmas day.

It was wonderful to get back to London again. After eight months of discomfort and worse it seemed a great place to be. As usual it was the simple things which gave most pleasure on leave. Eating meals off clean plates instead of chipped enamel ones smeared with a rancid rag. No tin mugs with their cordial of chlorinated water or tea made with water from a shell hole, with a dead body not far away. A hot bath and privacy instead of a canvas bucket with a minimum of dirty water possibly coated with ice. Sleeping in a bed away from other soldiers, and not on a draughty floor, or in a waterlogged trench full of rats crawling over our mud-caked clothes. Reaching out languidly to switch on an electric light, instead of groping uncertainly in the dark for a torch, or trying to light the candle you stuck on the ground last night -and discovering that the matches have gone astray. Of course there were other things too, but these elementary things were the foundation of what the joy of leave meant.

I felt like a prisoner making his way to the scaffold as I returned to Victoria station and set off for France. When I got back to my battalion, I found there were so many new faces I felt like a stranger. As Christmas Day drew near we weighed the possibilities of being either in or out of the trenches, as we had done the year before. To come back from London, where Christmas was in the air, and go straight into the trenches for Christmas Day seemed a little bleak, but we hoped for a quiet time and a-live-and-let-live-atmosphere suitable to the season. That seemed quite likely for the trenches had been quite quiet and no patrols had been seen. There had been no shelling or rifle fire from the opposite side. It seemed a farce to man our trenches fully. They were very uncomfortable and waterlogged, and we thought the Germans had probably had with more commonsense and retired to the Aubers Ridge which overlooked them. There they would enjoy Christmas, and probably make fun of us poor fools in the swamp below.

The sector we were in was known as the "Convent", presumably because a convent had once been there and indeed part of its walls remained. Another rumour was that in the early days of the war, a cellar full of wine had been discovered whilst some digging operations were going on. That news had been handed on to the successive occupants of the trench, who could at least conjure up a vision of what was no longer there. My own company headquarters in the front line had been decorated with some woodcarvings, meant to look like the mantelpiece of a room. A battalion of Guards had carved them, when they had been there shortly before us, and they gave the impression of being in a country mansion. H.Q. itself was a flimsy affair, built against the breastwork with a corrugated iron roof covered with earth and a few sandbags. It afforded no protection from anything but splinters, as we were to find out quite soon. It had a rough table and chair and, on one side, the usual shelf of rabbit wire on which an officer off duty might recline. The floor was simply a pool of water. We took over this position a week before Christmas day.

On Christmas Eve we heard that there was to be no fraternizing. The regrettable incidents of Christmas 1914, when German and English soldiers met in No Man's Land and exchanged cigarettes, were not to be repeated, though why anyone thought they would be after an interval of two years, was hard to imagine. On the contrary we were to show the offensive attitude so often mentioned in "Comic Cuts." We were to fire off our rifles all day long. Overhead machine gun fire would reinforce our efforts, but there would be no artillery - presumably because their officers would be attending the dinner given by the General in some chateau far behind the line, where they would be keeping Christmas in the good old-fashioned way.

Christmas day dawned quiet and misty with no hint of the foolery we were about to commit. I took a stroll along the muddy trench and thought how peaceful it was. It was very quiet indeed and, as I listened carefully, I heard a distant church bell. Then, at the appointed hour, pandemonium broke out. Machine guns, rifle fire and trench mortars all together. It went on all day without a stop, by which time, apart from the overhead machine gun fire, three thousand trench mortars had been let off and fifteen thousand rounds of S.A.A. had been fired on my company front alone. We wondered if there would be any retaliation, but it was all treated with good-humoured contempt by the Bosche and by nightfall we had orders to stop. Nothing whatever had come back but, just when we were beginning to feel it was safe, a missile did arrive. It was a rifle grenade, which fell into the mud and, fortunately, failed to explode. We thought it was probably a German attempt at humour and not a bad attempt either. We imagined feasting Germans passing round the wassail bowl and drawing lots for the job of going down to the front and letting it off.

Having carried out our programme, we heaved a sigh of relief and looked forward to the letters and rations coming up. We were told they would include an extra tot of rum. Our trench ration party had set off as usual to meet the people who brought the rations to a certain point every night. In the trench we awaited their return with a glimmer of hope. We waited a long time. Much longer than usual, but it was Christmas and perhaps that was why. At last our patience was rewarded. Dim forms appeared and we heard the subdued shuffle of feet. Saved at last, we thought! But the ration party seemed rather quiet, and we did not know why. We soon found out.

"There was no rum sir. Someone's pinched the lot", one of the ration party explained. And that was the end of a perfect day! I hoped the General's dinner had gone off well.

In the early hours of the next morning, when I was reclining on the shelf of rabbit wire in the Company H.Q., half-asleep and half awake, I was suddenly wrenched back into full consciousness by a slight disturbance. The habit of resting half-awake was such that it was possible to be on one's feet in an instant. In the split second if took to get to the floor, I had a vision of men in gray uniforms with red bands round their gray, peakless caps. So the Germans had not taken our Christmas attentions lying down after all? The officer I had seen lying on the ground by the light of a flickering candle was wrestling with them. It seemed very real, but fortunately it was not. I just was not properly awake. The officer was there but he was not wrestling with anyone. He had fallen off his chair and was shouting because a machine gun bullet had come through the back of the shelter and hit him in the neck. I went to find out what had happened and discovered that an Australian machine gunner, who had been told .to fire over our heads from just behind our trench, had fired into our Company H.Q. I was told it was defective ammunition from America (or was it Japan?) Wherever it came from it had stopped at once. It was enough to have been shooting at nothing all Christmas Day, but to have our own people shooting us in the back the day after! And no rum - I ask you!

Rum or no rum we were quite lucky to get away from the trenches before any retaliation took place.

We had no casualties at all. We moved to Laventie. The nearest place to go to from there was Estaires, two miles away, which still quite intact. We had got to know it well in the autumn of 1915. It was not much of a place but it was better than nothing, and we would imagine we were keeping Christmas there. Laventie itself had been heavily battered. The only inhabitants who remained were the few who made a bit out of the troops. Many of the houses had shell holes in them and bits of broken masonry littered the streets and made it look desolate and shabby. Here and there a substantially built house remained mostly intact. One had been taken for my billet and even the glass in the windows was intact. It was at the end of the street away from the firing line, and the other houses had probably protected it. There was no furniture in the house and I had a huge bedroom on the first floor looking out on the street.

Sunday came just after our arrival and as it was Christmas time I made an effort to attend a service of Holy Communion in the remains of a battered building which I was told was the place being used for Church of England services. When I left my billet it was nearly dark and spitting with rain. I plodded through the empty cobbled streets past the shattered buildings and at last found a dark little room at the back of a partly destroyed house. It had been fitted up as a chapel, by someone who had evidently taken trouble. I waited a little after the appointed time, but no one turned up. Not even a chaplain.

Another small incident I remember whilst at Laventie was a court martial. It was the first I had attended. It concerned a man who had been rude to acting lance corporal. I had to gabble the oath in a little room simultaneously with another officer, and was then told that I must give my vote for a verdict of guilty because discipline had to be maintained. The rebel in me did not like that and I remembered lance corporals that had not brought me much joy when I was a private. I thought was probably just a case of a man who had recently been made an N.C.O. and perhaps thought he was a little too important. The case against the man was that, when he got into billets bored after the Christmas in the trenches, the acting lance corporal had given some unnecessary order and he had cheeked him. Looking at the N.C.O. I decided that he was an ass and thought that it was a charge that need not have been brought and I said so. I was told afterwards that I had done quite the wrong thing.

We had spent Christmas day in the trenches but New Year's Day was to dawn while we were out. I thought I would stay up for it. I got back to my solitary billet towards midnight and, as the hour drew near I went to the window, opened it and leaned out in the darkness. I could just see a blurred mass of the houses opposite. Cold and damp air came in from the dark deserted street. I enjoyed the luxury of being alone in the quietness and meditated on the past two years, most of which had been spent in similar conditions. To have survived nearly two years of more or less continuous trench life was, on reflection, quite surprising. Not many of those who were still in the battalion had been in when I joined and none so continuously. Now another year was at hand. It was as impossible to know what lay ahead as it was to see the opposite side of the street in the pitch darkness where only the dimmest outline of the houses could be made out. It was better that way. In fact there was no other way of going on. When would it be midnight, I pondered. How quiet and still everything was. At that moment a series of loud reports broke the silence. The sky reflected the flashes. It was a battery of R.F.A. outside the village sending their best wishes for the New Year to the Germans. I drew in my head and closed the window. It was 1917 and I was still alive.

Part Two

from

War to Peace

Photographs on previous page:

Top: The author; Ypres campaign; *Middle Right:* Author conducting RAF funeral England 1960; *Bottom Left:* Author and wife Mary on their Wedding Day 1921; *Bottom right:* Author's daughter Mary

1917 – 1918

"Our physical endurance was flagging"

While we were celebrating the New Year, the Germans in their own deliberate way were taking measures in reply to our "Christmas hate." They brought up some guns, which quite destroyed part of our front line, including the company dugout, which had housed me on Christmas Day. When we went back to the same sector, we felt we had had a lucky escape, and were rather sorry that our absurd behaviour on Christmas day had been paid for by a number of casualties. The Brigadier, who came up one sunny morning to see what had happened, met me and greeted me in his loud and cheery way. By way of making conversation he said, "What a funny looking fellow that officer of yours is." He mentioned a name and then added, "Is he mad, drunk or what?" That seemed like a promising beginning for what could be an interesting a conversation and I wanted to make a suitable reply. Unfortunately the officer in question was only a few yards away, behind some sandbags, so I hesitated and said very little, which the Brigadier must have felt was an odd way to respond to his friendly efforts.

As the New Year progressed we hovered round the Laventie-Estaires district. We were now quite old soldiers compared with the time when we had been here last, eighteen months before. The flat and waterlogged nature of the ground made life difficult. It was different from the Somme area and we found it rather dull. We were also depressed by the feeling that the war showed no signs of coming to an end and no doubt our physical endurance was flagging.

The trenches were comparatively quiet once we were in them, but getting there was, as often as not, rather lively. The ground was so flat that it was easy to spot any movement and we had to be careful. We generally moved from our billets at dusk, and got to the trenches just after the time when we thought we might be seen. In some places the road was screened with curtains of camouflage to make us more invisible. Once or twice, when snow was on the ground, I felt that we were much too conspicuous and wondered why we were not shelled, as we were so near to the trenches. The conclusion we came to was that we could be seen, but the Germans were out for peace at the moment and did not want to be shelled in return. This period of non-molestation did not last long and any new arrivals or departures were greeted with a sharp bombardment by field guns. That generally happened just as we were getting in and others were getting out – the idea being to kill two birds with one stone. The timing was so precise that our suspicions were aroused and then someone told us that, when a relief came in sight, a column of smoke went up from a cottage, which somehow had remained for two years intact, and was quite close to the line. The accommodation was poor and my H.Q. consisted of a sandbagged shelter about 3 feet high, with the usual corrugated iron on the top and a layer of earth. During one relief, just before I arrived, a shell came through the side but it did not explode.   Here and there attempts had been made to construct something better and I was quite taken aback when one day I found myself taking over a company headquarters which had a concrete floor and two steps leading down into it.

There seemed to be a kind of suspense brooding over us at this time, due perhaps to the passing by of the great Somme push without, so far as we knew, any decisive result. We knew nothing of the exhaustion of the French Army, the intending collapse of Russia or the ideas that America might one day take a hand. All we knew was that we were still up to our necks in mud being shot after two years or so of the same kind of existence.

One day, in the middle of a long frost which had added to our miseries, I found myself crouching in a trench with some other officers, trying to shelter from a sudden, heavy bombardment. For some reason it amused those present when I quoted the statement which is to be found in Trafalgar Square at the base of Nelson's Column. It was a pronouncement by the King to the effect that we should not give in until the forces of the enemy were overcome (or words to that effect). Perhaps they liked to think of London, or maybe they were beginning to wonder, after two and a half years, if the war would ever end. The senselessness of killing each other was in all our thoughts. We agreed that in future wars the Governments concerned should have to spend time in the front line. Then perhaps they would realise the futility of war. I remember suggesting that Messrs. Thomas Cook & Son could bring parties to the battlefields so that, after all, they would serve some purpose. That was how we tried to make light of things, but the truth was that life in the trenches was hell on earth, and the weather was anything but helpful to us at that time. A severe frost had set in again and it froze everything. It put an end to the mud for the time being, but the cold was worse.

My company headquarters at this time consisted of a semi-circular piece of corrugated iron, with a little earth on the top, because the old one had been destroyed. It was not high enough to stand up in, and all eating and writing had to be done sprawling on the ground by the light of a flickering candle. I was always writing reports and a new one was called for at this stage of the war at 3 a.m., in order, I suppose to show that we were still awake. I remember groping for matches to light the candle and writing with frozen fingers some trifle about what had happened in the last few hours.

For some reason this was the time chosen to send us short rations. Apart from what I had brought with me, we only had bread. It was frozen solid and was as harder than a block of wood. It was impossible to cut. We were also told that the cold weather would not be accepted as an excuse for not shaving. One morning, when I put my broken bit of mirrored glass on the top of my shelter and began to shave with a blunt razor, I noticed that the thermometer was registering 23 degrees of frost. When the frost finally thawed, we were sent farther along the line to some trenches, which had been partly destroyed by a mine. It had left them so open we felt we could not approach them in daylight, so we made our moves at night. It was a very muddy business. Our route was almost impassable and we were so near the German line that we could hear a German sentry singing to while away the time and another who kept coughing.

Most of the time life indeed was so uneventful it was difficult to find anything to put in my reports, and when we said nothing we were told that it would not do. So in my 3 a.m. report, I noted down that a German sentry was suffering from a cough and the next day that it was no better. That amused headquarters for some time, so all was well.

We were so close the Germans that I sometimes felt that it was better to avoid even thinking of a subject for fear of suggesting it by telepathy. My company Headquarters in this new sector had a concrete floor, which was most up to date but unfortunately, it was always under water. I had to be there for eight days and nights and the only way to keep the level down to six inches was to have a man pumping it out by hand all the time. The roof was only four feet high so it was not possible to do more than crouch inside. The only way to keep out of the water (provided the pump was kept going) was to recline on a rabbit wire bed. It was there, by the light of a spluttering candle that my despatch about the German sentry's cough, which brought me so much fame, was written. I used to get out when I could, but generally that was the time for the telephone from H.Q. to ring, with a request for a report on whale oiling the men's feet, the rum ration, or why a spade was missing. I generally found it was best to stay on the wire bed most of the time in semi-darkness, and send for people I had to see; though it was not much fun in the gloom and wet. Towards the end of the week a Major, who had somehow managed to spend the first two and a half years of the war in England before being pushed out, came down to see me. I saw a shadow at the entrance and was told who it was, but I remained on my wire bed, explaining the difficulties of the position and hoping he would excuse my lack of enthusiasm.

The usual quietness of these trenches was sometimes disturbed by heavy shelling, which was sufficiently a nuisance for our artillery to say they would retaliate if required. As messages on the telephone were at this time reputed to be tapped, we were given a code message instead, which I remember in this case was "c o o g u n offend." I never used it because the shelling generally did not last long and I did not want to provoke an artillery duel. "Least said soonest mended," I found was a good motto in such cases. I knew it was heresy in the eyes of the higher command, which had just issued a booklet to encourage the offensive spirit. It was entitled "Some of the questions a Platoon Commander should ask himself on taking over a trench and at intervals afterwards." It included the following gems:

1.   I am here for two purposes. To do as much damage as possible to the enemy

and to hold my part of the line at all costs. Am I doing everything possible to ensure my being able to do this?

2. Do I worry the enemy as much as I might do and are the sniper scopes, rifle grenades, catapults and patrols at my disposal organised in the best way to affect this purpose?

And so on!

The Royal Engineers had obviously been busy in this part of the line for I soon found myself in another dugout with a concrete floor. This time it was dry. Not only was it dry but there was a brazier and I managed to scrounge a little charcoal for it. It was a reserve trench and my company, not being directly in the front line, had no night duty so I looked forward to a night of peaceful sleep. Having got the stove going I thought what a remarkable situation it was to find myself in. Not many yards from the front line, dry, quiet and alone and with a stove which sent up no betraying column of smoke. I felt sleepy almost at once and was just dropping off when I began to think that I was perhaps nodding off a bit too soon. I was certainly getting drowsy, which was unusual for me, and certain alertness bred of trench life made me think.

"Is it that really a charcoal stove?" I wondered and pulled myself together with an effort. With some difficulty I got on to my knees, crawled to the opening and put my head out in the fresh air, just before it was too late.

Life was comparatively uneventful while the winter lull lasted, with alternate turns of trenches and billets. Rest in billets was less restful than it might have been owing to frequent working parties, which were often carried out under fire. Most were conducted under cover of darkness but some were in daylight. It was on daylight one that I must have been feeling peevish. The troops behind me thought they would cheer things up by singing an obscene parody of the hymn "Holy, Holy, Holy, Lord God Almighty." I had not heard it before and it annoyed me, perhaps partly because I thought it might be meant for my benefit. Anyhow, I halted them abruptly and told them I would not march in front of rabble." They stooped and never did it again, which was perhaps surprising. If I had been older I should probably have taken no notice and realised that no harm was meant.

Another parody of a hymn, which is inoffensive, was:

We are but little children weak.

We only earn five francs a week.

The more you do the more you may.

It makes no difference to your pay.

It is rather curious how the British Public resorts to hymn tunes in difficult times.

Perhaps the most characteristic war songs were those with sentiments like

"Take me home to dear old Blighty. Blighty is the place for me!"

That was how men, who had come of their own freewill to the war and had no idea of quitting, expressed themselves in the face of monotony, discomfort and danger.

I remember marching a large party of Australians down to the train at Etaples, on their way to the front. The camp was drearier than most and the day was dreary too, but as we went down the slope near the line the sun came out and shone on our faces. It was then that they began to sing:

"Pack up your troubles in your old kit bag, and smile, smile, smile!

It came with a crescendo, as if they could face the trials and hazards ahead with the sun coming out to re-assure them and it really meant something.

Before March was far advanced, our dreary waterlogged period came to an end and we were not left in doubt about what was to be done with us next. We were to be taken out of the line and fattened up, for a push in the Arras region. With that aim in mind we were marched first to Sus St. Leger and then on to Monchiet – a village near Arras, which was just outside the area which had been shelled. Before we set out on that pilgrimage our old C.O. returned. He took over from me on March 6th at La Gorgue.

We spent some time at Sus St. Leger doing mild training in the more genial weather of approaching spring, which we found a pleasant change after trench life. It was there that we heard of the German retreat to the Hindenburg line. We wondered what it meant. Was it was a sign of weakness and that consequently the war was really coming to an end, or was it a catch and we would gain nothing by it? The fact that the Germans had retreated showed that the losses of the Somme had had some effect. On the other hand there was the Russian revolution, which meant an end of hopes of the steamroller, as Russia's slow and ponderous efforts were known. The news of America coming in was not yet public but we felt that at last things were on the move.

At Sus St. Leger one of my officers, who had enlisted as a private, was chosen to be sent to the United States as a kind of liaison officer. He was youthful and cheerful; though not much help in the trenches where his well-meant chumminess with N.C.O.s, combined with an almost childish appearance, ensured they took little notice of him. The C.O. asked me if I thought he would do for America.

"He would be all right in the mess, wouldn't he?" he said.

"Quite," I replied, "He'd do that very well." So off he went, out of the war and I hope he enjoyed the change. When I tried to find out more exactly what his job would be, I was told that he was going "to teach the American army" which I am sure they would have been delighted to hear!

At Sus St. Leger I suffered one of those periodical degradations from being a Company Commander, when an officer of senior rank turned up and was put in my place. I reverted once more to second Lieutenant. I thought it might have had something to do with my lack of a horse a few weeks earlier, for my successor was an expert rider with experience of the Wild West and could dash about anywhere. Had I lost my kingdom for want of a horse?

We moved on to Monchiet where we found there was little to cheer us up. The weather was very cold again and we lived in huts put up to house concentrations of troops for which there was no room in billets. There were no fires, scanty food and oceans of mud. The huts could only be approached through a quagmire and it was quite a business after arriving inside to get rid of the mud. Although the weather was cold, there was nothing to warm the huts and we were not near anywhere where we could get an occasional meal, to supplement our meagre and ill-cooked rations. Hanging about the wretched rain-swept village, which was swarming with troops, and having nothing to do, we became more and more bored, and were not sorry when the day came to move further up the line.

The Company Commanders made the customary journey to the front line to reconnoitre. We went as near to it as we could get but learnt less than usual by doing so. Some rifle shots showed us where the Germans were and we drifted aimlessly about some empty trenches before coming back. It was a fruitless venture but it did not matter because the next day (April 12th) the battalion moved off as a body. As we approached the front line we passed through the village of Beaurains which had been almost completely destroyed. The churchyard was still there but the little mortuary chapels, which had stood over many of the graves like streets of miniature dwellings, were all in ruins. Many vaults were now just gaping caverns, as if waiting for a premature resurrection. To complete the picture of destruction there was the carcass of a dead horse lying in a ditch outside, with its four stiff legs stuck up in the air like the legs of a table upside down. As we moved past we knew that we were back in the battle area again.

That night we halted just beyond the village, near a place which went by the uncomfortable name of Agny. There was an abrupt little hill, almost a cliff, sheltering a small grass area, which had not been discovered by the German artillery and there we rested peacefully for a time. After the scenes of destruction on the way, it seemed a curious and welcome contrast to be sitting there in the quiet evening sunlight for an hour or so after our long march. Battalion Headquarters remained hereabouts in the only building sufficiently intact. Our job was to go to some empty trenches farther on and get used to the place from which we would be required to make the attack. For the first night we remained in disused dugouts. Mine was very deep, and it seemed a long journey to get to the bottom. Not believing in being more uncomfortable than necessary, I thought of my camp bed and arranged for it to be collected and put up in the depths of the dugout. It was well worth the effort and I managed to get some sleep for the last time for many days.

Our new Company Commander, who had superseded me, shared our clammy vault. He had been to Rugby school, and had lived for some time in the U.S.A. His family owned a smart hosiery shop in Paris, which did not interest him in the least. Consequently he spoke French easily with a strong American accent. We heard of the entry of America into the war during the few hours we spent at this spot. I cannot say it conveyed much to me, partly no doubt, because one felt before a battle that nothing mattered very much except perhaps the purpose in hand. The chances were we would not be alive to hear any more.

From the dugouts we were summoned to attend a conference at Battalion H.Q. where we expected to find out what we were supposed to do in the impending show. It was Good Friday. The C.O. informed me that I would be put in command of the company for the battle. The new company commander would be left out along with several other officers. He asked me if I felt I could I could manage. It seemed an odd arrangement just after I had been downgraded to second lieutenant, but I told him that I had some very good N.C.O's and would cope with it somehow.

The plan was that the battalion would take the village of Neuville Vitasse and go over in waves composed of companies, the rear companies passing through those in front. My company being rear-most would therefore pass through the other three to take the farther objective. Having had this reassuring news, we departed.

I stood outside for a few minutes and watched an air fight. It was the biggest I had seen. There were a large number of machines and they were so high up so they looked like a little swarm of gnats, flying excitedly round. The German aeroplanes and ours were all mixed up. Little puffs of smoke dotted the blue sky, as shells from anti-aircraft guns burst and broke, like powder puffs on pale blue silk. One made a sudden dive on an opponent and another come falling down like a leaf, as if hopelessly vanquished, and then recovered itself at a safe distance. Another streamed across the sky in flames, leaving a black trail of smoke.

Air fight

The C.O., who had joined me and was watching them in silence, said "How dreadful," and shuddered. It did not last long and the German squadrons, which had come over to see what preparations were being made, were driven off.

Such were the happenings, which enabled newspaper correspondents' miles from the scene, to make the stereotyped announcement that "There had been considerable air activity on the previous day in the neighbourhood of Arras, resulting in so many enemy machines being driven off."

Actually what was happening in the air, though of course, we of the infantry did not know it, was that an attempt was being made by our Royal Flying Corps to gain mastery of the air, without which, victory on the ground was almost impossible. So it is interesting to know that in those days before the battle, we had in use on our part of the front 364 machines, of which one third only were single-seater fighters. Against these the Germans had 195 machines, of which half were equipped as fighters. It was that force which we had watched struggling for supremacy above our heads.

On April 9th, when the battle on the ground began, we were told that the total force in action on our side was 754 machines, against 264 German. And further, between April 4th and April 9th, while this battle for air supremacy was going on, we lost 75 machines in battle and 56 crashed of their own accord because of defects. Those were the days when pilots with a few weeks' experience went up in machines which were often unfit to fly, to do battle with numerically smaller but better trained and better equipped German air force.

At nightfall we were to move on to some disused German trenches overlooking the village we had to capture. It was there that the bright idea came to me that it would be nice to try and get some kind of a wash. I always did that before a show. I had not had a bath for some weeks. My underclothes were dirty and I knew it might be a long time before we got away from the line. I wandered away to the remains of the village, which was still being shelled at times, on the seemingly impossible aim of finding the wherewithal. The village was deserted and I began to think I should have to give up my quest when I came across a solitary soldier who had been left behind in charge of some pick-axes and other implements. He was hidden away in the remains of a small building. I explained my idea to him and before very long he produced a tub of hot water in a very restricted shed, which was just big enough for me to squeeze into. It must have been about the only place with anything in the way of a roof left over it. Here I performed a quite successful wash and put on clean underclothes. Having thus restored my morale

I returned to my dug out in time to move on to our next stage, which would bring our battle positions into sight.

When night came we left our sheltered glade and took to the road, which led to the old German trenches. There we made ourselves as comfortable as we could. The trenches had been vacated by the Germans when they retreated to the Hindenburg Line. Arras, on our left, was the hinge .of this retreat so only a small triangular area had been evacuated, but it enabled the British line to be advanced to within 400 yards or so of the Neuville Vitasse, which the Germans were still holding. The Hindenburg Line ran just behind the village and was connected with it by a communication trench. The trenches were deep and well made, with typical German thoroughness. They had their names in German painted on boards, which were still in position. Jackmann Stellung was the name of ours. Later on we moved into quite shallow open trenches which were a little farther forward. As there were no blankets and no possibility of making a fire, the frosty nights kept us from sleeping. Shells came over from time to time but nothing to worry about very much, though I remember one man who found them trying. I happened to notice him running about like a frightened rabbit, and wondered what was up. Oddly enough, the next day I had a message asking for a report on a man who was said to be suffering from shell shock. At that time, anyone professing to be shell-shocked had to be vouched for, because, of course, it would have been an easy method of getting away to peaceful surroundings. As it turned out the man in question was the one I had noticed, so I said I did not think he was pretending and away he went to safety.

The next day the C.O. paid us a visit to tell us that the attack, which had been planned for Easter Day (April 8th), had been postponed till the following Monday. He also remarked on my riding breeches, which he said he thought it would be inadvisable to wear in an attack because the Germans picked off anyone who looked like an officer. He always made us wear private's uniform for a battle.

We had been told rather casually that a tank would co-operate with our battalion, and that certain signals could be exchanged between it and the infantry. I used up some of the time while we were waiting by going over to its hiding place, which was in a sunken road, and talking to its commander. Our C.O. thought it would be more bother than it was worth, the use of tanks on the Somme not having so far, come to much. The Tank officer too, seemed despondent. This may have been partly due to his orders. He had been told to start off before the infantry and, skirting the village we were to take, arrive somewhere at its rear. During my conversation with him I discovered that he knew nothing about the prearranged signals. As that seemed to me to be quite important, I sent a message to an Adjutant, who arranged for the Tank Commander to meet our C.O.

More snow showers fell at this time covering the ground and increasing the cold and our discomfort. To make us familiar with the lie of the land we were then sent by companies down the slope in front of us to the jumping-off trenches. At night we wandered out into No man's Land as far as we could go, but to our surprise no Germans were met. We thought they probably knew our plans as well as we did and were saving their strength for the day of attack. We later found out that most of their men had been withdrawn from the village when the bombardment was going on.

At that point the attack was put off for another day. Easter Day was a gift to many, who now had another day to live. It was brilliantly fine and very cold. After spending a night in the jumping-off trenches, we were back again for the last day in the shallow trench on higher ground, from which we could study the village we had to take. With the help of maps and photographs, I showed the officers and N.C.O.s the various landmarks we were supposed to pass in our advance. We got to know quite a lot about the village as it then was. When my briefing finished, there was nothing left to do but wait till we went down to our battle positions. I remember wondering what the holiday crowds in England would be doing at that time. For some reason I remembered, that in former days at that time I would have been conducting a children's service in the slum parish in which I had started my church career.

There was an immense amount of shelling going on from our side in an attempt to smash up the village and the wire entanglements in front of it. Even 15-inch shells were used and, as we looked on, it seemed as if nothing could be left after so many shattering explosions. That, we were to find was not the case. The relentless pounding gave us confidence and we had hoped that we might have little to do but go in and occupy the place. There was little retaliation.

As darkness fell, we went down the hill to replace the troops in the front line. After weeks of under-feeding and exposure, we felt much less fit than we had been when we were last in the line. The arrangements were that my company was to be on the right. The other companies, which had to start first, had to bear to the right as they got out of the trench, so we could follow on behind them. We hoped that movement would be possible in the confusion and darkness of the attack. Having got the men in the required positions, there was nothing to do but wait.

As we waited our thoughtful C.O. suddenly appeared on the top behind our trench and made a few remarks to cheer us up.

I think he was hinting that I, who was then midway between 30 and 40, must know something about that too. He asked me if I understood about the flag going up. If the main attack on Vimy Ridge succeeded, a flag would be put up where we could see it. When that happened we were to advance and take our village.

I told him I quite understood but wouldn't be depressed if the flag didn't go up and we bade farewell to each other. It got colder and colder as we waited and it was inclined to snow. Lying down, inactive, as there was no room to move about, I found my heels were beginning to beat a tattoo ground which no doubt was largely funk. Waiting for zero hour in the snow, after many nights with little sleep or food, is not one of the more life's more genial occupations. Few people spoke.

At last my watch told me the hour of the main attack was approaching. Our bombardment began again some way off, to the left. The attack on Vimy had evidently been launched but there was still a wait of three hours or so before we had to go – if we did. By now the darkness of the night was giving way to dawn. In the first daylight, under heavy clouds, no Man's Land showed up as an indefinite expanse of forbidding grey. I looked at my watch at intervals. Nobody moved or spoke. As I listened I thought I heard, mixed up with 'the distant tumult, a subdued throb like an engine. Looking up in the distant gloom I saw a shadowy form slowly advancing towards the German line. It was the tank, already on its lonely way forward moving very, very slowly.

As the predicted time for our advance time drew near I said to my sergeant

"What about that flag? Has it gone up yet?"

He passed the word along to find out and we waited for ten minutes or so.

The message came back – "Yes."

"Are you quite sure?" I remarked.

"Yes," my sergeant replied.

"Well, we'd better be ready," I replied.

Our Zero hour still was one a minute off, by my synchronised watch.

We kept a sharp look out for the other companies we had to follow, because they had to start first. And there they were, in open order bearing to the right in the gloom. We got ready to move out as best we could with our half-frozen legs. Our own barrage had started and our front companies were advancing over No man's Land. As soon as they were seen advancing, the Germans replied with field guns. The fogginess of the morning and smoke from bursting shells combined to provide a murky haze to cover our movements. Added to it all was the sleet and snow. There was a certain amount of rifle fire but no machine guns. As shells burst they made a red glow in the mist. I did my best to make the men keep a safe distance from each other, and advance in the right direction, but the din of the bombardment made any orders impossible to hear so I picked up a rifle and went on in the middle of the line. We advanced slowly, so as not to run into the barrage and as quietly as if we had been taking a stroll in the country. It was a relief to be out of the trench after the long wait, and to be doing something.

We were now quite close to the German Front line, which, I assumed had been taken by our first company. I saw some German soldiers coming through the smoke with their hands up, looking very scared and shouting "Kamerad." We took no notice of them and they passed through us to safety. I thought they were the lucky ones.

Then we came the German wire. It had mostly had been destroyed, but here and there a tangle of it remained. At one point, I saw one of our men half sitting on the wire, with his face turned towards us as we came along. I thought he was resting and watching us with his eyes wide open and was anticipating some remark as we approached. It took me a few seconds to realise that he was dead. After that I had to pick my way through the broken wire.

A sunken road ran behind the first objective, which had been taken. Thanks to aerial photographs; when we got there we knew that, so far at least, we were heading in the right direction. At that point there seemed to be something holding up the advance and we waited longer than I liked. I knew that our creeping barrage was going on ahead of us. At that moment a shell burst at my feet between another man and myself. I wondered how it was that we were untouched. I remembered that moment eight years later when I revisited the place and identified the spot. There was a solitary and meagre little red poppy growing on the exact place, as if to mark it. On that occasion I did not have a company of British infantry with me. Just my wife and a portable pram containing my son.

Clambering up the bank on the other side of the sunken road, we discovered the reason for the delay. There was a ruined building surrounded by a wall and wire, where a German machine gunner and some 70 men still remained refusing to be dislodged. They stayed there for two hours. That, of course, brought our prearranged plan of attack to an end and soon a heavy German barrage was put down to stop any further advance. There seemed to be quite a crowd surrounding the ruined building, where the Germans were holding out. It consisted of men from the two companies, which had preceded ours.

After a while I sent one platoon off to the right to try and get round the point of resistance. I then took another party myself to try and get round on the other side. That left the greater part of the company staying with the others in the centre. The platoon I sent to the right ran into a very heavy bombardment and we lost, amongst others, one of our best sergeants. On the left I got into even worse trouble. It was the more exposed side of the village and it was under heavy bombardment and being continuously swept by machine gunfire. I had not gone far when I encountered the German barrage, which was focused exactly on a trench I knew I had to cross. As the trench had once been their own, they knew exactly where it was. Amongst the wounded in this trench I soon noticed my best runner. He was lying down with both his legs broken below the knees. The lower parts pointed at right angles to the upper parts. He caught sight of me and laughed, as if it was a good joke. I tried to move nearer as it was impossible to hear anything in the prevailing din. I managed to get close enough to bend over him to catch what he was saying. He wanted water badly, so I leant across and poured some into his mouth. The shelling at that point was very heavy and accurate. As I leant forward there was a loud explosion immediately overhead, which left me stunned. I knew I had to continue my way forward and try to get through the barrage. With a final smile from my wounded runner, I clambered up the steep side and ran forward but the bombardment, far from stopping, actually increased. In addition I found that on the top I was exposed to heavy machine-gun fire, so I waited, in a shell hole, hoping for the best. I could watch the shells during the last part of their flight and they came down with clockwork regularity.

By now I only had only one man left with me and he was in a bad state. To fill up the time I shared some chocolate with him and had a look round. The ground fell away sharply to our left and I could see for some miles across to the horizon. A mile away a few stragglers were making their way across open country heading for Monchy. Monchy itself was being attacked and the smoke of bursting shells was clearly visible. I could see farther still, where transport on the move stood out against the skyline. The Germans were making a hurried retreat. They had not expected a heavy attack in this sector.

At last the German fire slackened and I was able move on, as were the others. On reaching the Village Street we met. There was not much to see. Just piles of debris and here and there bits of broken wall with a few German dead, who had been left there to hold up our advance. Amongst them there was a very badly wounded German officer. He was still alive but only just. He said in English – "I beg you to help me."

I had some painkilling tablets I gave him to one to put in his mouth.

A little farther on a German machine gun team on the far side of the village came out of an immensely strong concrete fort and surrendered to one of my platoons. By now the whole of the village was in our hands. One of our N.C.O.s was astonished to hear one of German prisoners calling out his name. It transpired that before the war he had been a baker in Twickenham where he had then lived.

The only thing left to do now was to make some sort of a line on the farther side of the village in case there was a counter attack. The battalions on either side of us now made their appearance. We were squeezed out, and they became responsible for the front line. I sent back a report on our activities and set out to stroll through the ruins of the village. I wanted to see if there were any Germans lurking in dug outs, which might join in any counter attack, as was sometimes the case. It had not been a great battle as our own casualties showed. They were two officers had been killed and five wounded, 17 other ranks were killed, 121 wounded and 3 were still missing. In the village we took 510 prisoners and captured 7 machine guns.

Walking round the village it was interesting the results of our bombardment. Every building had been reduced to piles of rubble. The church was the largest pile of all. Only reinforced concrete dugouts were intact. Fifteen-inch shells had failed to break them down. From one such dugout smoke was proceeding. Petrol had been poured down it and lit to bring out any occupants. There were comparatively few dead Germans in village itself, which must have been evacuated except for those who had been meant to delay our movements, but on the far side there was a considerable number who may have been caught when retiring. I thought I would go back to the scene of the morning bombardment, where we had been held up. On the way I passed a wounded German in a shell hole. He was a middle-aged man with blue eyes and a fair, old-fashioned moustache, which drooped, over his mouth. At his side hung a bloody mess, which had been his arm. He looked doubtfully at me at first and then asked for some water, which I gave him. At that moment a party of German prisoners was passing under the command of a British N.C.O. They were searching for wounded and they had a stretcher. I pointed the man out telling the N.C.O. to come back for him.

All was quiet when I reached my shell hole of thereabouts in the morning all was quiet and I sat down and looked out on the altered scene. I looked towards Monchy, so distant that it seemed almost impossible to believe that our troops had got there and back amidst acrid smoke and bursting shells. At that point something caught my eye. Coming down over the slope, which was still white with snow, I saw what looked like a long black snake slowly winding its way. The light was failing, but at last I could distinguish horses. Could this, at last, be the long expected break through and the cavalry advancing? And that is exactly what it turned out to be. They were the 'Lifeguards' and they had been hastily summoned to follow up our unexpected success.

Unfortunately they were attempting the impossible, moving over ground broken up by lines of trenches and an endless tangle of barbed wire. They could not get through, so they halted where they were. They had lost great many horses to artillery fire and, when it started again, they turned and took back what was left. Six years later I preached to them in London more than once and their band played at my wedding, but I could not see that far ahead as I watched them move away in the gathering gloom of an April day.

I was not the only person who was curious enough to wander through the village to see what it was like. One of our officers, who had been left out of the battle, had come up too. Unfortunately he was killed by one of the shells which still fell from time to time amongst the ruins.

It got very cold that night again, and I was glad to find some shelter. I discovered a German officer's dugout on the far side of the village, just where our objective been. It was a pleasant surprise to go down many steps and find that there was a place to lie down and sleep after so many nights without any rest worth mentioning. The Germans had obviously left in a hurry because all the officer's kit was still there, though I was much too exhausted to look at it. I lay down and enjoyed the luxury of gradually dozing. I must have been asleep for some time when I found someone leaning over me and violently tugging at my shoulder, as if he had nearly decided to give up trying to wake me. As I lay on the ground I heard the orderly talking. I wondered if I could possibly force myself to wake up and take in what he said, so complete was my exhaustion. I think I was dimly aware we could be in trouble. The orderly delivered his message. Company Commanders had to meet early next morning at Battalion Headquarters, which had now moved up into the ruined village. From there we were to make a further advance.

When I struggled to my legs a few hours later I was still so exhausted I found it hard to stand up. The morning was cheerless. Emerging from my dugout I went to find out where the meeting was, moving past the bodies of dead Germans lying on the melted snow. As we crouched in a temporary shelter I heard the plans for the new advance. They were fairly vague, with some mention of cooperation on the right by another battalion. All we knew definitely was that we were to start off from our last stopping place and go on till we go no farther. As I left the meeting I made a little detour to the shell-hole where the blue-eyed old German with the shattered arm had been. He was still there, sitting up as if looking for the stretcher-bearers who had not come, only this time he was dead. As I walked back to my dugout I passed numerous dead Germans, whose bodies lined the road. I noticed that our chaplain was methodically covering the faces of each man with a handkerchief. It hardly seemed worth the effort.

By now the officers who had been left out of the battle had come back and the proper Company Commander automatically took over from me. At the beginning of the road we had to travel down, there was the body of a very youthful and rather pleasant-looking German officer who was really no more than a boy. Having got the men together we moved along the road. It had a bank on one side and I made the men line it, facing what appeared to be a strong German defensive position. Presently we saw some grey uniforms moving there so I told them to fire. It is curious how different shooting at a target is from shooting at people, when you are under fire yourself. Two men next to each other were firing and one shot so carelessly that he blew off the wood under the barrel of his neighbour's rifle. He didn't notice until I pointed it out.

We had been told to wait where we were, as we were going to be joined by another battalion, but they didn't turn up. We thought we ought to do something about that, so we went on down a slight incline to the end of the road, which was still under the cover of the bank. From there we could see across an open stretch, which ended with a steep bank, behind which we had seen some Germans moving. The officers began to stroll across the open space, wondering what would happen. The men followed. To our surprise nothing did happen. We clambered up the bank and, just inside a trench a little further on, came upon a dug out. It had been so recently abandoned that there was still some bread and potted meat on a table. Being really hungry I sat down and ate some. I also put on some grey gloves I found and borrowed a German officer's walking stick. My colleagues said they thought I was mad. The remains of a German breakfast might have been poisoned but no evil effects followed and I wore the gloves until fingers wore through. The potted meat and bread was remarkably good too.

The next stage was not so easy. We agreed that we couldn't just stay where we were. We must make some sort of advance, so we clambered once more to the top where the ground began to rise gently. There we had to stop as shells began to fall thick and fast around us. We decided to advance by making short rushes and then lying down but even that proved difficult to accomplish. As we ran forward a blinding snowstorm started and hid our movements. It was lucky it did. That was about all we thought we could do. As the light was failing we lay down with what cover could find until it was dark.

It was during this last advance that I lost another good sergeant. I was particularly sorry about it because for some weeks he had been due to leave the battalion and go home as a specialist. He was an electrician. The usual delays had prevented his name coming through, and I saw him getting more and more depressed and feeble until he was not really fit to stay. Alas for his wife and family.

The night, which now began, was a change from our usual trench life. As soon as it was dark I tried to get the men on the open ground into some sort of line facing what appeared to be the German Front. The moon had risen and not far away I could see silhouetted against the sky, the forms of German soldiers who were hurrying about. I hoped they were not coming our way. Meanwhile a brisk bombardment was kept up. It went on all night. We were told it was to cover movements they were making to the rear in view of our advance. I thought I had better move along the line as I could see no other officers and needed to show the sentries that someone was awake beside the Germans. I soon found I had been expecting too much. All the men, without exception, lay like logs, fast asleep on the snow in the moonlight, and nothing could wake them. I shook one or two of them, but there was no response. Perhaps they were the dead ones I shook? More probably absolute exhaustion had overtaken them and they lay there, "dead to the world" as they say. There they were, asleep on the snow, within sight of the Germans who were evidently on the move, with shells intermittently falling a few yards away from them, as if there were nothing whatever to bother about. I thought it was useless to try and rouse any of them and went back to my shell hole to wait for the dawn, or for anything else that might happen in the meantime.

By now it was freezing hard and the sides of my muddy shell hole were stiff with frost. I had no food left and had eaten nothing since the morning when I had finished the German officer's breakfast for him. My liquid refreshment was nearly finished too.

Only a dribble of rum was left in a small aluminium flask. I drank the last few drops of my chlorinated water, with grit and a hair in it. It seemed the most glorious drink I had ever had. From my shell hole I looked out across the snow. The landscape was dotted with the bodies of men who were all dead or asleep. Shells fell intermittently as I wondered what would happen next. It was then that I realised that I was the only man awake. It seemed so funny that I laughed out loud.

Presently it began to get lighter and the indefinite things I had observed in the moonlight took shape. On the previous night the rifle fire had been so close and accurate that it had not been possible to look about before it got dark. Now that there was no firing I could see that ground fell away a little in front. It then rose again with barbed wire entanglements between us and the point where I had see Germans moving about. It was easy to see why they had had no fear of being attacked from our side. I made use of the dim light to crawl back point from which we had advanced in the snowstorm. That was where I had last seen the other officers. They had now found a communication trench, which led to a little lane. The lane gave us an entrance to a trench on the higher ground, where the Germans were still holding out in their main position. That was probably the way we ought to have come in the first place. It must have been a pretty little country lane in peacetime, winding up the hillside, with hedge and spring flowers. Now it was blasted with shells and a number of dead Germans were lying about. One very big fellow lay on his side with one leg up in the air. Beside him was a machine gun, which had toppled over. As I moved along I was surprised to see what appeared to be a live German soldier, standing up in his grey overcoat with his back to us as we approached. I wondered what he could be doing there. He was a sniper, evidently intent on spotting anyone who advanced towards his carefully concealed hole. Now we were coming up behind him. It seemed odd that he should be there with his binoculars still held up to his eyes. And then I realised that he too was dead. His elbow, balanced on a ledge had kept him upright after he had died. To all appearances he was still on lookout.

At that point the trench turned to the left and we were soon at a block, where we rested for a few minutes after our exertions. I posted a sentry in case of attack, telling him not to look over the top. After a time I thought we had better do something so I

Out of petrol?

told one of the men to throw a bomb over the barricade to see what would happen. He threw a German stick bomb – one of a supply, which the Germans had left behind. We did not have any of our own.

As nothing had happened since we arrived, one man thought it would be all right to have a look and see if the Germans had departed. What he saw we did not discover, for the moment his eyes were above the top of the trench, he was shot neatly through the forehead. The men, who by this time had sat down to rest, were dozing. I knew that if they were not kept on their feet they would soon fall asleep. They had nothing to eat for more than 24 hours and had long ago finished all their water. Looking around I noticed that, quite near the top of our trench, just to the right there was a stationary tank. It had evidently been put out of action and smoke was pouring out of it. It must have been the one I had seen starting off the morning before. A few moments later an officer emerged and strolled towards me. I was surprised the sniper who had just killed one of our men had not shot him.

"I've run out of petrol," he said, as if we had met casually and he wanted a match. Do you have you any?"

It seemed rather an odd request to make to the infantry who at all times were weighed down with the things they had to carry. As patiently as I could I explained that we did not carry tins of petrol with us in an attack. It was about as much use, I thought, to ask him for water, but I found myself saying

"I don't suppose you have got any water you can give us. We haven't had any since the day before yesterday."

"I can give you a petrol can full", he replied. And that is what he did.

Shells began to fall round the tank, we wished it would move elsewhere, but we appreciated the water which revived us at once.

The next unexpected thing to happen was that English aeroplane arrived and flew lazily over our heads. It was very low down, and it flew along the trench we were hoping to go to, sounding its klaxon horn as it went. It was a very welcome sight, and we felt that we really being helped. An angel of deliverance? As the sniper had so far been too good for us, I decided to leave that trench alone and see where we could safely head for next. I moved to a trench, which ran parallel to the one we were in, and wandered down it for some way by myself. I met no one at all. There was a dugout on the right, which sounded as if it still had some Germans in it, but I thought it would be unwise investigate on my own. I picked up a nearly new German overcoat, which I found nearby, and made my way back. Perhaps the remaining Germans had seen the tank and the aeroplane and decided it was time to pack up. Now it looked as if an advance could be made if anyone came along to do it, but our tired remnants were not fit for any more.

I was wondering what to do next when news arrived that we were to be relieved. We were told to stay where we were until reliefs arrived. An officer of another company who had been left out of the battle brought the news. I told him that the trench seemed empty and he went along it and investigated the dugout where I said I thought there were still some Germans. He found several that had been wounded but were still alive.

At nightfall we stumbled away to comparative safety. We got as far as battalion headquarters, which was now not far away. It had been moved up to a dilapidated dugout in a sunken road near the front. I should have gone in and reported on the day's events, but I was so totally exhausted I lay down in the snow outside while the other officer; who had come up when the work was done, went in and passed on my report. It would have taken longer if I had gone in myself, because I had been there when it all happened. I was too done up to talk much, so I lay down on the snow in the dark outside. Eventually someone came and told us to move to some sandbag shelters where we were to spend the night. That was the end of the battle for the present, as far as we were concerned. We had had a second dose because it was thought that the casualties we had suffered in taking the village were not large enough to warrant a withdrawal. In two days two more officers had been wounded. Eleven, other ranks had been killed and fourteen wounded. Four were still missing. One of our officers told me that on the first day he had been hit but a bulletproof waistcoat had prevented him being wounded. Unfortunately he was killed later on.

The next morning was sunny, which drew attention to my week's growth of beard. The Adjutant was not impressed and told me that I must shave. My efforts to treat his comments as a joke upset him so I once again had to endure the painful task of removing a week's growth, using a blunt razor and a broken mirror propped up on a snow covered sandbag. We spent the next night in a village in the suburbs of Arras. We were billeted in a small house on the edge of the village. It was well maintained and appeared to have been and abandoned in a hurry. Everything was exactly as it had been left. As we sat at table in a furnished room with the plates and cutlery of the owner we felt like burglars. I was sorry to move out the following day and even sorrier when I heard that an enterprising mess cook had replenished our collection of chipped enamel mugs and tin spoons with some nickel-plated items he had found in the house.

We moved on next day to another ruined village. There was little of it left. The ruins included what had once been a church. All that remained was a brass crucifix lying in the rubble. From there we moved on to Mondicourt – a rather shabby place on the way to Doulleus. We were glad to be there, with the prospect of being out of the line for a while, but we soon found that once again we had expected too much. In a very short time we were back on the road and heading for Arras. As we moved off I must confess, I was very disappointed. I reflected on the fact that, after two years of the life we were enduring, I was the only officer left of those who were in the battalion when I joined it, and that there were hardly any of the original men. I was exhausted physically and mentally.

When we had done the first spell of marching and had fallen out on the side of the road, I was handed a written message from the Adjutant. It said:

"Report at Warlencourt where you are to be Town Major."

I asked if anyone had heard of such a place. No one had so I started off by myself, looking for signposts as I went. There were of course none.

I really felt rather a deserter leaving my battalion in this way, knowing what they were going back to. I wandered on, meeting no one and eventually found myself in a street of a very small village with a few shabby cottages down one side. The officer whose job I took over as Town Major was in a hurry to be off.

He showed me his billet, which I quickly decided would not be mine for long. It was a shabby cottage reached through an untidy yard and inhabited by aged couples, who were not at all glad to see me. I asked to see the bedroom and was shown a bay windowed room which could only be reached by passing through their accommodation. At night I was expected to knock and, after waiting for a sleepy "Entrez," stumble over a huge feather mattress rather like a balloon, with the old couple perched on top.

The next day I walked round the village and found that it adjoined the little town of Pas-en-Artois which at that time was a rather tidier place. My duties as Town Major appeared to involve doing a nothing at all and after one day it became very boring. On Sunday I attended Mass at the village church, rather hoping to be greeted with a nod or two from the inhabitants. Evidently my predecessor had not paved the way for me and I received none at all, and was evidently regarded as an interloper. I decided to try and find a better billet and eventually found one on the top of the hill. It was in a house in which a woman and some children were living alone. She seemed quite agreeable about my going there so I decided to move. By now the aged couple had found that I was not troublesome and did not want to lose the payment for my billet. When I asked about the house I had discovered they told me that the woman I had met was a bad lot.

When I woke up the following day I heard one of those terrific bombardments in which numerous explosions merge into a long, murderous rumble. I then knew that another attack started and that this time I would be out of it. Habit made me feel I ought to be there and I wondered what my battalion was doing. The noise I had heard turned out to be the start of the third battle of the Scarpe.

I later heard that about this time my company had been ordered to take a trench in the small hours. There had been an ineffective scramble across No Man's Land just before another order came to tell them not to go. One of the platoon officers and my good sergeant major were both killed. The American-French officer in command was wounded and taken prisoner in the German trench. He was later sent to Switzerland.

Several years after the end of the war, I was suddenly reminded of one of the officers who died that day. I was passing through Surbiton by train. That was where he had lived.

When I was in hospital some months later, holding on to life very precariously, a letter from his wife had eventually reached me. I found very hard to answer. He was always such cheerful man. A typically good citizen and family man quite unfitted for warfare. He looked at everything from the point of view of an efficient clerk, who caught the same train to town every day and was welcomed home by a good wife. In my reply I explained to his wife how he had been killed so far as I knew, though I was not there she could not understand why her husband's body had not been recovered and buried. It required a little imagination, I suppose for people only accustomed to English life to picture the scene of a night attack and realise that an undertaker could not be rung up on the following morning.

A few days after I arrived at Warlencourt I had my first piece of business to transact as Town Major. A rather pleasant young Irishman in civilian clothes accosted me. At that time civilian volunteers were being sent over from Ireland to work behind the lines and replace soldiers who could occupy the trenches. In Ireland there was no conscription. They were paid for what they did and well paid too. He had a question about billets and explained quite politely that he didn't think his men were satisfied with the ones they had got. Could I find something better? He told me he had trained as a carpenter and we chatted about that and other general topics. Gradually I led the conversation round to the war. I explained that I had temporarily left it but had only heard that morning, that my sergeant major had been killed. I mentioned that that he too was a carpenter by trade. He did not press the question of billets.

He was better than some, for I later discovered that on May 9th 1917, a few days before that conversation took place, there were 100,000 munitions workers on strike in England and a general strike was feared.

Shortly after I moved into the family house at the top of a hill, I received orders to move to the neighbouring town of Pas-en-Artois. It had a Mayor and a Grande Place, with a miniature Hotel de Ville. It also enjoyed a quiet style of life as all the male members of its population of military age were then elsewhere. To anyone fresh from the din and turmoil of the front line, it was an oasis of peace. There was very little traffic and hardly anyone around. Only the distant rumble of guns to reminded me that there was still a war going on.

My first business there was to look for a billet. I hoped to do myself well and be able to enjoy comparative luxury, but my efforts to make the most of the opportunity did not prove successful. I went first to a large house, which stood by itself away from road. I thought it would be quiet and might be comfortably furnished. I was shown a bedroom, which was clean and furnished in a gloomy way and decided to stay there for a start. It was a pleasant change to sleep in a decent room, but soon the gloom of the place soon became oppressive. There was never a sound in the house and I rarely saw anyone. One day I did meet the owner on the stairs and he struck me as being the last word in gloom. He was dressed completely in black with a tailcoat and a black tie. He spoke in a low voice with his eyes on the ground. In a few words he explained that his son – his only child – had been killed in the war and that his wife would not leave her room. As for him, he went off daily to a factory a few miles away. It belonged to him and it was there that he worked. He was polite and I gave him no trouble, but the day came when I felt I could stand the gloom any longer. Making some excuse I moved out, hoping to find something brighter. I achieved my objective quite soon when I discovered a widow and her daughter who had come from Paris. They were much more cheerful and I stayed with them till they went away.

My new billet was a few doors away, in the house of a retired farmer who had also been the town's mayor. He was a widower who lived with his only child – a daughter, of whom he was naturally very fond. They had a super correct lifestyle, which I found oppressive. The situation got worse when my batman conveyed (as he always did at the first opportunity) details of my clerical origin. That always had a freezing effect on a continental mind. The farmer's daughter was a nice girl, but she was so thin that her bones showed through everything she wore. I discovered later that she suffered from consumption.

The great thing about this billet was its fairy tale beauty. My bedroom was painted a delicate pale blue. The furnishings suggested quite good taste and there was a very comfortable bed. It was a pleasure not only to sleep there but also to wake up and see so much brightness after the filth I had endured for the last two years

Of the town's other inhabitants I can only recall two. I remember an old Count. He was a dull, grumpy old man who lived at the Chateau. I also remember the parish priest. They were both unpopular in the town. The count was said to be grasping and people shook their heads when I mentioned the priest. Perhaps he had not always approved of them. The priest wore a dirty cassock, marked by years of slobbering and was so unwashed and horrid that it appeared he had given up hope. His niece kept house for him. I recall him partly because, on a previous occasion when my battalion was marching through the town he came to the gate of his house, and stood there hat in hand as if wishing us well. I thought it was a pleasant gesture and waved to him in return which was not thought to be militarily correct. Le Comte de Pas, to give him his full title lived at a pleasant old house a little removed from the other dwellings. A glimpse of it could be seen through the trees surrounding it as one passed by on the main road. It was quite well furnished in a bygone style and adorned with the portraits of his ancestors, mostly eighteenth century, who with their wives and the typical French faces of the well-bred gave the place an air of distinction, somewhat lacking in the Count himself. I had a conversation with him only once, when he came to see me about a visit to the area by Bishop of Arras, who was a well known at that time. He had stayed in his house at Arras long after it began to crumble under the fire of the German guns. I had heard him preach to a large crowd in a church in Boulogne. As Town Major I had to give the Count permission for his lordship to stay at the Chateau, but I mischievously suggested that he should stay with his unhygienic old parish priest.

I knew the Chateau, not from being his invited guest but because it was requisitioned to house a Signal school and I used to visit the officers occasionally. They had appeared suddenly from nowhere and my landlady – the Parisian Madame Ste Croix – had risen to the occasion and given them their first meal in her home. My job was to go round to every house and find out what they could do in the way of billets, in case troops came that way. They were all loud in their protests explaining how limited their accommodation was and how impossible it was to put up as many as they were supposed to do. That was how I became acquainted with everybody, and it passed the time better than just sitting in my office where there was nothing to do.

Now and again odd people turned up with jobs of a vague description. There was a Colonel Atherton, who was very pleasant to me and took me to a County Sports, presided over by one Lord Kavanagh, to whom he introduced me. We took with us another new arrival who was MP from somewhere. Col. Atherton told me that he had been "pushed out by his constituents." On another day, a whole London bus load of pleasant elderly people were decanted outside my office and asked me where to go. They were retired army and naval officers, some quite senior. Feeling they ought to be doing something to help they had volunteered for France and had come out with the rank of Second Lieutenant to do some job behind the front. I sensed in their arrival some danger to myself because mine was the kind of job they had come to do.

Another day a tiny little General appeared and marching into my office demanded peremptorily how many I could billet. I told him how many and he replied that I would have to billet his whole brigade. I said I would do my best, which seemed to annoy him. He started to rant and rave and told me I would have to do it, not just try, as if I had been guilty of gross insubordination. It amused me inwardly to see anyone behave in such a ridiculous way but I remained silent and he disappeared. Neither he nor his troops ever arrived.

On another occasion a little dark skinned person suddenly appeared and asked me some questions. He gave me his name and I guessed at once that he was son of a judge I had known when I was working in Burma. He was surprised that I had spotted him and had known his father and Burmese mother. He told me he was in the Intelligence department. I did not see him again until after the war, when we met at a college in Cambridge. Letters denoting two decorations he had received for distinguished service followed his name on the list of undergraduates.

One day, when I was feeling rather bored; I spotted an artillery sergeant who was moving down the street with uncertain steps. It was fairly unusual to see a British soldier from outside and I wondered what he was doing on his own. I decided to stop and interrogate him. I asked him what he meant by coming into town and getting drunk. I think I even threatened to report him to his C.O. That upset him and next morning, when he had sobered up, he came to beg me not to do so because he was a prewar soldier with a good record and all sorts of things might happen to him. He told me he had come into town to buy beer for his battery, and had decided to sample it first. He went away very sad when I repeated that I should have to report him. Of course I never did.

A few days later an officer, who spoke French very well, arrived to investigate claims for damage done by British troops. He asked me to join him. One claim was for the collapse of a barn wall. The wall was made of mud, which had been plastered on laths of wood. That claim was allowed but it struck me as odd that a flimsy piece of rubbish, which would have fallen down by itself at any time, should be paid for by the British taxpayer.

I received a number of visitors in my time as Town Major. I recall two Anglican clergy who came to me for looking for a billet. They had given up their livings temporarily in order to do Y.M.C.A work somewhere in France. I explained that I did not know of any Y.M.C.A establishments in the area, and they seemed surprised. I arranged a billet for them but, when they found they had to pay for their food and nothing happened day after day; they became decidedly upset at the thought that their volunteering had attracted so little attention.

After a month at Pas I had some villages added to my domains, which meant that I had to go farther afield to inspect them. My kingdom increased so rapidly during my three months as Town Major that, if I had remained there longer, I might have ended up controlling a large part of France! Much as I loved the peace and quiet of Pas, there were times when the living there was boring. I was getting restless. Should I put in for leave? I debated the question and realised that if I did, my hope of being forgotten would fade, if not vanish. Boredom won and I decided to be bold and apply. To my surprise leave was almost instantly granted and off I went.

I set out in brilliant sunshine with my valise, and took up a position on the Arras road to wait for a lorry that would take me to Amiens. As I stood at the roadside I looked up and saw a string of cars coming along in an orderly procession. They were all stuffed full of Red Caps, who looked like a very sober bank holiday party out for the day. I had been told that the King was in the area and assumed this must be his entourage, so as they passed I sprung to attention. The staff officers all turned towards me as they passed, with anxiety on their faces wondering if I would salute. I had no intention of doing so until the last car passed, as I assumed that was where the King would be. The big moment came but my best salute was unnoticed as he was earnestly conversing with a staff officer as his car shot by.

I eventually arrived in London in brilliant summer weather. There was an aura of untroubled prosperity and the eager pursuit of gaiety, by people who seemed to have come into unaccustomed wealth. Having marched everywhere in France, with heavy loads to carry, I decided not to walk anywhere. Even for the shortest journeys, I took a taxi. Once I went to a theatre, which was crammed to the roof and very hot. I came out before the end of the play, which was just called "Romance." Somehow the drama of the stage seemed flat and unreal, when there was so much first-hand drama on the other side of the water. There our task was just the opposite of the theatre. We set out to undramatise life as much as possible, and to regard the most trying things as commonplace and ordinary.

London was still a great place for a carefree holiday and I enjoyed the simple things of life and being able to shut out the atmosphere of war. I was aware that my leave would not last long and wondered what I would find when I got back to France. I hoped I might be able to return to the comparative peace of Pas, but it was not to be. Ten years were to pass before I went back there. When I did go back the war had ended and the whole world had changed.

Ten years later, I took a slow train to Mondicourt on the Arras road. It was a very hot summer day. Arras was then as far as it was possible to go by train so I strolled out of the station hoping to find something that could take me the few remaining miles on to Pas. As no conveyance was to be seen I reconciled myself to walking, but I was soon overtaken by a farm cart, in which was a young priest who let me get up beside him. It felt rather odd, in the brilliant sunshine of a quiet summer day, to be jogging along in these wartime surroundings with no major anxiety on the horizon. Quiet, safe and free.

I tried to recapture the old atmosphere. I recognised the houses we passed and some of the roads, though they somehow seemed to have lost their life without army lorries and khaki-clad soldiers. It all seemed so quiet and rather dead. I noticed one new building – a pink modern little house, which I was told was a new police station. Apart from that was little had changed. It just felt as if the place had lost its object in life.

The priest did not go far and when he got down I was left with the driver. I talked to him and mentioned that I had lived in Pas for a time during the war and asked after some of the inhabitants who were there then. I thought it would be interesting to hear how they had fared. I remembered how they had all looked forward with so much longing to the day when the war would be over, and they could resume their old way of living. What had happened to the Priest with the slobbered cassock who was living with his niece who looked after him? How was he?

I was told that he had died some time ago and his niece had married a man who kept a small hotel. Then I thought of the owner of the bright bedroom, and the emaciated daughter, of whom he had been so proud, no doubt hoping that she would marry well. I asked after them. He had also died and his daughter had married a. young man in Government service, who had subsequently absconded with some public money. Soon after that, she too had died – of consumption.

Next I asked timidly about the old Count. I explained that I had hardly known him but seemed to recall he was a bit of a stick. I was told that a fire had destroyed his pretty Chateau but my driver did not know what had happened to the count. Then I thought of the people in whose house I had stayed first of all. The sad old people, whose only son had been killed in the war, I felt the atmosphere too oppressive to stay. Did my driver know what had happened to them?

He did and here the story was a little longer. The old man had gone on much as usual after the war running his business. He set off regularly every day. Seven years after the war, and ten since his son had been killed; people noticed that his habits seemed to be changing. To everyone's surprise, he then bought a car. It looked as if he was beginning to take an interest in life again. He learned to drive and went about a good deal, but one day he set off on a journey and never came back. A search was made and the car was found, just a few miles from his home. It was parked up in a quiet lane where it was almost entirely hidden by high hedges. The old man was still in the driving seat when they found him. At his side was a revolver with which he had shot himself.

As we travelled on, I remembered how the place had looked during the war. The utter devastation all around and the longing for peace, which had kept people grimly hanging on for all those years. Now peace had arrived but it had clearly not bought all the happiness they had sought and deserved.

Ten years earlier, in 1917 I had come back from a spell of leave in Britain to join my regiment at Ypres. I was greeted by the C.O., as always, with a kind of welcome that seemed to make up (if anything could) for the gruesomeness of returning to the hardship and drudgery of the front line. He was cheerier than usual and introduced me to a major who had come as second in command and was later to succeed him. I was told that the battalion was being fattened up for the new offensive had been launched on July 31st. It was to drag on at enormous human cost through Passchendaele.

Ypres campaign

After the Pas district, the country was dull and lifeless. In a couple of days we moved on and arrived in an area packed with troops on their way to the active volcano of Ypres. The name of the place we found ourselves in rather suited it. It was "Ouderdom." We were accommodated in tents that had been put up behind some trees, which were meant to hide them. Loathsome as a crowded bell tent is, we were no doubt lucky to have any shelter at all so near the battlefield and to escape the bombs which fell on another camp which was quite near. The place itself was so full of men and transport it reminded me of an ant heap. Walking in the street was a slower process than going along an Oxford street pavement in the rush hour. Moving men into a battle area was rather like pitch forking them into a seething cauldron. They were swallowed up so soon that the problem was to keep up the supply. In the short time we were there, final preparations were made for the attack. We had the usual officers' meetings at which it was decided that I should once again be in command of a Company instead of the proper Company Commander.

My Company was to be a few yards behind the others at the beginning, in reserve. There were therefore no complicated instructions, as there had been at Arras in April, but we still had to reconnoitre the positions. Those who knew wartime Ypres will not need to be told that that was not easy, at any time. In daylight it was virtually impossible. The only thing we could do was to get as near as possible to them and find the road we would have to take. We were due to start early, in the hope of avoiding as much shelling as possible. We knew that the Germans had precisely charted the layout of all routes to Ypres. We met in a hut to discuss the situation as soon as it was light. The hut had some tables and chairs and there were faded posters on the walls, promoting the delights of a number of English seaside resorts.

The C.O. arrived and we sat in silence and ate some food. We were all very depressed and I had had no sleep. The C.O. noticing that, made some jocular remark to me and I replied saying that I felt as if I had a heart of lead. We knew each other well enough now not to pretend. No other battle area was ever as grim as the appearance of Ypres. It was hard to resist its atmosphere of death and destruction, even though we were well accustomed to such things. No doubt the discomfort of our crowded tents and lack of sleep had also lessened our powers of resistance.

The other officers rode their Company horses, but I chose a bicycle, which I could discard easily and perhaps find again. I did not fancy myself dodging shells on horseback. So off they went, and I followed later. I got as far as Hell-fire Corner on my bicycle, left it there and set out on foot to find the others. The gloom of the early morning had now turned to rain, which made the dreary shell-pitted waste even less inviting. Just behind Hell-fire Corner was a little tramline, which some men were repairing after the night's bombardment as a few shells continued to burst overhead. I joined the rest of the party and for some distance walked with the C.O. who, unusually for him, had not shaken off his low spirits, For some reason, he talked to me about his early days as we went along, as if he was trying to forget the present.

The ground was waterlogged and the only way through it was by corduroy roads, which seemed were well worn and had clearly often been repaired. At the side of the track were many shell holes, full of stagnant green liquid and here and there, there was a dead horse. A bogged down tank completed the picture of desolation. Beyond us there was a low ridge. It was so low it was hardly a ridge at all but it was important to us because it commanded a view of the ground beyond. Away to the left was the place that gave its name to this devastated hell: Ypres. By now all that remained of it was a remnant of a once white wall. Its broken outline suggested the jagged remains of old discoloured teeth, sticking up out of a gum. There were no buildings left inside the wall.

We pushed on and crossed the Menin Road, which was often a target for heavy bombardment. We then turned left and came to what we were told was battalion headquarters. It was a sandbagged shelter above ground. The floor was covered with hay and it was empty. We had reached Hooge – the scene of a major battle earlier in the war. We could not go any farther in daylight and there was no point in staying so we went back, with sundry shells bursting overhead. We returned a different way and when we had travelled some distance I realised that we had passed the place where I had left my bicycle. It was getting noisier and more shells were coming over. Hell Fire Corner was living up to its reputation, but I did not want to lose my bicycle and disliked the idea of walking back. I made a special effort, found the bicycle intact and hurried off.

Two days later we were due to move up to the line and take up our positions. There was nothing to do but hang about near the tents. We were not allowed to do anything else in case there was a change in our orders. There were Company Commanders' meetings too, and the troops had to be fitted out with bombs and other impediments. On the afternoon before we moved off, our Chaplain arranged a service of Holy Communion at 5 p.m. It was held in a small hut and it was quite well attended – mostly by officers. There is no doubt that this service, under conditions of imminent death, has poignancy. In that respect it perhaps recaptures the spirit of the occasion on when it first took place.

The following afternoon at about 3 p.m. we paraded, rather like beasts of burden with our extra attachments of food and other things. Our C.O. on his horse addressed us as we stood there and exhorted us to "keep our powder dry." That, as it turned out, was good advice for ammunition ran short during the next 36 hours and at one point we had to get some more, fetching it under a crushing bombardment. Heavy of foot and heart we then set off. Our acting Chaplain, who had just joined the battalion, stood at the roadside as we moved off and waved to us. He was a pleasant man and he was going back. I was told he had a stomach complaint. I never saw him again.

We were lucky enough to get a long way along the road without any shelling. At about teatime we arrived at the spot beyond which it was impossible for us to proceed in daylight. We had come, as one would expect, by a different route from the one we had reconnoitred. I was glad to get my many impediments off and lie flat on my back.

Just above us, quite near to each other, there were three captive balloons keeping watch on the German lines. In about as long as it takes to write these words, without any warning, the bursting of a salvo of shells dispelled the quiet of the evening. They must have been accurate for all three balloons rapidly collapsed. One descended in flames. We expected more shelling would follow after that but nothing happened. We sat down in little groups and ate some of the food we had provided ourselves with.

It soon got dark and eventually the stars came out. It seemed wonderfully quiet and peaceful. More so, perhaps, because we knew that zero hour was less than half a day ahead, and then things would be very different. In our little group of officers sitting on the ground, there was a man I had not seen before. He seemed very quiet, not joining in, and I remember thinking that he and I would probably get on well. He too, had noticed the stars. After looking at them for some time he remarked:

"How far away they seem!"

"Yes," I replied. "It makes you wonder what's behind them."

He was killed the following next day.

So far the whole battalion had remained together but the plan was for three companies to go and take up their front line positions that same night. My company was to halt near the Menin Road and go on the following night and take up a position just behind the others. So, when we got to the Menin Road we stopped and the rest went on. Unfortunately when they reached their front line position they were heavily bombarded and had many casualties. We didn't escape either for at the same hour; we too were bombarded with a mixture of heavy and gas shells, the latter arriving like damp fireworks with their characteristic "phut." We were lying down on the bottom of our trench when the gas shelling started. We felt for our respirators and put them on hoping it would soon stop. When it had ceased I was able to look around. I discovered that, in addition to being next to the Menin Road – the exact position of which was well known by the Germans – there was a fleet of tanks anchored just in front of our trench, waiting to go up. No doubt German aeroplanes had noted that and marked it down for shelling.

Another day passed without further incident and in the darkness we began to move up to our final positions. We moved on the hour at which they had shelled the Menin Road so heavily on the previous evening and I was glad to get across it without casualties. Just beyond Hooge, we were to pick up guides, whose job it was to lead us by duckboard tracks, across the swamps, which lay between our battle positions and us. The swamps

Duckboards

were quite tricky and we knew that, if we strayed off the duckboards, we might be drowned in gallons of liquid mud. Before we met our guides a heavy barrage closed down on us as we were passing Bellewarde Lake. We all flopped down and, as luck would have it, found ourselves behind a high bank amongst some remnants of trees, which gave us good protection. From this comparative security I watched a great many of the shells dropping into the water a few yards on my left, where they did no more than send up cascades of liquid mud.

When the shelling stopped I was astonished to find that we had had no casualties at all. As we emerged into the open and began to go across the swamp, I looked out for a red light, which I had been told would mark the spot we should make for. It was actually a bicycle lamp put down at the bottom of the bank on our side of the trench, where Battalion Headquarters was positioned. On the maps, for some reason, which I never understood, it was called "Jabber" trench.

The guides who were to meet us at this point were late. We had to wait for them, balancing on duckboards in the dark in the middle of a swamp, with a very good chance of being shelled. When they eventually arrived we wasted no time in moving off. For the last part of the journey I had got the men into single file and put an officer in front with the guide. I brought up the rear myself, to prevent the usual straggling, which always led to aggravating stops. We proceeded at a snail's pace, hoping that no further bombardment would descend upon us in this uninviting spot.

It was very dark indeed and easy to go astray. I had been told that, as there was now no wire between the German positions, and us we must be careful not to accidentally wander into their trenches. The men, with rifles and heavy with kit, had to balance themselves in pitch darkness on the narrow duckboards and move forwards, without making any noise, and trying not to fall. One or two found that was asking too much and we had to stop while they were pulled out. At one point we stopped altogether for some time, which was exactly what I had wanted to avoid. I had to scramble to the head of the column to find out what was up. When I eventually arrived I asked the guide what was going on. His reply was brief.

"I've lost the way, sir."

"Good God!" said I, knowing the battle was due to begin very shortly and having no wish to be drowned in the mud or be blown to pieces. At that point an officer who had been in front said he thought he could find the way. As there was no alternative, I told him to try. We trudged on once more but I confess I had very little hope until at last the red light appeared. We felt we had been saved.

It was now nearly midnight and it had taken us several hours to do cover a very short distance. I positioned the men at the bottom of the bank, where we were to be in reserve, telling them to get what cover they could from it, in the absence of a trench. I then went up the bank into "Jabber" trench, where battalion headquarters was, to tell the C.O. that we had arrived. I found him walking about in the trench with something less than his usual composure. His headquarters was a little shelter in the angle made by Jabber trench and another, leading to the front. Both of them were so blocked with men lying on the ground that it was almost impossible to move around.

"Pretty awful isn't it?" he remarked in a quiet voice to which I replied that it I hoped a bombardment would not start while we were so packed together.

Having reported in, I moved back to the place where I had left the company, which was only about twenty yards away. I found that some of the men had scooped out holes in the bank, which gave them about two feet of protection if they sat with their backs against it.

Zero hour was not till 4.30 a.m. and so we knew we still had several hours to wait.

Having nothing more to do I sat down too to get what rest I could, with my back to the shelter bank, which protected me a bit except for my head and shoulders. I was facing the treacherous swamp we had just come through but it could not be seen in the pitch darkness. It was very quiet now, with the ominous stillness, which often precedes a battle. It was so dark that it was impossible even to see who was next to me, but I could feel there was someone on my left, in the same position, facing the swamp. I thought he had his knees drawn up and his arms resting on them, so he was probably asleep. There was also an unpleasant smell, which was not unusual in these situations.

Time dragged on, and at length my luminous watch told me we did not have long to wait. The darkness became less impenetrable. When at last zero hour came, it was impressive, even for one who had seen similar things before. As the darkness dwindled, the outline of the protecting bank behind us became more clearly defined. In front of us we could now see the men-acing swamp and the end of the duckboard track, by which we had arrived. The morning sky was overcast and there was a mist, which soon turned to drizzle. I could now see my companion on my left and understand his silence. His head had been neatly blown off, without otherwise disturbing his position and congealed blood had dried on the decapitated trunk. That also explained the smell. From time to time I looked at my watch. There were only a few more minutes more to wait. I wondered if the Germans knew as well as we did that something would happen then.

When zero hour came, it was as if someone had pressed a button. Simultaneously uproar broke out all along the front. As far as you could see there were pinpricks of light, where guns were being fired into the early morning haze. Miles and miles of it could be seen from where I was and the ground quivered, as if an imprisoned giant lying underneath was struggling to escape. There were no individual explosions for all were merged in one Titanic rumble. The noise was so deafening that it was useless even to shout. When shells burst quite near they were seen and not heard. The ground wobbled like a jelly.

At first there was little retaliation, but that did not last long. Occasionally dense puffs of black smoke appeared overhead and then there was one explosion, which seemed very close. I was winded and felt as if I had had a heavy blow on the chest. I knew I had been hit but I couldn't see anything, even when I undid my coat. It was only after the battle that I found out what had happened. I had been hit on the brass button of my breast pocket, which had been bent. Behind the button there were two clean handkerchiefs put there for emergencies and a thick wad of very tough French bank notes. Even so, the buckle of my braces was bent into a bow and had been driven into me right through my clothes. My fountain pen too was smashed but it had had played its part in protecting me. The pen had been mightier than the sword! In fact the chief result of this incident was the strange hue of my whole front, which afterwards turned completely purple. I realised that I must have been struck with some force. I picked up the piece of shell and kept it for years.

It was becoming very uncomfortable where we were, with so little to protect us, and there were casualties. On my right, a man who was sitting in the same position as my silent companion on the left had his head removed in exactly the same way. So now there were two headless men, one on each side of me. It became more necessary than ever to keep my own!

Fortunately most of the shells fell a few yards beyond us. They landed in the swamp sending up columns of black mud. If the ground had been hard, their fragments would have demolished us. So the deadly traps, which at times drowned wounded men, were to some extent our salvation. In the middle of all this a man suddenly appeared to report that ammunition was running out just up the line. I sent two of our men across the duckboards to fetch what was required. The men noticed my decapitated colleagues and took the pay books out of their pockets. They seemed glad to have something to do and to get out of the area of intense shelling. Soon after they had gone another man made a brief appearance in a lull during the hurricane of shelling. He had come from was from the C.O. who wanted me at once.

I covered the short distance to his position without being hit and found him in his small sandbagged shelter in Jabber trench. He seemed very worried and asked me what I had been doing. I explained that, as ordered I had waited in reserve not many yards away, where heavy shelling had caused some casualties. I told him that I had sent for more ammunition but that was all. He said I had better go forward with what men I had left and try to find the other companies as no one knew where they were.

We set off went down a trench which was almost filled with dead men and eventually got into another which seemed to face the German front. In the middle of this terrific bombardment a German aeroplane suddenly appeared and swooping down just over our heads machine-gunned us. I flopped down; hoping the earth might open and swallow me up. As it didn't, I tried to look as if I wasn't there. I then discovered that I had flopped on the partly buried body of a man who had evidently been lying sometime in the hot sun. He was on his face and earth covered the upper part of his body, but his behind, now bereft of trousers, was sticking up above the ground. It was a case of any port in a storm but I was glad when I hadn't got to stay in there any longer. The aeroplane, which was, painted pale green like a dragonfly, hit the ground with its wing and crashed. An officer, who was somewhere behind us at that time, told me afterwards that as it swooped down he and some others had shot at it with their revolvers.

I got up as quickly as possible and decided that we must bear to the left. Using what protection a shallow trench gave, I moved off and before long found myself at a point where I could over look the German positions, and even see beyond them to the horizon.

A short distance away there was a place called "Nonne Boschen" or "Nuns Wood, in English. I remembered it because I had made a feeble joke about it when we were told about it earlier. I had said that wondered if we would find any Germans there. When we eventually arrived we found that the place was no longer a wood. The few blasted tree stumps that remained could not hide a rabbit. Polygon Wood, which lay a little further on, was in the same condition. The ground sloped away, from where I was to where our other companies were supposed to be (if any of them still existed). Somewhere between us there had once been a wood. I waited for a time in my new position hoping that the men would straggle forward to join me. They arrived one by one. I had never known such heavy shelling as now descended upon us with even greater fury. It was a marvel that anyone could remain alive.

The bombardment threw up so much dust and dirt that I expected our Lewis guns would be useless, so I told the men to clean them. Keeping watch from my forward position I could see some movement far away on the horizon. I thought it might interest the C.O. to hear about it and to know where we were so I sent a runner with a note back to battalion. Much to my surprise he not only got there but also managed to bring another message back. It said ""Hang on old man, and look out for a counter attack. I'm looking after you."

The guns were cleaned and we now had five in working order. When the shelling slackened I was surprised to see some men coming towards us from a position away to our left. They had run out of ammunition and were coming back. They passed through us.

"It's no good stopping," one of them remarked.

Those men, who I think must have been the stragglers, were sighted by our C.O. when they got level with him. By that time a direct hit had demolished his shelter. His batman had been killed and he and the adjutant had been dragged out from the debris. The C.O collected some men and began to lead them forward in my direction when he was shot through the lung. It was at that moment that we moved forward down the slope.

I started off and found that in the open the shelling was less, though there was rifle fire to contend with. I ran in short spells and dropped down making a zigzag course, which I hoped the men were following. I looked round after the first stop but could only see a German field gun, which had evidently been brought right up to the front to deal with tanks. I moved on again and when I looked back saw a few men coming after me. After a couple of hundred yards, I came to a place where a bank fell away, with a swamp beyond and decided that was as far as it was possible to go.

When the men came up, I put them on either side of me, making them wriggle up on their tummies, until we had made some sort of line facing the direction where the accurate rifle fire was coming from. It was now late afternoon and I thought we would probably have to spend the night where we were. No Germans could be seen but it was clear that we were being watched. When one of the men, whose heel I could touch, raised his head a little he was shot dead. No movement – not even a quiver – marked a German sniper's very accurate shot.

As the light faded a number of German aeroplanes flew slowly just above us sounding their klaxon horns, which was the signal our own aeroplanes gave to the infantry who had to reply by showing their positions. They wanted to know where our front line was. I remained still and hoped the others would too, but a misguided soldier shot at them with his rifle, so presumably they got the information they required. There was a lot of pretty accurate shelling soon after that. Before it got completely dark I thought I would try to pen a few words of comfort and, if possible, send them back to Battalion H.Q. I did not then know that Battalion H.Q. had ceased to exist. I settled down in my shell hole and, pulling out my book for writing messages, felt for my fountain pen. It was then that I discovered it had been broken by the shell fragment, so I had to do my best in pencil.

I had just begun when to my astonishment someone, who must have crawled towards me, sprang with great nimbleness over the side of my shell hole and crouched down in it with me. Before I had time to think whether it was a German or not, I recognised the spare form of the Commander of "C" Company, whom I sometimes called "our only soldier" because of his apparent relish for war and his great efficiency.

As he sprang in he said, "Anyone at home for tea?"

He asked me how we had been getting on. I told him and asked if he could tell me where his company was, as I had been sent to find them. There were not many left and those that remained had come to a point on the edge of a swamp beyond which it was impossible to go.

"I'm pretty well done in," he replied, which was an odd remark for him.

I told him what I proposed to do that night and we discussed the possibilities of relief. We stayed quiet for a bit, and he seemed to recover his usual spirits. Seeing a dead German just outside my shell hole, he reached out and felt in his pockets. He drew out a pair of spectacles, put them on and surveyed me sternly. We had to laugh at that.

"I must go," he said suddenly, and then he was off, as quickly as he had come.

I resumed my interrupted note to battalion H.Q. As darkness fell I spaced the men out. A few faced our original front and a few at right angles to them – parallel to the Menin Road on our right, where I had seen some Germans coming up before it got dark. They had been only a few hundred yards away and the light gleamed on the wood of their rifles, which showed that they were fresh troops with no dust of battle to dull them. I thought they might creep up nearer under cover of darkness or, as we had no one either on our right or left, might get in behind us. I was expecting a counter attack and that was the best we could do and with five Lewis guns.

At intervals we could at least fire them off if we were attacked. With everyone in position I went to one end of the "L" shape they formed with my sergeant major and there we remained on the lookout. A very heavy bombardment then began, which was perhaps due to reports from the low flying aeroplanes, which had spotted us. By this time I had altered our position and the shelling fell mostly behind us, though that may have been with the idea of preventing reinforcements coming up.

After a time I thought I must go along and see if the men were awake. We had had no food or sleep for 36 hours and during most of that time had been under a continuous heavy bombardment. My acting sergeant major had been lying down at my side with his head on my leg and I had let him stay there, thinking he would be better for any sleep he could get. He was very young. But now I had to wake him and take him with me, so I said into his ear, quite close, "Wake up", but he didn't move. He was too done up, so after a bit I gave it up and went alone. I had a word with each man as I crept along as quietly as I could. It was wonderful how self-possessed and cheerful they were, in their cockney matter-of-fact manner, taking things as they came. I dared not speak above a whisper because it had now become quiet.

The shelling now seemed to have stopped. That could indicate that the Germans, who had seen us moving forward in daylight, thought that we would not move any further. Alternatively it could mean a counter attack was coming. I went back and lay down at the end of the line and kept a sharp lookout, listening for any movement. It was a difficult night and my second without any sleep and hardly any food, with continuous heavy bombardment and many casualties. We were also out of touch with other troops and I did not know how far behind reinforcements were. It seemed impossible to stay where we were indefinitely without food, so I decided to try and find battalion headquarters before daylight came.

There was just enough light at daybreak to help me to stumble in the mist up the slope leading to where our headquarters had last been. I spotted the German gun I had passed the evening before, so I knew where I was. A little farther on the number of dead bodies increased. There were so many that it seemed pleasant to notice amongst them an officer who seemed to be only asleep. It was his position, which made me feel he was only sleeping. He was lying on his back with his legs straight out and his arms by his sides. His uniform was so clean, and his boots too, suggesting he had probably joined us late in the day. His hat was off and his fair hair was well brushed and tidy. He looked as if he might wake up at any moment and look down on the valley, where the battle had raged. It seemed almost a pity to wake him up but it had to be done. I leant forward to tell him that it was getting light. It was only then that I realised he was dead too.

I moved on to find myself in a trench, which led into another at right angles, at the point where battalion headquarters once was. It was impossible to move without treading on dead bodies. Now, after all the hubbub, there was complete and utter silence. Not a shot was being fired and, as far as I could see, there was not a living soul to be seen.

I found our H.Q., which had been patched up enough to be used again, and went inside. It was still quite dark so I did not see anyone at first, and then I became aware of a bent figure sitting on a box with his back to me. It was the C.O. of another battalion, which had come up to relieve us. I spoke to him and explained our position and said that it seemed rather useless to remain where we were. He didn't take it in very well and sounded tearful and upset but I gathered that his battalion had come up to relieve us and that there was now no further need to stay.

The trenches were now so full of dead bodies that it was impossible to move without treading on them. The silence was oppressive after what had been happening. Was there no one alive at all? Two nights ago this trench had been buzzing with conversation and crammed with men.

I had almost given up hope of finding anyone alive when I heard a voice. Looking up, I saw a young signaller who I remembered had recently been attached to our battalion H.Q. He was standing in a gap between some sandbags, at the side of the trench.

"What on earth are you doing here?" I asked him.

He said he was the only man from battalion headquarters who was still alive.

"Have I your permission to retire sir?" he asked, rather formally.

"Well, there doesn't seem much to stay here for does there?" I replied.

I moved back to the place where the evening before I had sheltered between two decapitated men. Their bodies were still in the same position – sitting up.

I moved away and began to thread my way across the swamp. At the side of the track I noticed a new officer's haversack stuffed with papers. Thinking they might be of interest I stopped to pick them up. They were all messages about our own battalion and they had evidently been thrown away in a hurry. I took them with me and moved on; passing a stretcher on which two men were carrying a wounded sergeant. He was gasping for breath, and had been shot through the lungs.

I crossed the Menin road without lingering and hurried up the slope on the other side. I was back in the place where we had been bombarded with gas shells and heavies two days before. Now the sun was shining and I began to feel better, away from the atmosphere of death but the unexpected lull did not last long.

As I hurried on, the shelling started again, and I hoped I would continue to be lucky. It was at this point here that the real Company Commander, who had been left out of the battle and come up unofficially to see how things were going, had himself been hit. I carried on until I was out of the immediate battle area and then saw some huts and lorries, which I made for. I was hoping I would be able to get a lift. It did not matter where it was to. Anywhere would be better than where I was.

I climbed aboard and waited for the vehicles to start. While I was sitting there a smart staff officer came up to me and had a few words.

"Are you an officer?" he asked, as well he might for by this time I had a few days growth of very black beard. I was also wearing a private's uniform, outside, which was a leather jerkin, a tin hat with a canvas cover, and everything was smeared with the dried mud of the trenches. He asked me how things had been going and I explained that we had gone on until we had hardly any men left. If there had been a lot more men I thought some farther advance might have been made. It was a misleading statement in the light of what happened at Passchendaele, but I was no doubt feeling exhilarated by the prospect of getting away from it all. I had also just had my first food for days and one is liable to be hopeful in situations like that. I later learnt that this was how they sometimes collected information. By asking people who had actually been in the battle.

My Royal Progress then began. Jolting along by the side of a lorry driver, going through peaceful countryside heading for anywhere. It didn't matter where, so long as it was away from the war and its atmosphere of death and destruction. Those who have escaped great danger will be familiar with that exultant feeling of escape. An instinctive clinging to life, beyond all reason.

As the lorry rattled along I asked what troops were in the neighbourhood and where my own battalion was likely to be. I eventually found them in a field in tents.

Battalion H.Q was now in a cottage on one side. As I approached I felt rather like the last survivor coming into Jellalbad, but I thought it would be rather amusing to walk in unannounced.

The Adjutant was there as I opened the door and he and some others looked at me in silence.

"I think this is yours," I said handing him his haversack.

They seemed very silent and the Adjutant opened his mouth as if to say something.

I suppose, when he had left the day before, he had concluded that no one had survived and there I was, complete with beard, not to mention his haversack!

That night there were tents to sleep in and I got one to myself, thinking that it was peaceful, if dull and hoping that soon we would move to somewhere more interesting. Thoughts of peace, however, were dispelled by a German aeroplane, which flew over us when it was dark. Searchlights picked it up, and it looked like a frightened little silver moth as it tried to squirm out of the betraying beam.

Next day we moved on and were rejoined by "the survivors", as they were sometimes called. That is those who had been left out of the battle to form a nucleus if there were a lot of casualties. The officers were all strangers to me, having come when I was away as Town Major and I found that rather depressing. When night came I felt I didn't want to crowd into the unattractive billets so I looked for a barn. I eventually found one and I climbed up into the loft and lay down on some hay. I congratulated myself on the peace and quiet I had found but it wasn't as good as I had hoped it would be. Some bug in the hay got into my clothes and set up such an itching that I spent a wakeful and unpleasant night and rejoined the others next morning having not slept at all.

We were now near Poperinghe. Although it was out of the war compared with where we had been, German aeroplanes regularly passed overhead. We could still hear the rattle of machine gun fire and the dropping of bombs, which made the area far from the completely restful place I had been hoping to find. We were only there one night. Early next morning we were ordered to move to the region of Steenvoorde, on the frontier between France and Belgium. At that time it was quite out of the war. I got the order the later than everyone else, having slept in my barn, and it was impossible to verify the map references we had been given, which told us where Companies were to meet and prepare to march off. I had to do a bit of guessing and. Fortunately, I guessed right!

As I was marching along with my company "survivors" I saw another body of men on the main road. As luck would have it they proved to be ours, so I fell in behind them in the nick of time, as if our meeting had been carefully planned. Fortunately the C.O. was a major, who had just arrived from England and I hoped he thought I had arranged it all and fallen in behind the others according to plan.

At last we found ourselves going away from the war. In the brief but eventful time since I had returned to the battalion, three officers and thirty-six other ranks had been killed at Ypres in less than 36 hours. Ten more officers were wounded and 228 other ranks. We had suffered 274 casualties out of around 400 men.

Some months later I saw the events of the day referred to in a newspaper as the Battle of Westhoek Ridge. Only then did I know where I had been!

After a short march we found ourselves in the pleasant little town of Steenvoorde which I now saw for the first time. It was big enough to have a few shops and an improvised restaurant for officers, run by enterprising people who saw the opportunity of making a bit out of the crowds of English troops who were thronging the place. It seems difficult now, after so many years, to realise the intense pleasure of sitting down in such a place eating well-cooked food off plates and being waited on by civilians.

As I sat there I dreamed of more visits to this unmilitary place but, as I emerged, I ran into an officer wearing a red cap who called out cheerily saying I must come next day and dine at Brigade headquarters – an unheard of distinction. My spirits sank, but I could not refuse. The staff officer had been our Adjutant and was now on the Brigade staff, hence the invitation. We had not met since I went to be a Town Major, when he had been quite a friend. While I was away and he had attained his present eminence.

I duly presented myself at the required time, feeling as if I was on parade. The Brigadier arrived, breezy and undimmed by war. He was the same Brigadier who had come up cheerily to me in the trenches in the preceding January, remarking that one of my officers always seemed so odd that he must be drunk or dotty. My response to his evident wish to be friendly had then been somewhat marred by my knowing that the officer in question was listening to what was being said. On this occasion the Brigadier, who, no doubt was bored with the thought of having anyone to dinner, greeted me with enthusiasm as we all sat down. There was some rather forced conversation, and our late Adjutant and I eagerly bent forward to listen while the General recounted stories of India and how he had kept a pet mongoose. I always felt that in the presence of a General one was supposed to behave like a very small boy who was not quite all there, and I never quite managed it. I left at the earliest possible moment, hating myself for having been caught and not being able to go to the restaurant I had discovered and enjoy the civilian atmosphere by myself.

I did not get another chance for the following day we moved to a place called Watten, which I found was rather depressing. Flat fields intersected with little canals for irrigation and there was very little else. The place had a kind of gloom I did not associate with France. That, on the top of my dinner with the General, took a toll of my spirits, but

I think it was probably a reaction after so much nervous strain that was now making itself felt.

We stayed in Watten for a day and then found ourselves even further from the war on the main road to Calais. Our spirits rose and we felt quite near to home. We wondered why we were being moved this way and felt it was probably because the areas we had been in were wanted for concentrations of troops who were heading for the Ypres slaughter house.

Soon after we arrived in the Calais area I was told that I could go on three days leave to Paris, if I liked. I did not feel particularly joyful at the prospect, being too done up to do much but rest, but it takes a bold man to refuse an offer of even three days' leave. I also heard that I was to be accompanied by another officer who had not been long with us. He had Great Britain written all over him and regarded the French with good-humoured tolerance. He was also rather very deaf and I shuddered at the thought of bellowing at him continually. The dark design of dropping him as soon as we got there entered my mind but at this point yet another obstacle loomed on the horizon. It proved to be an even greater deadener of joy than my good-tempered, deaf companion.

Our Medical Officer was given orders to inoculate us. Should I let him do it and get it over, or put it off and deal with it when I returned? I thought any side effects would be negligible, as they had been before, and decided to have it done. I am not sure if it was because the room our Medical Officer worked in had once been a pig sty, or if the was some other explanation, but the effects of receiving my injection, far from being slight, afflicted me almost at once with violent diarrhoea. I was unable to eat anything or to go many yards without having to pull up with violent tummy ache and hurriedly search for a refuge. The effects lasted for some days and had such a weakening effect that I could hardly stand up. Only the fear of having my leave cancelled made me go ahead with my plans.

I had to get to Calais first, and the only way of doing that was by getting a lift on a lorry. My condition made that more difficult than usual but eventually I got to Calais station. It looked very woebegone with every window shattered, but there I managed to board a train and was soon sitting in a first class compartment, where I met the deaf transport officer, who beamed with goodwill from the opposite corner.

The civilising effect of the train, which was carrying passengers from England, was great and thoughts of war quickly receded from my mind. Opposite me was another emblem of peace in the shape of a very good-looking and fashionable lady whose expensive handbag, which she opened for purposes of toilette, showed a number of luxurious fittings, which I studied with care. I compared her life with that of the shell stricken swamps I had so recently left behind and thought how wonderful it would be to be pleasantly attached to the war, as she appeared to be. I was wrenched back to reality by looking up and seeing that the eyes of the other officer were fixed on me. My dark designs became a certainty.

Getting down at the Gare du Nord I was interested to see that my distinguished and beautiful acquaintance was followed at once by a British officer, who was careful to find her a taxi. He had appeared from nowhere and stepping nimbly in front of me offered his services. Who says the British are slow? I did not see what happened next. I only heard that the taxi was going to the Ritz. Meanwhile my companion, who was deaf, but not blind, winked at me, and I took him off to a quiet hotel where I thought he would be all right and then fled. The fact was that, although he was a nice man, I did not want to witness his reactions to the Paris scene. I wanted a rest and I felt I simply could not shout for three days at the top of my voice, with a continual pain in the tummy as well.

I went, by myself, to the Westminster hotel and had a very good room with bathroom and sitting room attached, where I thought I would be comfortable for the short time and hoped to rapidly recover. My investment in luxury proved to be a waste, for I found I could eat nothing at all and dragged myself around with the utmost weariness, having to suddenly disappear into any house I happened to be passing for a certain imperative purpose. I tried to eat an ordinary meal at a restaurant, which at other times would have been an impressive event, but had to give it up and live on milk, and not much of that.

There were meatless days in Paris at this time and meals seemed to consist chiefly of sauces which, in my state, were nauseating. Indeed I became slightly alarmed at my condition and repaired to a British M.O., who I managed to locate after a long search. He evidently disbelieved my story of the inoculation and concluded that I had been living it up in Paris and knew the remedy without coming to him. So I went off and bought some castor oil, which had cured me in the past, but by now my leave was almost up.

I only saw one person I knew during my visit to Paris and that, oddly enough, was the C.O. of the Battalion, which had relieved us at Ypres. When we had last met he had been tearful and undone in a wrecked sandbagged shelter. He probably did not recognise me as I saluted. If he did, the spot where we met, outside Rumplemeyers, was a long way from the hatefulness of the Ypres, which neither of us would have wanted to remember. At night there was a very brilliant moon and that accounted for the ceaseless drone of unseen aeroplanes patrolling the sky. It seemed strange for an Englishman to lie safely in bed in Paris, after so much that had been otherwise. I thought of the pilots. Frenchmen patrolling overhead in the darkness, going backwards and forwards all night, until the morning light made it unnecessary. When they faded away into silence. Guardian angels, unseen and un-thanked.

As I was only beginning to recover when my three days leave was up, it required a good deal of strength of mind to drag my tired body to the Gare du Nord, and leave the delights of civilisation largely untried. I glanced (but not too carefully) about me when I arrived at the station, but my companion, deserted three days earlier, had not returned. He had probably got fed up with the absence of a cup of tea and an English breakfast and gone back before his leave was up.

My battalion had been on the point of packing up to go back to the Somme area when I had left them, and my instructions were to make for Albert and there find out exactly where they had gone. Albert then was a small agricultural town. Arriving in wartime after a crawling railway journey I was to see it at its worst. The tall battered red brick tower of the church still kept its Madonna and Child on the top. It stuck out at right angles where a shell had bent but not broken it. It was to remain in that position until 1918. The other most noticeable feature of the town was a restaurant for officers. Some very business-like French women kept it and they ran it very well, providing a facility I was glad to make use of. At that point Albert was out of the war, but in 1918 it was severely damaged. When I returned there in 1919 it was little more than a heap of ruins littered with rusty barbed wire entanglements. It had become a hunting ground for salvage parties.

My next destination was to be Beugny, a farming village in the Bapaume district. Like so many other villages in the devastated regions, when we arrived it hardly existed except in name. There was no sign of human habitation and troops were housed in huts on either side. Bapaume, through which I also passed, was just as desolate and the effect of seeing so much destruction was very depressing. Our new C.O who sent for me when I arrived, explained how my leave companion had, like a good boy, returned some time before. He seemed to be waiting for me to make some comment. I explained I that I had been ill but my explanation was not well received. In retrospect I suppose it may have sounded rather unlikely.

The Germans did a thorough job when they retired to the Hindenburg Line and devastated the country they left behind them. Anyone, who lived there for any length of time, felt the depressing effect of being in this forbidding area. When we were not in the front line trenches, we lived in huts and sometimes not even in them but in reserve trenches. There was consequently no change when we were out of the trenches and supposed to be resting. The civilian atmosphere of what had been a delightful French village had all but disappeared, and that had a depressing effect on our minds and spirits.

By way of cheering us up, from time to time we were given reports to read to the men. They were accounts of the outcome of recent court martials. They included details of the sentences that had been handed out to unhappy people, who had failed to turn up for some show or other, and had later been found wandering about behind the line. The people concerned had often been shot. The men did not like hearing these reports and I did not like having to read them out.

When we moved up to the line, we went most of the way by light railway, travelling in small trucks on a little tramline. The train made quite a lot of noise and sent up showers of sparks, so we were all expecting to be shelled at any moment. When nothing happened we were surprised and grateful. Perhaps it was a case of live-and-let-live, or maybe the Germans were just busy elsewhere. While sitting in one of the small trucks awaiting our departure, I remember having a very strong presentiment of impending disaster. I put it down to accumulated fatigue. In the event it proved to be much more than that. Another two months would see my exit from the war and, very nearly, from everything else.

When we made that journey our terminus was a point between Lagnicourt and Moeuvres. When we arrived there, we got out and walked. We made the same journey several times. On one occasion when we got out, it was so dark no one could decide which direction we should take. We knew by then that our guides were useless. I had to guess the way and, fortunately, my guess was right.

A sergeant who was with me remarked, "That some people could tell others what to do, without always being able to do it themselves." I took as a compliment, which I hope it was.

The trenches we took over were dry and chalky, unlike those in Flanders. Looking over the top we could see undulating, pretty country with little sign of war. In the distance was Cambrai. Its buildings looked white and unattainable on a sunny day, as if they belonged to a world of dreams. My company headquarters here, was, at first, a long way from the front line, and hidden away by itself in a kind of dell. It was very pleasant to sit in the September sunshine, surrounded by wild flowers and a few lingering bees, and imagine that the war was only a dream. The dream, it is true, was dispelled at times by sharp little bursts of shelling by someone who knew the exact location of my one-time German dug-out, but it was very deep so that it was quite safe if we got there in time.

One day, when we were caught by surprise, I noticed an oldish fellow who I had not seen before. He didn't seem to take much notice of the shelling, so when it slackened I stopped to say a word with him. I asked him how old he was, but he did not reply. Guessing he was deaf I bawled out the question once again, closer to his head. He said he was afraid he was rather deaf. When I asked him his age he said he was 44.

"What on earth did you come out here for?" I yelled, thinking of some stalwart people I had seen elsewhere. He surprised me by saying, "I would rather be here than at home."

I saw him again ten weeks later, when we were both lying on adjacent stretchers. On that occasion I was not so successful in making him hear. His head was heavily bandaged, and so was mine. Perhaps my bawling was a little subdued. I saw him once more five years later, in London, on the day before I got married. He approached me in Holborn and asked if I would mind accompanying him to the Prudential Insurance Building, where he was having a little difficulty, He had allowed an insurance policy to lapse and they were refusing to renew it. I explained who he was and how long I had known him, and they said that they 'would make a concession which would put the matter right.

During our first tour in these trenches, I was admiring the view when a message came to say that I was to go on a course at an Army School. It would have been sensible to go, but at the moment I remembered the boredom of my last course and said I wasn't keen, so someone else went instead. That decision let me in for my next and last battle. The man who took my place survived the war as an unwounded major.

The trenches at this point were very deep. Deep enough to be traps if anyone came over the top, but no Germans were ever seen and there seemed to be a kind of mutual agreement to keep quiet. Only once did they raid trenches hereabouts, and that was a little on our left. Suddenly one night a German appeared and flashed an electric torch in a man's face. He was so surprised that he was lifted unresisting from his place and carried back to the German lines.

We took over the trenches where the kidnapping had occurred, but the only event while we were there was my unsuccessful attempt to shoot a pheasant with my revolver. It persisted in coming back till someone shot it with a rifle. He told me later that it had tasted good.

The line was held by a number of isolated posts, and it was quite a journey to walk along the deep trench from one post and another. On one particularly dreary day I was making my way along in pouring rain. As I splashed through the half-flooded trench, I passed some men sheltering in a hole scooped out of the side. I knew they were there because I heard voices coming from behind a waterproof sheet, which hung over the opening with rivulets of muddy water trickling down. When they raised it like a curtain, I made some remark and they roared with laughter.

"I hear we are going to be relieved by the submarines sir," one of them said. Cockney soldiers were always good in conditions like that.

At Beugny, when we were not in the front line, we found ourselves in huts instead of the usual reserve trenches. We thought that better because we were less likely to be called on to form a working party. When reserve trenches were used instead of billets, we were not allowed to leave them, which added greatly to the boredom. When the weather got cold I remember trying to pass some time by building a fireplace in the trench's earthen wall. It was not a great success. It just filled our shelter with blinding smoke. After a while we smelt like kippers. I wrote "Kipper Factory" on the door, which was my melancholy attempt to squeeze a joke out of our discomfort.

Even in these dreary substitutes for billets, we did have some distractions. One evening, after a particularly dull day, I looked up and saw an aeroplane approaching. That was not unusual and the arrival of a plane would hardly have been noticed if it had not been such an uneventful day. As we were in the equivalent of billets we did not have to post sentries, so no one took much notice as it moved slowly towards us. It flew lower and lower, until I thought it must be going to land. When it was just above our heads, and so near that the pilot's face could easily be seen, I awoke to the fact that it was a German plane with black crosses and all. It turned and flew swiftly out of sight.

We of course knew that this isolated visit had not been made for the pleasure of calling on us in our quiet retreat. Its true purpose became apparent from what followed. There was a battery of eight-inch guns a few yards behind us, and that was what they had come to see. Any doubts about that were dispelled next day when the Germans began shelling it early in the morning. With Teutonic persistence they went on all day and, by evening, there was nothing left but a smoking ruin. The shells passed just over our heads with clockwork regularity, so although the noise was a bother, we did not worry as much as we might.

When the shelling stopped, I thought I would go and see what had happened. That was a mistake for as soon as I arrived at the smouldering ruins my ears, which had learned to recognise ominous sounds over many months, detected the distant whine of more shells on the way. I guessed that the best thing was to run at right angles away from the scene and not straight back to the trench, because any shells not on the target would probably fall short rather than at the sides. I managed to get clear and reached my trench in a very breathless state after a record sprint. Some people thought I had been spotted and had drawn the German fire. I think it was more likely that they thought someone would probably go to inspect the damage and felt it was worth firing another salvo.

By this time church parades had become so rare that I had almost forgotten they had ever taken place but one day, while we were in our huts at Beugny, it was announced that there would be a parade, which we were expected to attend. Shortly afterwards a rumour spread that a gas attack was being made on the front line trenches some miles away. It was a fine morning with no wind, so to be on the safe side – the very safe side – the parade was cancelled. It never took much to cancel a church parade. During my two years and a half years with my battalion as an officer in or near the trenches, I remember can only remember two ever-taking place. They had consisted of some subdued singing of unaccompanied hymns, a few prayers and no sermon, so I cannot say that we overdid it. On both occasions we stood in a ring in a field holding army prayer books and were not too sorry when the service was over.

Another diversion while we were in the same huts was a Divisional Sports' meeting, and for that our Divisional General was present. It had probably been arranged with the aim of keeping up our morale in depressing surroundings. Our new C.O., who had recently arrived and was brimful of energy, kindly, invited me to go with him so no refusal was possible but the walk to the ground at his pace left me out of breath.

He made fun of that, thinking I was lazy, but the fact was that I couldn't go any faster and the depressing conviction came to me that I was getting very used up. He also chaffed me about being improperly dressed, because I lacked a ribbon, which could not be obtained in the devastated regions.

We were told that the Divisional General would be glad to make the acquaintance of any officers who liked to speak to him, which was civil enough. I got close enough to see quite a pleasant-looking man but my British shyness and general fatigue kept me from doing anything more. A happy thought came to me later on and I suggested taking a day's leave and going to Amiens to deal with my missing ribbon. My suggestion was approved but getting to Amiens proved to be quite difficult. There was no railway and comparatively little traffic, but at last I found an officer with a car who gave me a lift. It was a joy to get away for a few hours.

From time to time notices came round asking Company Commanders if they had anybody who they could recommend for a Commission. The supply of suitable men by at this stage was pretty well exhausted and it was difficult to find anyone you could honestly recommend. We knew that if you had a well-tried N.C.O. and sent him off to be an officer your company might suffer. We also knew that good N.C.O.'s did not necessarily make good officers. It was thus tempting to send up the name of someone you would not particularly miss. These problems were specially in evidence in the autumn of 1917 when the drafts of men were not as good as they had been and good N.C.O.'s were more important than ever. After much thought I put forward one man's name and sent it off with a brief note of rather faint praise. Our new C.O., who in normal life was an experienced businessman, quickly noted the brevity of my comments.

"Did I or did I not think he would do for an officer?" he asked so I said "Yes."

Three weeks later the man concerned was to figure in an episode which was important for me. During an unexpected bout of shelling, he shouted to me – "This way, sir!"

I followed him and ran straight into the shell, which put me out of the war, and very nearly, out of this world. Was that perhaps a sly dig of fate?

I met him again in England several months later. At that point I was crawling uncertainly back to life and he was on the way to his commission. I don't think he went back to France again because the war ended a few months later. So my recommendation did not really matter, except to him. It may have saved his life.

By the middle of November rumours of an impending push on our front became more persistent and we were told that everything was very secret. It was so secret in fact that we suspected that everyone knew about the plans except ourselves. There was some special activity at night, not far away on our right. Cambrai, which was almost in front of us, was also mentioned. I hoped any activity it would be on our right and that we should be out of it.

As often happened when a major push was planned, we were warned that there would be a party of Staff officers coming round the front line – an event rare enough to be considered important. Having received that information I summoned the sergeant major and told him to be careful to see that the sentries were in their right places, facing the right way and able to give an intelligent answer if they were questioned about their duties. To make quite sure everything was in order, I made a preliminary tour myself with the same object in view. I also arranged for a runner to be at the only place where an entry to the trench was safe. He was told to report the arrival of the cavalcade as soon as it appeared. The sergeant major would then hurry along and wake up the sentries. It was rather like the story of getting the pig over the stile, but of course, it depended on each chain in the link holding. It seemed to be a foolproof plan anyhow!

When the staff officers arrived everything started splendidly. The runner arrived and I went to meet the party, as if it happened every day and we were just carrying on as usual with no special preparations of any kind.

"Take us as you find us and of, course, we are pleased with the honour of your visit."

I hoped it looked like that anyway.

It was an imposing troupe that arrived. Larger than any previous one I could recall, except perhaps when General Allenby had come round one day in another part of the line. But he was an Army Commander. Then as I was only engaged on a working party and had hidden in a deep dugout till he had gone. On this occasion I watched as the V.I.P.s approached in their unhurried way, with clean uniforms, bright with red tabs, well-polished buttons and gleaming boots. They looked well cared for and as if they had had a hearty breakfast and a good night's rest. I saluted smartly, or as smartly as I could having lived 33 years before beginning army life and having survived for 21 years since, mostly in filth, dodging shells. Stifling the rebel in me, which always rose when staff officers were about, I led them slowly along the trench.

"You are the Company Commander?" the General asked at last, rather clipping his words as if he thought I didn't look like one.

I gave the only answer possible and waited for the next question.

He paused and said, "How are you holding your front?"

"By detached posts sir, at intervals," I replied and there I should have stopped, but I became chatty and added – "There is no other way because we have so few men."

"Oh!" said the General with a note of interrogation after it, and then he stopped walking and turned to me.

"And where are your reserves?" he added.

"We don't have any," I blurted out. "The nearest men are at Beugny, several miles behind the line."

The General glanced at the nearest red cap and my C.O., anxious that the battalion should avoid trouble, assumed a mask-like expression.

"It's not going too well," I thought. I was never any good at these inspections. No more was said and the solemn procession moved on. My sergeant major had not appeared and I earnestly hoped he was waking up the sentries. I continued to lead the procession along the trench, feeling fairly confident. We had not gone far when a man without a tin hat suddenly appeared. He was not where he should have been and he was blocking the way. I recognised him at once. He was a hopeless little fellow, quite unsuited for warfare He had fishlike eyes and a toothbrush moustache and was always dribbling with rum. I had always known that he would do something awful one day. He was quite unimpressed by the General staff but they immediately took note of him. I think he rather fascinated them. They were suddenly interested and everything stood still. They noted that the man was evidently a sentry. His rifle was there, but what a sentry! We moved on and I knew I would hear more of this. Our C.O. emerged at this point.

"What is that fellow doing without a hat?" he asked.

"I would like to know that too," I replied, adding that he was always hopeless and did everything, badly, probably in the hope of being sent away. I also explained how I had sent the sergeant major along to wake up the sentries just before the General arrived. I had left no stone unturned in my efforts to make the visit a success.

My C.O. had not finished.

"Why did you tell them you had no supports? You should have made the best of it."

It was the absence of supports, and having so few men in the front line, that made the German attack on this front in March the following year so successful. But perhaps the shortage had been kept dark – from all but the Germans.

The V.I.P.s visit produced some results. The defaulting sentry got what he had always wanted. We didn't feel we could stand him anymore. The next thing I heard of him was that he had been made a military policeman and put on traffic control.

It was during this last period of my trench life that I spent eight days in a very deep dugout. It was furnished with a shelf of rabbit wire and, in the centre, a table made out of a few rough bits of wood. There was also an old packing case to sit on. It had been an old German dugout so the entrance was the wrong side, facing the direction from which any shelling was likely to come. A candle, stuck on the table by its own grease supplied illumination. If a shell exploded it went out. Being in this sepulchre for eight days and nights had a weakening effect, so I went up pretty often, to tour the front line and get some air. Our Adjutant, who was a diligent telephoner having spent his life in a London office, found me out more than once. On one occasion he rang up about some returns and upbraided me for my absence! After that I had to spend most of the time living like a mole underground.

One day I heard that some new officers were coming. The news did not fill me with enthusiasm, as we had done without them for so long. In due course, in the semi-darkness I became aware that the sergeant major was standing at my side while I was writing a report.

"Three officers are here, sir – to report to you." he announced.

In the light of the candle all I could see was a dim outline of the sergeant major, so I merely told them where to go and asked if they had had anything to eat. They then went away to take up their first positions in the front line and I went on with my report.

Five years later one of the officers who reported to me that night reminded me of that occasion when he stood by my side again, as best man at my wedding.

As November advanced there remained no further doubt of an impending attack, though the exact nature and place of it was still unknown to us. One of our Company Commanders left us at this time. He was one of the best we ever had, but he had always been frank about the war and said he would give it a miss as soon as possible. He had spent two years as an officer in England and when he appeared in France had immediately taken the place of an experienced Company Commander in the front line. Now he had developed a cough and disappeared. The next time I met him was in the London the following summer, after I had been in hospital for many months. He was wearing a green band round his cap and I asked him what it meant.

"Oh, I'm in the Intelligence Department," he answered brightly and then added "I'm on the staff."

The main trouble on our part of the Western Front appeared to be occurring at a spot just on the right of our position in the line, not far from Cambrai. We hoped that with luck, we would be able to avoid it. We were worried because our battalion was still well below strength. It had not been made up since Ypres and we were now only about 300 strong. For a long time we had also been promised a rest.

We did not know what was going to take place on our right, but heard rumours that an attack by tanks in large numbers was going to be tried out. It eventually took place on November 20th. We watched from the higher ground on the left, where our trenches were, but we were not allowed to be idle spectators for long. At that point the Higher Command had another of their happy thoughts. While the main attack on our right went forward, we were to make a demonstration. Our demonstration was to be organised as follows:

On the night of November 19th we were to carry a dummy tank forward and deposit it in front of our wire. It was a kind of film-prop tank, made of camouflaged canvas on a wooden frame. Not easy to hoist over rows of barbed wire when it is dark. We were also to have dummy soldiers, to make up for the shortage of real ones. They wore khaki uniforms stuffed and tied to the barbed wire, to look like a menacing host about to advance. To make them even more so, strings were to be attached to them, and we were expected to pull them and make them behave like marionettes. In case the intelligence of the Germans should cause them to think they were not real men, we had to light a good number of fireworks, which gave off dense smoke and partially hid them.

When the Germans saw the stationary tank and the joggled dummies shrouded in smoke, it was hoped that it would make them think the attack was spreading. During these preparations one of my officers succeeded in spraining his ankle, He came and told me that he would have to go away so I bade him farewell and he did not re-appear at the front. He had been disapproving of the war for some time, so the sprained ankle came in just when it should.

Up to the morning of the attack, we had not been told that it was to be made by tanks, without the usual preliminary bombardment. It was only when zero hour came that we began to realise that something was happening, Even then the barrage which preceded the arrival of the tanks seemed a mild affair. We began to wonder if the attack was taking place and whether our smoke bombs had been lit in vain. I left out the joggling of the dummies and told the men to get what shelter they could, because, if the Germans were taken in, (which I felt was very unlikely) there would be retaliation and casualties. Fortunately only a few stray shells came our way. They seemed to explode rather contemptuously as much as to say, "You didn't think we were such fools as that did you?" So we had the unusual experience of watching a battle from quite near without much hindrance. As everyone now knows, this new form of attack by 70 to 80 tanks was the first ever conducted on such a scale. It closed the experimental stage of the use of these weapons. The army authorities had not been convinced that they were much use. The Army Commander on this front had however been converted and it was with his approval that the attack was made. One unusual feature of this attack was that the Tank General led it. After the war the Dean of Clare College, Cambridge told me, that as chaplain he had followed his example and rode in a tank too.

Several miles of German territory were over-run and, with the help of the infantry who followed, 120 guns were captured and 8,000 prisoners taken though the guns were to be mostly re-taken in ten days' time. The advance stopped short of Cambrai but the ground that had been captured could not be held, so the only thing gained was a demonstration of what tanks might do. A lesson which was no doubt not lost on the Germans.

We knew that there would be a counter attack but before it could come we were taken out of the line. We could thus only speculate on what kind of reply would be made by the Germans and when it would come.

Mid November in these devastated regions offered very limited recreation. As I had not been able to get a bath for six weeks I decided to have some kind of a wash. Someone found a tub and brought me a few tins of hot water, so I covered myself with soap and poured the hot water over. The only towel I had been by now very dirty but I used the extreme ends only. With a clean shirt I felt I was more able to face the fray, which I was sure would be coming shortly.

Our next move up to the line, which turned out to be my last, took us to some trenches in very wet and depressing weather. When we arrived we were summoned to an officer's conference. That invariably meant trouble was in the offing and we assumed that our overdue and long promised rest was likely to be off. We trudged gloomily to our meeting place in driving rain. It turned out to be a bit of roofed-in trench on the side of a road. The roof was so low that we had to crouch down when we were inside. There we listened while the C.O. outlined the probable course of the events that were to take place in the next few days.

Since the tank attack, there was a big bulge in our line. On the extreme left was the uncaptured Hindenburg Line, which was still held by the Germans. From that point to our old front line position there was a defensive flank, to prevent the Germans coming across No Man's Land and getting behind our new front. On the night of November 29 my company was to hold that defensive flank. On the next night the whole battalion would move up and occupy the captured Hindenburg Line itself, up to a point where the Germans were still on our left. As my Company had held the defensive flank, we would be in reserve the following night, in a trench some yards behind the captured bit of Hindenburg line. The other Companies would be holding.

We were far from happy with the news that we were to go into the line again. Our numbers had been so drastically reduced and we were all completely exhausted. We knew that the Germans would probably not stay where they were, but would counter attack almost at once. As I walked away from the meeting I overtook the Company Commander, whom I have already referred to as "our only soldier" His cheerfulness was generally proof against anything. He agreed that we were due for a rest and thought it unfair to send us into the line again. I had not seen him much since he had jumped into my shell hole at Ypres and said, "Is there anyone at home to tea?" and I felt that my own misgivings were reasonable if he had some too.

We set off that evening. As the light began to fail we made a winding approach down a pleasant little valley, which hid an advance. By this time the battle had died down and there was no shelling when we started to move. Our little disjointed snake of men, in single file at intervals, wound its way along as a brilliant moon began to rise and, with its quiet splendour, to take charge of the sky.

We got to the end of the defensive flank and moved out of the protection provided by the valley. Now the moonlight became a menace because it made us conspicuous, so we flopped down and crawled up to our positions. Shelling started almost at once. I took up my position at one end of the line and hoped for the best, but it was not a pleasant time. The continuous bursting of heavy shells, missing us by a few yards, was rather shattering when it continued for hour after hour. The moon remained bright all through the night. Its placid beams seemed at odds with the noisy attempts that were being made to kill us.

We watched for the first streak of dawn and then eagerly crawled away. We went on till we reached a point where we were able to stand upright again, and then walked back, under the cover of the valley. We eventually got back to our front line, where we planned to get what rest while we could, before the whole battalion moved up in the evening.

Resting in a trench, when everyone else is busy getting ready for a move is difficult. I lay down on a rabbit wire shelf for some time, to compose myself after the night of shell dodging and almost continuous explosions. As a result I felt more used up than usual when the time to start came. This time we had to go further, bear right and cover a stretch of rising ground before we could reach our positions. The last part of our course was often swept by machine-gun fire and the brilliant moonlight, which illuminated our progress, did not reassure me. I did not think we could proceed unobserved. We were also heading for a trench, which we would be sharing with the Germans as they were still holding an adjoining part of it. I was not optimistic about the outcome.

We had crossed a good deal of the exposed plateau, when our disjointed snake of separate parties of men in single file, stopped altogether. Of course the men, some of whom had never been in a trench before, did not know how near the Germans were. We were very obvious in the moonlight and one burst of machine-gun fire would have wiped us out. As I was aware of these points I lost no time in going to the front of the column and telling them to get a move on.

Just outside the trench there were rows of dead soldiers whose bodies had been lifted out of the trench to make room for us. In the moonlight their immobility suggested rest and made me think how much out of it they were. Perhaps they were to be envied on that account. The sight of them all neatly arranged, as if asleep in the moonlight, must have impressed someone else too, for as I waited a few seconds I heard the man next me say thoughtfully, "How still it all is."

That rather roused me and putting my mouth close to his ear I said in low but decisive tones, "About as quiet as you will be if you don't get into that trench pretty quick."

We moved on, with the greatest deliberation, until we managed to get in safely. I heaved a sigh of relief at such unexpected luck, which was possibly explained by the fact that the Germans were also moving up troops for the attack next day and did not want to provoke retaliation.

The reserve trench, which my company was to hold for the night, was about 50 yards behind the front line where the other companies were. It was joined to it by a communication trench. Battalion Headquarters was to the right of my Company, in a trench, which was a continuation of our own. It was therefore not necessary to post the usual number of sentries, but I took the precaution of collecting all my bombers and putting them together on my right, as near as possible to Battalion H.Q. I did that because long experience had told me that any ominous stillness without a shot of any kind being fired was always the prelude to something unpleasant. I then looked about for a place to lie down in, and get some sleep and told the men to do the same after the trying night we had all had.

I found a new dugout, which had been taken for Company H.Q. and descended into it. It was about the size of a small WC It had a concrete floor and was not big enough to let more than two people at most lie down at full length. It was also (as most German dugouts were) full of lice. After squatting for a few minutes and realising that sleep would be impossible I began to itch violently and decided to give it up. Extricating myself from a tangle of arms and legs, I set off in search of some fresh air. One of the officers I left behind had timed his first visit to a front line trench for this occasion. He no doubt, preferred my room to my company. It was better in the fresh air and I talked to the men, who seemed to be making no attempt to rest.

I moved along the communication trench to the front line, where there was another company. On the way I stopped to talk to a tall officer who was by himself in the trench. He was a quiet, rather reserved person who I thought I should like. He had just come to us by from the Guards where he had been a private but in peacetime he had been an actor by profession. I went on to the dugout where the other officers of the company were. Just beyond their dugout there was a bombing block, which separated our part of the Hindenburg Line from the Germans. There were just a few strands of wire across the trench and German voices could be heard coming from the opposite side. A sentry stood on guard with his bayonet at the ready. We talked in a whisper and then I left him to visit the officers in their dugout.

I had a surprise when I walked in. It was furnished like a room. The earth walls were hidden by curtains, on which pictures had been hung. There was a real table, covered with a table cloth and chairs which were real furniture. Not the makeshifts of rough wood we had got used to. In one corner there was a crate of mineral waters, which had just been opened. The owners had evidently left in a hurry, not expecting to be pushed out of a dug-out in the second line (as it had been whilst the Germans were here).

The effect of seeing our own officers in this apartment, which was meant to resemble the more regrettable type of middle-class German abode, was quite comic. They seemed to find it amusing too and were in very good spirits. There was the smell of burnt brown paper and rubber, which was always a distinguishing feature of German dugouts (as well as the lice!) I felt I could not be away from my own trench any longer and, with many cheery "good-nights", I went back.

Again, the silence impressed me and I felt sure that something unpleasant was in the air. As a trench dweller of long experience, I did not have the energy of a newcomer, but I had developed a certain instinct. November 30th began pleasantly enough. Everything seemed normal as I walked along the trench. The men were having their food and cleaning rifles. There was no obvious reason why the peacefulness should not go on.

It was at 9 a.m. that the German bombardment began. It started without warning as if someone had pressed a button and it was heavy and precise. It came down on our trench and behind it, to cut off reinforcements. We knew then that an attack was imminent. With that in mind I moved along the trench seeing that the Lewis gunners were posted at intervals and getting what cover they could. I told them that on no account were they to use their guns until they saw Germans actually coming over. The trouble with Lewis guns was that they easily got dirty, with so much mud and dust flying around. They could easily prove useless when they were needed most. With that in mind I made them cover everything but the muzzles, because bits of the trench were being blown up in the air and showers of earth were descending all the time. Almost as soon as the bombardment began a fleet of twenty-six German aeroplanes appeared, flying overhead along the trench. They were moving very slowly in formation and were so low the faces of the pilots could be distinguished. They were of course directing the fire of the batteries and informing the attackers that we had no reinforcements on the way. As they flew over us, one solitary English aeroplane made its appearance from behind our line. It came ambling slowly forward, as if it was making its usual morning tour of inspection. Compared with the German machines flying in formation, this single English one seemed old and shaky. Perhaps it was, only being meant for taking a daily look at the front to see if all was quiet. But the pilot did not turn back. I watched it coming nearer very slowly, and then it crumpled up and fell not many yards away. The German squadrons had not moved a varied a yard off their course and continued their formation flight as if nothing had occurred. That was the only English aeroplane I saw during the day.

The bombardment of our trench continued to be heavy and showers of earth and dust flew up. I was talking to my sergeant major when a big lump hit him on the arm. He had been wounded several times already. Going to the left of our line I discovered a machine gunner who had been sent there without my knowledge. Evidently he had been spotted because shells repeatedly hit the parapet where he was so valiantly sticking to his gun. As clouds of dust and muck were scattered, I wondered how long he could last. It was at that point that another stranger appeared.

"Where on earth do you come from?" I asked but the noise was too great to hear his reply. The shelling, which cut us off from the rear, was so heavy that it seemed like a miracle that anyone passing through it could possibly have survived. Rather breathless he handed me a pink signals form on it were written these words:

"From Corps Headquarters". "Is all quiet on your front?"

No doubt the hubbub of 'the bombardment', had been loud enough to penetrate some way back and Corps H.Q. had begun to wonder.

I handed the message to my sergeant major and we both laughed – glad of a little comic relief.

The Bombardment began to slacken after about an hour, and then I expected we would see the grey green uniforms coming over, if they decided to capture our front line first.

I got the men in position with uncovered guns and kept a sharp look out but nobody came. We found out later what had happened. They had captured our front line and then, perhaps finding the machine gun fire uninviting, had turned half left and followed their other troops who had broken through. I saw them some way on our right, streaming through like a football crowd going away after a match. That of course, meant that my company was left in a little island with Germans on our, left, in front and streaming through on our right. For all we knew they may have been behind us too.

About this time Battalion H.Q., which was just on our right, was attacked and a few bombs were thrown down the dugout. The C.O, who bad escaped a few minutes earlier, came towards us shooting a German he saw coming over the way. He then sent an S.O.S. asking for bombers. That was where my men came. As they were ready and in one place, there was no delay in sending them to drive out the few Germans who were still in the trench. The Adjutant, who was imprisoned there, was using his best German with no effect when my bombers arrived to rescue him. There was an amazing aside to all this. My sergeant major went with the bombers. A few days earlier, The Adjutant had told me that he felt the sergeant always had too much to say. He wanted me to get rid of him. Fortunately I did not. For his part in rescuing the Adjutant he was later awarded a D.C.M.

In their advance the Germans had come over the top and passed through the bombing block I had visited on the previous evening, taking a number of prisoners. Then, finding it easier, they had turned half left. Amongst other things they had killed the new officer whose acquaintance I had made the night before, who had refused to surrender.

In the middle of all this I got a message from the C.O. who said he wanted me to take over the trench, which an officer who was totally exhausted was still holding. The C.O himself seemed in good spirits. He told me in some detail about the rescue of the Adjutant and how he himself had shot the German. Our conversation took place in the communication trench, which I was to take over. It had been very much knocked about by artillery fire and there were a number of dead bodies lying about. One at my feet attracted my attention, because there was a neat hole about the size of half-a-crown in his head, from which four little spiral of steam was still ascending. It dawned on me that the temperature of the blood was still higher than the autumn air.

The C.O. explained that a few men from other units had got mixed up with ours and the Colonel of one had been killed. When I asked where he had died a very Scottish Chaplain, who had come up since the battle had died down, pointed to the body at my feet and said, "He lies here."

"Oh," said I, in my unimpressed English way.

I proceeded to my bombing block and took over. There was nothing at this post which would stop anyone coming along and, as I was told that the Germans were just round the corner, we stayed there with rifles and bombs ready, just in case. What troubled us most was our own barrage, which was being put up to discourage any further attacks. Shells were falling like clockwork all around us. If I had been sensible I would have moved farther back, but having been told to hold that particular place, it didn't occur to me to do so. My mind was probably too tired to work. It was all very trying and how we avoided being hit was a mystery.

A rather nice young officer who had just arrived in France was at this bombing post when I arrived. I had not seen him before. As shell after shell burst and shook us up it became too much for his nerves and he began to cry. While the bombardment was going on I looked up and saw a man crawling on the top. For a split second I thought it must be a German, worming his way round. Actually it was a man of my own company who had gone to help a wounded friend. I yelled at him but in the din he did not hear so I beckoned to him to come back at once. When he returned he explained what he had been doing adding, "He was so dreadfully wounded." The man who had risked his life trying to save his friend was normally the despair of the sergeant major, who generally thought he was "not quite all there." He had such a huge head that it looked deformed and his tin hat was always sliding off, whilst his large red face wore a fixed and benign smile. I had always been rather lenient with him because he seemed willing and good-natured and I was glad to hear later on that he was given the military medal, which I had recommended him for.

After a longish spell of this, another message came to tell me that the C.O. wanted me at once and I was not sorry to quit. When I went down into the H.Q. dugout, he told me that he had been wounded and was going away and I should have to take over from him. He had, in fact, been smitten in the hinder parts but seemed as lively as ever. He stayed a moment or two before he left and recommended me to try some port he was leaving on a shelf. I am sure it was good because in private life he was a wine merchant. I left it where it was, as I felt I had at least one pressing reason for being wide awake just then.

A little light still came down the dugout steps in the late afternoon, as I watched the Adjutant and him slowly climbing out, leaving me in command of the remnants of the battalion. In the dugout itself it was completely dark, apart from the light provided by one candle, which simply seemed to accentuate the gloom. It was quiet down there down there and I sat down to rest. It was so quiet that I fancied I must be alone. But after a while I could see shelves, which might have men on them and presently, somebody spoke. It was a tired voice and it belonged to a man with a bandaged head, who told me that there were shelves all along the side and that they were full of wounded men. When I looked round again I thought I saw someone else. He was squatting on his haunches at the bottom of the dugout steps. His right arm was reaching out in front, as if he were pointing the way. As the light that had come down the steps had now failed, only the dimmest outline could be seen. I moved across and started to speak to him but he did not reply. I thought he must be dozing and bent down to check only to discover that he had died.

While I was sitting down hoping for a little rest that I received a message from an officer belonging to another unit, which must have come up after the attack. He wanted me to go and see him, which I did, rather unnecessarily. He cannot have understood the situation very well, for he proceeded to give me orders to attack the Germans down the communication trench. He was a young man who I am sure meant well and he may have been puzzled by my private's uniform covered with dirt. I think I went so far as to explain that I had only a handful of men left, who were very done up, and that I had no intention of doing so. Having wasted time and energy I returned to the Bat-talion H.Q. and stumped heavily down the steps of the dug-out, past the dead man pointing upwards, and sat down again amongst the quiet wounded men to get a few minutes rest.

While I had been away, the three remaining officers of the battalion had come in and were now sitting silently in the gloom at the other end of the dugout. Presently one came up to me. I had never seen him before but he said he had been in that part of the trench all day and might be able to help. He was full of energy and cheerfulness and lacked the subdued manner, born of long endurance, which belonged to those who had had stood the bleak and unforgiving existence of trench warfare for any length of time. I felt glad of his company and told him we would go round shortly and explore. I explained that I would soon be going to visit what posts there were, and he could point out any places he knew already, which I might otherwise miss. He seemed pleased with the idea, indeed even cheerful, and asked when I would be ready.

"In half-hour if that will suit you," I replied.

We set off when that time had passed. We moved up the steps together. Outside the moon was shining brightly, except when an occasional cloud hurried past. When the moon went in, it was quite dark. Someone, with the idea of being helpful, flashed a torch to show me the way. I immediately made him put out, knowing that only new arrivals from England did silly things like that.

First we went to a place which overlooked the bombing post, in the communication trench. It was an important position. Silence was essential. We crept up to the solitary man who was lying there and I spoke quietly to him. When he had first joined us he had been rather a namby-pamby type. An impression that had perhaps been accentuated by his fresh complexion and the spectacles he wore. As time had passed he had developed and was now a very useful person. I had once asked him what he did in civilian life and he told me he was a church organist. Anyhow, he did well on that day. He was cool and collected when there was every reason to be otherwise, and I put him up for a medal too.

We then went on our way visiting the other sentries. Coming back we got as far as the entrance to our headquarters dugout. As the position had been captured, the opening faced the Germans and its position was well known by them. They did not need a torch!

A few moments after our return, a brisk salvo of German shells came over exactly on the spot. I heard them coming, unexpected as they were, and instantly dived in one direction hoping to get some cover in time. It was then that a corporal next to me shouted – This way sir", and I turned back. The next thing I knew was a big explosion, smoke and a stunning blow on my head. A large piece of shell had hit my tin hat. It had partly come through it to make a dent in my (fortunately thick) skull and it had knocked me over. For a moment everything turned black and I felt as if an enormous giant had hit me on the head with a beam. I was not unconscious but was glad to have someone help me up and presently I was dragged down the dugout steps. My field dressing, which I had carried about for two and a half years, now came in useful and it was clapped in the required place. Very little blood trickled down my face and I began to be more hopeful and sat on a chair, but when I got out my report book and tried to write an account of the day's happenings the words would not come out.

I became aware of two officers who had been sitting in the gloom farther along the dugout. They came to me and advised me to depart. There seemed to be little point in hanging on but I waited a little longer to see if I got better. It occurred to me to ask what had happened to the young officer who had been with me. I had been talking to him when the shells came over. The shell that knocked me over had blown him to pieces. Nothing what-so-ever could be found of him. Not a single button.

As my condition did not improve I reluctantly decided to go. I was annoyed that the extraordinary good luck, which had enabled me to escape so often before, had failed at last. That was the chief impression I had at the moment. I was also annoyed with the man who had said "This way, sir" and would like to have put the blame on him, but of course, if I had gone the other way the result might have been worse. He was the man I had put up for a commission. Was it a sly dig of Fate! And I had lost my revolver, which I had been carrying in my hand and looked upon as an old friend. Altogether it was a bad evening's work, at the end of a day of many escapes.

When a stretcher came I nodded to the two officers I was now leaving behind and wished them luck. They were the only ones left out of the whole battalion. I had never been on a stretcher before as a casualty, but I had slept on one once, in some waterlogged trenches. I knew it was so narrow the wooden sides had caught me just where my shoulder blades were. On that occasion it had bridged a hole full of water in a trench swarming with rats. I coped with the narrowness by lying on one side, but now I had to lie down flat.

After a few yards of this assisted passage, the trench became very narrow and we arrived at a place where a tangle of barbed wire had been pushed in to make a block. I remembered this because we had put it there. They lifted me over with many groans and then decided that going any farther in the trench was not going to work, so they got out on the top. We went a little further then they put me down and disappeared. The problem was that I weighed 12 stone and was not much fun to carry, so perhaps a little refreshment was required. It was exactly in the same spot where we had dawdled twenty-four hours before, amongst the rows of dead men.

It was peaceful now as I lay there; looking up at the stars and the war seemed to have become rather remote. That was partly due to the fact that the concussion had broken one of my ear drums and made the other ear very deaf, so that every noise which reached me sounded as if it came through a bale of cotton wool. I managed to distinguish the occasional sound of guns, which may not have been as distant as they then appeared. I was on my way out of the war, for some time anyway, and it now seemed to have become someone else's job. It was 30th of November and, after a while; laying on the ground at midnight it is apt to be chilly. I was not sorry when my stretcher-bearers returned, and with a few subdued grumbles about my weight, lifted me up again. The ground was very uneven and I didn't like the jolting very much. After a while I suggested getting down and walking. I had not yet reconciled myself to being a casualty. My offer was very definitely declined so on we went. At last we reached a sandbagged shelter where I was taken inside and dumped on a table.

Two doctors appeared at once out of the shadows, and one asked me quietly what was wrong. I told him I had been hit in the head and he very gently examined the wound but said nothing. After that he stepped back, looked at me for a few seconds and asked what I did in civilian life. I knew I would never see him again so I gave him the usual cold douche, which he received without comment. He then stood aside while I was moved to an ambulance, which was waiting outside. It was a horse-drawn ambulance with two horses. I had never seen one before and it looked so prehistoric-that I almost felt I was back in the Crimean War. When they at last began to move they ambled slowly over the fields across uneven ground until we came to a stop outside a hut. There I was left on the floor with a large number of other cases, all on stretchers. And there we lay, in complete silence. There was no movement at all We might all have been dead. Perhaps some were.

I looked at the man on the stretcher next to me and found it was a man from my own company. It was the very deaf man of over 40, who had told me he enjoyed being in the war. I called out to him but he made no response. It was now about 2 a.m. and everyone seemed to have forgotten us. Eventually someone came and put me in another ambulance. It was a motor one this time and before long we arrived before long at a hospital of wooden huts at Achiet le Grand. There was no delay there. I was taken at once and put on an operating table where a very cheerful doctor came and gave me an injection. He dabbed my front with iodine and jabbed me with a needle.

"What's that?"" I asked

"Anti-tetanus," he replied. He then shaved my head round the place where the wound was. I do not recommend using a blunt razor and no soap to shave a place made infinitely tender by a wound. It is not a pleasant pastime. My clothes, which I had not taken off for three weeks were then removed. And so to bed!

It all seemed very tame and I began to dislike the ward immensely. What made it worse was that I could not sleep even for a moment. I suppose the head wound, which was thought to be a fracture, and the severe concussion had shaken me up a good deal. I seemed even wider awake next day and, from habit as much as anything, called for a pencil and paper to write down as many names as I could remember, of men who had been useful during my last day. I laid it on pretty thick on purpose. Our former C.O., who was a professional soldier, always used to say that no one should be given decorations and that it was a soldier's duty to do his best. As time went on and I realised the wear and tear of long service in that kind of life, I began to think that the men who were, after all, amateur soldiers, deserved rather more. On this occasion we had emerged from Ypres after suffering a great many casualties and our numbers had not been made up.

We had been sent to what were supposed to be "quiet" trenches for that reason. Our total strength was under 300 men when the battle began and of those 244 had become casualties. So we had not had too easy a time.

I asked about the other patients. One had come down in a blazing aeroplane and had been badly burned. Another was not even in bed and I saw him coming in my direction. It was our energetic C.O. whose wound, he told me, was only slight. He was anxious to get back to the battalion because if he failed to return by a certain date he would lose his command.

I was not sorry to leave that depressing place and made my next journey by train. It was a splendid train and, as we left on a sunny afternoon, I felt rather as if I was having a continental holiday at someone else's expense. I could not move to get a better view, and more cases came through a door in front of my place. At one point I thought I saw a stretcher with my batman on it. I did not then know that he had been wounded. I had last seen him when the big bombardment began and had advised him to go down into the dugout and stay there but he must have come up. Later, I was very sorry to hear that he had died. A few months later I thought I ought to make the journey to his home, where I could say how sorry I was and how much I had appreciated his work. My meeting with his young widow was not easy and I came away feeling that perhaps it might have been better if I had not gone. He had suffered from asthma and had problems seeing things at night and was totally unfit for life at the front.

At length our train began to move. It was such a gentle, gliding motion after the means of travel we had recently some to expect, that it seemed as if it were floating on air. I felt that I would not mind if the journey took a very long time. Others, who were in a worse condition, could not have thought the same and one kept calling for help, which was not forthcoming, which made us feel helpless and very sorry.

The afternoon passed quickly and darkness fell while our train continued to move in its stately way. It was in the small hours of the next morning that we finally stopped. Judging by the grandeur of the station, we had come to a town of some size. I was taken off the train and put into a Ford ambulance. As the doors were being shut I asked if they could be left open so that 1 could look about. After months in the devastated regions that would have been a joy but my request was denied. I did manage to catch a glimpse of some street lamps, which for me meant civilisation, and I asked where we were.

"Rouen," said the ambulance man who clearly did not want to start a conversation, as it was then 3 a.m.

The hospital I now found myself in made me feel I had been born into a New World. When I first arrived the patients were still mostly asleep and I was swiftly deposited in a bed in the centre of a ward. It was, I suppose, an extra bed, because the other ones were in rows down each side. The isolated position made it seem as if I was lying in state. Almost at once a youngish man appeared and said he would massage me if I liked. I said "All right" and wondered why he was not in the army. The hospital, I discovered, was known as "No. 2 Public School Hospital." After what I had gone through before, it was the last word in luxury with a staff of nurses who were marvels of elegance and efficiency. The chief trouble was that I still could not sleep. When I tried to put my head on a pillow it was more painful and no sleeping draughts seemed to have the desired effect. I began to wonder how long it would be possible to continue without any sleep at all. If it hadn't been for my inability to sleep, I would have enjoyed this change to civilisation more, but I did not feel I was getting on much. I ate the excellent food, evidently cooked by a Frenchman, chiefly because I thought it would be better for me to keep up my strength.

Time went by and then one day I was told that I was to have an operation. I had guzzled my way through an excellent lunch and was not expecting anything to happen, when a nurse suddenly came and stood by my bed. She pretended to be tidying me up and then bent over me and quietly said, "You won't give me away will you, because I should not have let you have a full meal before your operation."

Soon after that a stretcher arrived and I was helped on to it. As I passed down the ward I caught sight of the officer I had succeeded at the bombing post in the trench and waved to him. He did not seem to recognise me in my many head bandages.

The operating place was across an open courtyard in another building. The roof extended beyond the walls and was supported by some pillars. Under them a doctor was waiting in his white garments with his hands behind his back. I first saw him as the winter light was failing and wondered if that would be my last sight of life on this earth.

No time was lost. Next moment I was deposited on the operating table and another doctor quickly came to me and said with a strong American accent –

"Ever had dope?"

To that I replied, "No, but I have had gas quite often."

He adjusted the gauze and told me how to breathe. I put my hands together and hoped for the best.

When I came round, I was back in my bed in the centre of the ward. Four nurses were in attendance, one at each corner. I held out my hand to the best-looking one. They knew then, that I had returned to consciousness and all vanished as if by magic.

Later that night my own nurse returned and bending over me said quietly, "You didn't tell him, did you?" I shook my head.

A few days later I was moved from my bed in the centre of the ward and took my place between two other patients whose beds were next to a doorway. I later learned that this was the place where cases on the danger list were usually put. The door was handy because if things went wrong a patient's body could be removed without disturbing anyone else.

On my right there was a rather nice man who seemed to be wounded all over and could not move. He became very depressed at times because he did not get better as quickly as he hoped. Next to the door on my other side, there was a patient who had a severe head wound. He was always unconscious and sometimes delirious. One day two very quiet people came in and sat by his bed. I thought they were his father and mother. Soon after they had gone his condition got worse. The following day his nurse, who was a very a pretty girl, gave him a very thorough wash and put his bedclothes straight. When she had moved away he suddenly sat up in bed and began to talk very fast indeed. He called out a man's name and shouted for him to come at once. I was not in a fit state to do anything, being completely swathed with bandages and very deaf indeed, but when no one came, I went over to him and told him it would be all right. Someone said that he was calling for his batman, so I told him he was coming. That seemed to calm him down. Then his nurse reappeared and he put out his hand to take hold of hers. She put it down and left him again.

He was very quiet and still after that and I looked at him once or twice, wondering whether he was still alive. Then quite suddenly he sat up in bed, stretched out his right arm pointed, as if to some place in the far distance. In a tone of interested surprise he said: "Look at all those people over there." And then he fell back, dead. His body vanished through the handy door in no time at all.

In own case things were marking time. One day an army doctor of the old type came to carry out an inspection and there was a tense atmosphere amongst the staff. The patients were vigorously tidied up so that no bedclothes were out of order and then the great man arrived. He spoke in staccato tones and the staff who followed him round listened deferentially. When he had gone the normal atmosphere returned to everyone's delight.

On another occasion I was wheeled off to have my skull X-rayed, to find out where my fracture was but I was told the results revealed nothing. On another occasion a doctor came round to examine my head. "I am going to hurt you," he said, and, without further warning, tore the gauze off the wound with a rapid jerk."

"You did", I said.

One defect in this otherwise excellent hospital was the noise. Perhaps it was unavoidable. Many of the patients had injuries to their limbs, which left their vitality unimpaired. Their high spirits and talking did not help sleepless me. I thought that if only I could get some sleep I might make some progress but I still could not put my head down and to stay awake indefinitely in a sitting position was wearisome to say the least.

Then the day came when, with the usual lack of warning, I was told I would be returning to England at once. After being in such a good hospital, I was not sure I wanted to go. It would not be like going home on leave, and I thought that if I got well soon I might be pushed off back to the trenches. So I hoped my return to England might be delayed a little longer. The man on my right, who had been so badly wounded, had not progressed very much. He asked me rather earnestly if I thought he was getting better. When my stretcher came, I was lifted on to it and said good-bye. I felt rather like a deserter, and very much hoped that he would not go through that convenient door.

Lying on a stretcher in an ambulance is not the best way to go sightseeing and, as the doors were shut, I had to reconcile myself once more to missing a view of Rouen, which I knew quite well. During my week there as a private, two years and eight months before, I had been confined to camp and now I was in a conveyance which was only one degree better than a hearse.

When we got to the quayside they had to open the doors but I only got the briefest glimpse of cafes, where many years before I had sat for hours.   It was at about the same spot where we had paraded in full kit in 1915, after many hours of vomiting on a cross channel ship. On that occasion we had marched off to a camp where we had been expected to survive without tents or food.

On my return to England via the hospital in Rouen, I was once again put on board a ship. I was deposited on a deck just below the top one. It was December and a brisk wind blew. It was not the ideal place to be after a nice warm hospital. After a while a rather grumpy young doctor came along and asked me if my wound needed dressing. I said "No," not wanting to be hurt just then. He came back later and asked if there was anywhere special I wanted to go to in England.

"It doesn't, of course, follow that you will actually go there," he hastened to add.

I said "London" because that was the place where I knew people, and it was where I thought I would want to be in when I was able to get up.

The ship moved off and went slowly up the Seine to Le Havre, following the route I had come down on that a Sunday in May 1915 when I had first arrived in France. This time the sea was calm and the voyage was uneventful but we were lucky. Another hospital ship had recently been sunk on the same route.

As we sailed home I vowed that I would return and re-visit the places I had known in wartime France. Seven years later I found myself in Rouen once again. The inhabitants still remembered the hospital and the first man I asked directed me to it. The building seemed empty when I got there, but I discovered a man in charge who was able to tell me what was had happened. He explained that had become a seminary for priests but was now being done up and was about to become a hospital again. He had been there during the war and knew all the different wards including my own, which I was able to identify by telling him about the corner that was reserved for "danger" cases. I asked him if he knew where the operating theatre had been and he took me there. Like the rest of the buildings, it was in the hands of painters and decorators. The room had already been washed down and was ready to be painted. In a more hours I would probably not have recognised it. On one of the walls I found some well-drawn sketches. They were of the medical staff who had been there in the war, with ribald remarks attached. One caricature was of the doctor who had operated on my head. The name "Austin" had been written underneath it. It was surely an odd thing that, after seven years, I should have drifted into the room only a few minutes before those works of art were obliterated forever. It was as if a special greeting had been reserved for me.

When we got to Southampton there seemed to be hardly anyone about. Stretchers were taken off the ship in leisurely fashion and deposited on a platform, where we were left for quite a long time. The wind was colder than it had been on the ship. There seemed to be nothing going on and then it dawned on me that we were in England and it was a Sunday.

My sea and train journey, added to my long spell of sleepless nights, had not made me feel very pleased with life. I was eventually put into a bed in a small room full of a lot of noisy convalescents, who were playing a gramophone. It seemed an odd place to put a patient who was supposed to have a fractured skull. After an hour or so I decided I could not stand it anymore and asked if the row could be stopped. A doctor was called. When he arrived it was immediately clear that he was he was in a bad mood. I told him that I couldn't hear very well so he shouted at me and then disappeared. I found myself wishing I was back in France.

I was eventually moved upstairs and put in a room by myself. The doctor who had seen me when I first arrived came to visit me every day. After the first visit he just put his head inside the door and said "All right?" and was then off again to see patients who mattered more. I was in fact left alone for most of the time apart from a very old volunteer nurse who came in and fumbled with my head wound each morning. I thought I had been forgotten then one day I was suddenly told to get up. As I had no kit of my own, I was given a uniform many sizes too small which had belonged to an officer who had recently died. I squeezed myself into it and sat about for an hour or two and then began to feel even less well than when I had got up. I announced that I was going back to bed. There I got worse still and things about me began to take on a different look. Eventually they took my temperature. It was 105.2! After that I got steadily worse and my wound became septic, which made my face swell until I would have been unrecognizable if my head and face had not been completely swathed with bandages, leaving only slits for my eyes and mouth. As well as all that, a substance, which smelt of fish, was smeared on my face. I had now become an "interesting"' case. The doctor now came right inside the room to see me and brought other doctors with him. One day there were six of them, all standing round my bed in dumb bewilderment? I was clearly very ill indeed and the hospital people, by way of cheering me up, telegraphed for my relatives to come-and pay me a farewell visit. I was annoyed at that and managed to tell them they had no business to do that without my consent.

Christmas Day was my worst and they put a "danger" notice on my door as a gentle hint to other patients, who were up and about, to keep quiet outside. They were rather apt to be rowdy and the worse for drink. I hovered in that state for some days and one evening, when I had been alone for many hours, I asked to see the Chaplain, whom I knew slightly. He arrived after a long delay and asked if I wanted to make my confession.

I said "No," as I did not feel I had much to confess. He seemed rebuffed and I think he was only partly appeased when some time later I asked him to come and celebrate Holy Communion.

As Christmas passed my condition continued to deteriorate. The septic poisoning affected my sight until I could hardly see. Some bright carnations, which had been sent to me by the mother of another officer, were now just a smudge. When a new day broke, after a long and sleepless night of sweating, I could just distinguish a smoky glimmer of light where a window once was.

At this point I was considered important enough for a nurse to be instructed to sit with me all night. She was an Irish Roman Catholic and a very good nurse. She never spoke and never moved, except to come to me, but I felt she was there and had not gone to sleep. With my temperature so high, I was pouring out sweat so that my pyjamas had to be changed many times. My heart going like a steam engine and I was glad to have her there. Once she got up and, leaning over me, took up my hand and let it drop from the wrist to see if I was still alive. My committee of doctors was surprised that I was still around. They could only say that I must have been a man of temperate habits. Then they frankly announced that they had no idea what was the matter with me. They were giving me 60 grains of quinine a day, with brandy and caffeine, but even so my temperature obstinately refused to go down.

"Have you any phenacetin?" I asked one day, remembering that it had brought down my temperature once before when I had been very ill with malaria. They gave me some and it dropped at once. Unfortunately it did not remain down. Every seven days it went up like clockwork and stopped at exactly the same point. By now my strength was giving out.

The committee of doctors no longer came. They seemed to have given me up. Now there was only one doctor who regularly turned up. "Let me see," said he thoughtfully, one day after examining my chest. "Your temperature is lower but it will be up again on by the end of the week." I tried to turn my swollen and bandaged head towards him and look at him through the slits. "It will not go up again", I said and, much to my surprise, it never did.

I drifted on and sweated my way in semi-consciousness from one year to another. As 1918 began I gradually, and at first almost imperceptibly, started to recover. Before long I was well enough to have another officer put in the same room. He was a Belgian staff officer with a florid Flemish look and a good-looking wife who came to see him one day and burst into tears. He didn't seem very ill and he soon went away. They tried to change the nurse who looked after me, who was very pleasant. I was told a gawky female who was Irish and a staunch Roman Catholic would replace her. According to some of the other patients, she spent most of her time trying to convert them to her religious beliefs. I cannot say she tried it on me, but I told the hospital people I wouldn't have her near me and they moved her somewhere else.

Concerts to cheer up the patients took place at intervals. I was taken to one on a stretcher soon after I arrived. I was put on the floor beyond the front row of the audience so I would miss nothing. What it was all about I never knew because my head wound had disorganised my hearing. Everything I heard was completely distorted. Soon after the concert began, I found myself wishing I had not come.

As the New Year progressed they arranged another concert. I thought I would see if I could survive that. Cheering up the troops had become an obsession with so many well-meaning people that the sparse amount of talent available was running out. The performers romped around the stage enjoying themselves and seemed to take the derisive applause of the audience as if it were real, redoubling their efforts.

I hoped my slow improvement would go on but my temperature rose again. There was also more evidence of septic poisoning, so some painful swellings in my neck had to be lanced. They came in after breakfast one day with a bag full of gas and a special instrument and lanced the offending glands. The gas was enough to take the sharpness of the pain away but the doctor told me afterwards that, when they jabbed me, pus had shot out and sprayed across the room. Anyhow I was relieved and my temperature went down. Just before that performance began, a venerable figure appeared in the doorway and came and sat down on a bed beside me. He congratulated me on winning the military cross.

(Editor's Note: In his original manuscript my father was far too modest to say any more than that. His citation for the award stated that "he led his company through heavy shell fire to an exposed position with great gallantry and ability. Though short of ammunition and suffering many casualties, by his fine example he inspired his men and held the position until relieved. He sent in most valuable information and set a splendid example of courage and resolution".

When I was eventually allowed to get up again, the boredom of the hospital was killing me and I felt far from well. Our greatest excitement was being allowed to help iron bandages in the evenings. Eventually the day came when I was able to creep to the hospital gates and see the first undamaged street with traffic that I had seen for six months. It looked unreal and I was rather scared to see a world I had so nearly left. My first day out was spent in a bath chair, which was wheeled around by a very old fellow who was anxious to help. He wheeled me for an hour through the gloomy streets of oxford and then took me to a party in a room stuffed with people who were keeping trying to be cheerful, but I was not well enough for that and managed to escape. I decided that I would not go out in the bath chair again so next time I tried to walk. I was so feeble that I had to hold on to the railings. On the first day I only got a few hundred yards but it was surprising how soon I found I could go farther and I was eventually able to explore the town.

I knew that in due course a decision would be taken on whether I was or was not fit enough to be discharged. One morning I was summoned to have my ear examined. The drum had been broken when I was wounded. I arrived at the appointed place to find a doctor sitting rather nervously amongst some elaborate apparatus of lights and mirrors, which he did not seem to understand. He was quite an old man in uniform and the equipment he was expected to use had probably been invented years after he had reached his prime. His object it seemed was to prove that my deafness was imaginary. After a cursory examination, he announced very curtly that he could find nothing wrong with me.

Winter turned to spring and I heard that I might be pushed off somewhere to convalesce. I was eventually sent to a country house near Windsor. It was a large place with a neat garden, an artificial pond and the usual crazy paving stones. It was pleasant enough, but for anyone not well enough to do other things, it was dull to the point of suicide. The nurses had little to do because most of the patients were well enough to look after themselves. The only exception was a badly wounded airman who we never saw but whose very pretty nurse we admired from a distance. There were about a dozen patients and we were as ill-assorted group as you could ever find. We had nothing in common but our war experiences, which we all wanted to forget.

There was a typical prewar sergeant who had been promoted to second lieutenant. He was very chatty. Another patient, who was always referred to by the staff as "The Honourable...." never spoke at all. The food was very scanty and meal times were particularly depressing. I found the well-kept empty garden particularly dreary and longed to see lots of people and something going on, after months of dreary life in the devastated regions. I escaped and went up to London as often as I could. I went there by train. The few trains that ran were slow and often packed with munitions workers. The journey was long and tiring in my weak state, and only the boredom of the convalescent home drove me to it.

Once or twice I went to St. George's Chapel Windsor, which was about a mile away across a park. Wounded officers could get in without a permit and sit in the stalls, which were still adorned with the coats of arms of their owners for the time being, and look up at their banners overhead. The Emperor of Austria's coat of arms, on a little metal shield, was still affixed to the back of the stall where I sat on one occasion. When the King was at Windsor he attended. We knew when he was coming because a little knot of sightseers gathered in the cloisters. As soon as he had gone through to the Chapel, they ran round to a grille in the wall opposite my seat, and peered through as if they were in a zoo. They looked through the bars and beatified the meaning of being "lionised" as the King quietly took his seat. Only a few members of the Royal household were there and it was a little like family prayers.

My convalescence eventually came to an end and I was told to report to Reserve

Battalion Headquarters to be re-posted. This was the first time I had reported to my regiment as an officer since I had joined it from the ranks in France, and I did not know what to expect. They were very kind to me and, perhaps realising that I had done long spells in France and in hospital, seemed willing to forget me, which suited me well. Believing that out of sight was out of mind; I absented myself from the camp as much as possible and hoped that no one would notice. My ploy seemed to work until one day someone politely approached me and asked me if I would care to do a job in a clothing store. I did not fancy fiddling about with old uniforms and must have appeared lukewarm for the matter was dropped. Meanwhile I lived in a tent, which I had to myself. Being summertime it was no great hardship but I could still hear the guns distantly rumbling in France, in case I forgot there was still a war going on.

One day I was instructed to attend the court-martial of a conscientious objector. I found it hard to forget that, while the objector was living in comparative comfort and thinking about himself, so many men had suffered terribly and had been killed and wounded. The president of the court was Colonel Nacre-Brabazun who went on to become Minister of Transport. I sat on his left.

The prisoner was marched in with an escort and ordered to halt and turn left. He refused to obey the order explaining that he did not recognise any military authority. He then produced a written statement, which he started to read out. The Court President cut him short and said to me quietly, without looking up,

"What do you think?" My reply was, "Can you send him to France?"

He murmured something to the sergeant who took the prisoner away, probably to resume his safe occupation. I imagine that interest in conscientious objectors in the fourth year of war was-not very great.

My only other military activity at this camp was to take the battalion out for a route march. It was the first time I had even given an order in England and I felt rather out of it. Marching on the left side of the road made me feel nervous too, as did the horse upon which I rode. I was not sorry when we got back to camp and I saw the last of the men and the horse.

One Sunday there was a Church Parade. It was the first and only one I ever attended in England. We paraded at the roadside a long time before the service and everyone looked very polished up. There seemed to be a feeling of suspended animation in the air, which I suppose was a normal English Sunday. I had been away from it so long that I had forgotten what it was like. When we arrived at church we sat in dumb boredom during the service, while a long formal sermon about nothing in particular was preached to the air.

After about a month I was beginning to wonder how much longer I would remain in semi-retirement when a note was given to me ordering me to report to the War Office. I did as I was told and was interviewed by a very polite man who asked me if I could teach. I told him I did not think I knew anything to teach. They apparently wanted to send me to a Cadet Battalion as an Officer Instructor. When the interview ended I did not expect to hear any more about it but a few days later I received a letter telling me to go to a certain School for Instructors where I would learn what to do.

The prospect of yet another school did not appeal to me. I reported to the address that I was given and found it was even worse than the schools I had been sent to in France. We lived in bungalows and our meals, which we ate altogether, were badly cooked. The rest of our time was spent listening to lectures and doing drill to smarten us up. Squad drill, for officers who had endured three and a half years of war and who were mostly recovering from wounds, seemed hardly sane. The man who stood next to me in the ranks, who was a baronet amongst other things, found it as hard to see the funny side as I did, though we managed to exchange the occasional grin.

The lectures were mostly quite absurd, especially those given by one officer who we all liked personally very much. He knew that he was quite hopeless as a lecturer. Before he began one day, someone drew some very good caricatures on the blackboard he was going to use and added some of the stock phrases he always trotted out. "By and large" was one of them. He used to say that whenever he got to a point in his lecture where he realised that what he was saying did not make sense. The only lecturer who was any good was a one-eyed officer with a D.S.O. who lectured on military law. Why we should want to know about military law, as we were not going to be officers after the war, was hard to imagine but at least he succeeded in making his talks interesting.

Perhaps the fact that he was a barrister by profession had something to do with it.

One day, when the course was drawing to a close, we were each told to stand up and deliver an imaginary lecture. The man who performed best was one put a lot of energy into everything he said. His message was rubbish but it was delivered with conviction and he was awarded top marks. When my turn came I felt I ought to know something about it, having had to talk to people in public in various world parts of the world, but I had not done it for four years. Perhaps I would be no good at all. Our examiner told me afterwards that I had not "put it over". I did not have anything to put over, which may have had something to do with it. The man who got the highest marks was bright about nothing, which was of course was so much better.

My next destination was the Eastern Command Gas School at Crowborough in Sussex. It seemed that they were still determined to make me an instructor. There we lived in huts. There was quite a good mess and there were even hot baths, which were much in demand every morning. We attended lectures on the composition of various gases and practised putting on gas helmets in a few seconds. Once again I had to give a mock lecture. I did better this time and acquired the 75% mark I needed to pass out as a qualified instructor. From that day on I have never been asked to say a single word about gas.

Our mess was presided over by a quiet South African. He was a chemist in private life, and the officers were the usual collection from every unit imaginable. One evening the conversation became serious and the question arose as to whether such a thing as Providence existed. After various opinions had been given, none of them much in favour of the idea, I ventured to suggest that it was difficult to rule out the existence of Providence because, when it seemed very likely that He did not exist, something happened which looked like an intervention. I was interested to see how this remark would be received because at this school it had not leaked out that I had had a clerical past. No one said anything for a moment then the quiet South African remarked:

"Yes, that's what I feel."

One night we were sent for a two-mile march in the dark, wearing gas masks. It proved to be too much for me in my weakened state and I shifted the apparatus to one side, after a time to get some air. It was not nearly such a dull school as my last one had been and one weekend I escaped to Eastbourne. I had not been to an English seaside resort for many years and it was quite a surprise to me to find the sea front was packed with people. I wondered why this was happening in England, while attractive places in France like Le Touquet, were generally quite deserted with their hotel windows still boarded up.

After a few days' leave I was sent to report to my O.T.C. which was just outside a rather dreary town in the midlands. The place I was told to report to was about three miles from the nearest railway station on what Shakespeare would probably have described as a "blasted heath." It was a prewar barracks, built with in red bricks. The blasted heath was used for training purposes. As I approached it for the first time I saw the familiar row of stuffed sacks, suspended for bayonet practice. I knew then that, even in this fourth year of war, some sturdy sergeant would be instructing recruits about "giving them cold steel" – something that in my experience hardly ever happened.

From the outside the barracks had the forbidding air of a prison. Inside it was even worse. I was allotted a huge and dirty bedroom with hardly any furniture. It looked down on a large barrack square. There was a general air of gloom, which was quite menacing.

I took a walk around. There were very few people about, in the slack time between tea and dinner, but I knew at once that it was a place I could never like. The war was bad enough but this was far worse. I took a swift decision and sought out the C.O., to whom I had I any case to report my arrival. At the same time I decided to tell him that I did not want to stop.

I found him sitting quietly, alone, in a gloomy office. He was a very prewar old soldier who had probably been dug up and put in his job.

"I have come to report sir," said I and then added –

"Could I put in for a transfer? I am sure I will be no use here."

He moved very slightly and then looked up at me. After a pause he remarked that it seemed rather soon for me to be going. I explained that I had been on the move so much I could never stick in one place and would be grateful if he could arrange it. I felt slightly better after my bid for freedom, but I could see from the C.O's manner that I would have to do a lot more to secure my release.

Later that night we assembled for dinner. We met in an anteroom of the mess and waited until the Colonel arrived. When he walked in, conversation ceased and we all stood up and followed him in like lambs. He took a seat at the extreme end of the table but not at the head of it, and there he remained, without a word, throughout the meal. I soon learned that here silence was the general rule.

The officers at this establishment were very pleasant people. Some had been too badly wounded for further service and were now content to mark time. There was also one or two who played up to the old Colonel, in the hope of being thought indispensable and getting promoted. The old man was replaced by another C.O. quite soon afterwards, and I had to attend a lecture that he gave. I thought it was unusually good because it was quite entertaining. I was never put on to give a lecture myself, possibly because the only military thing I knew about was how to hold a trench and organise its defence. As most of those present were N.C.O.s, with a good deal of service, any instruction on that subject would have been superfluous.

One evening I sat with on a seat in the barrack square with an officer who had recently arrived. He told me that he felt he could not stand another minute of the awful boredom.

"I can't either," I said and then asked, "What are you going to do?"

"I shall apply to go back to my regiment," he replied and shortly afterwards he was gone. I saw him later when had been awarded the D.S.O.

My own modest idea was to become an army R.T.O. (Railway Transport Officer). I felt I had now had enough of the infantry and knew I could not stand much more from a physical point of view. Being responsible for running railways, particularly those that linked France, Belgium, France and Germany sounded like an interesting job. As I spoke French reasonably fluently and knew the countries well, I felt I would stand a good chance of being selected for an R.T.O. post in those areas.

My plans appeared to be dashed when I was summoned before a medical board and told that I was only passed fit for service at home. I had no wish to be an R.T.O. in England but refused to give up and continued with my plans. Having heard nothing from my C.O., who no doubt had forgotten all about me, I wrote directly to the war office disregarding the "usual channels'" and a little to my surprise was, summoned there for an interview. The interview went off quite well and left me hopeful. Then came the Armistice.

Armistice Day was the day after my interview, so I was in London at the time. I had got up late, after a leisurely breakfast in bed, and had left my room in St. James' Place to saunter up towards Piccadilly. I had got half way there when I heard a few explosions and saw people pouring out of the shops and offices on to the pavement. I thought for a moment that some public event had been arranged and I had not heard about it, so I stopped a passerby and asked what was happening. He told me that the war was over and looked as if he thought I ought to have known. My first thought was, "Dear me! What is going to happen to my application to be an R.T.O.?"

The streets soon became blocked and buses and taxis came to a standstill. People stood on top of buses and beat the tin advertisements displayed on their sides, shouting anything to make a noise. Taxis, with people standing on the running boards and sitting on top, looked as if they would collapse. I watched them through the drizzle, which was now beginning. As it was lunchtime I made my way towards my favourite restaurant – an Italian one in the Haymarket. It has since been pulled down but it was there then and, of course, it was full – of very excited people drinking each other's health. To me it all seemed a little unreal, as if it might not be true that the war was over. I went on towards Buckingham Palace, thinking there might be something to see. There was such a large crowd it was impossible to get near.

"We want George!" they kept on shouting. And George appeared, so I had not gone for nothing.

It is difficult for a crowd to express itself on such an occasion and, as the King represented the nation, the crowd felt they were doing something when they cheered him. He had become identified with the War and was an object of affection through his unassuming ways. All this was, of course, preliminary to a night of celebrations. If I had been sensible I would have stayed in London but, as I was due back at my barracks that night, I returned to them. It seems strange at this distance of time to think that I did not stop, but it only shows how four years of obeying orders had affected me. So I spent the evening on a slow train crawling away from London on an historic night and, when I got back, I found that there was really no reason for me to return. I had however been in London when the Armistice came, and that was something. At the barracks only one thing seemed to have happened that day. A very quiet and respectable old man – a former N.C.O, who had been given a commission – had consumed a few drinks more that he was equal to, and had been found, dead, outside the barrack gates.

Soon after my return I performed the one notable act of my career as an officer instructor. An officer had died in hospital and a big funeral was to be staged. No one wanted to be in charge of the troops attending it and, perhaps because it had now leaked out that I was a parson by trade, the job was given to me. No one had any idea how to behave but some of the N.C.O.s undertook to practise the men in marching with reversed arms, leaning on arms reversed, and how to fire a volley in the air. All I had to do was to borrow a sword, walk in front and learn a few commands.

Zero hour for our party was when we met the body in the neighbouring town, not far from the church and churchyard where the service would take place. We managed to get there on time and took up our positions. A line of men on each side of the street, leaning on arms reversed. They saluted the body as it approached in a hearse. Up to this point I had managed to avoid doing anything, but now I had to order the men to move from this position, turn inwards and follow the body to the church.

But this time the Band which was in attendance had got into its stride and the noise a military band can make at close quarters playing Chopin's funeral March, is considerable. I realised that it would be impossible to make myself heard, except by who were relatively close. Fortunately, in spite of their downcast heads, they saw me out of the corners of their eyes as I advanced with my sword reversed, guessed what was happening and did what they were supposed to do perfectly.

When we arrived at the church we waited outside during the first part of the service. We then moved to the grave side, where the rest of the ceremony was to take place. It was carried out with such efficiency that those who were involved looked as if they had been doing it all their lives. My own anxiety was my sword, which I carried on this occasion for the first and only time in my military career. It was a very big sword, which belonged to a Canadian Officer who had been trained at the Canadian equivalent of Sandhurst military academy. I was glad when it was over and we marched back to the barracks to a merry tune, and the sword safely back in its sheath.

It was around this time that we were involved in a great Influenza epidemic, which was sweeping across the country. I was usually pretty good at escaping infections but perhaps my weakened state made me more liable and once again I retired to bed. Fortunately it was only a mild attack, and did not delay my departure, as I had feared it might. I was up and about again when, to my joy, orders came through that I was to report to a school for R.T.O.s which was near London. It was good news because it meant that I had surmounted the last of the many obstacles I had faced and could now escape from the hated barracks.

The R.T.O. School consisted of a camp of wooden huts surrounded by a miniature railway, complete with signals, level crossings and various tracks. It would have delighted the heart of any seven-year-old, but I confess I felt rather too old for it all. I had been sent there to acquire the skills needed to control railway traffic but, as I did not have any instruction in my time there, I was never able to see it at work. I had hardly arrived when I was summoned to the War Office to undergo an examination in French. That was quite sensible because, if my request to return to France and Belgium was granted, my work would often have to be conducted in French.

I arrived at the appointed time, for what was to be the second war office interview of my military career, and was told to go to a small room at the end of a long corridor and wait for my examiner to arrive. When he turned up he said something in French. I replied quickly enough to show that I was used to the language. He told me I had passed before I could sit down.

Now nothing seemed to remain in the way of my appointment and I was instructed to be ready for orders to proceed to France. I also had to provide myself with blue tabs and a blue band to go round my hat. Christmas was approaching and, as I had nothing else to do, I decided to go down to Bristol, where I had once worked as a curate in a very poor parish. As soon as I had finished arranging the trip, orders came through telling me to report at the War Office on December 25th! I thought that perhaps the authorities had forgotten that December 25th was Christmas Day and, as the war was over, I might arrive and find no one at home so I queried the date. It was duly revised and I was told to report on December 26th, at a very early hour. I found that would mean leaving Bristol on the evening of Christmas Day and returning to London on a very slow train.

On Christmas day I decided to go to Bristol Cathedral for the 8 a.m. service. It meant walking for three miles but, as I had been ordained there, I felt it was worth the effort. To get there I walked through Clifton, along the streets I had known well as a small boy when I used to go that way to school carrying my books. Perhaps that was why I had decided to make the trip. I must have been in rather a dreamy state, reflecting on years gone by, because I was quite startled when I heard a voice and realised that someone was addressing me. The voice came from a very old man in a black and green uniform, which I did not immediately recognise. I think it may have been the Rifle Brigade.

"What do you mean sir" roared the voice, "by passing me without saluting? You young fellows in the Flying Corps don't know how to behave." I might have replied but I felt annoyed and had little time to spare so I held my peace and saluted. He probably only wanted to be chatty but It was too early for me.

When I arrived at the cathedral I found that the service was being conducted by a friend, who until recently had been Headmaster of Marlborough school. In my earlier days he had tried to persuade me to work as a teacher there. I had to leave Bristol just before dinner and returned to the station, where I boarded a slow train and ate some sandwiches in gloomy solitude.

As the train rattled its way slowly towards London I dreamed of getting a meal when I arrived. I made my way to Piccadilly with that goal in mind, but all the places I visited were shut. My last port of call was a restaurant called The Florence, which I had visited several times before and had always enjoyed. On this occasion it too was closed, but I could hear sounds of merriment coming from inside. I pushed open the door and looked inside. It was full of people who were evidently enjoying themselves with their families. Someone came to the door and invited me in. It turned out that a Soho shopkeeper had hired the place for the evening. He had brought his children and friends there to celebrate the first post-war Christmas as cheerfully as possible. When I sat down some people were already standing on tables, singing and I was given my food while they entertained each other. I was very tired and did not stay long. They asked me to remain but, as I had to be at the War Office early the next morning, I knew I needed to get a good night's rest.

Next day I reported as I had been instructed to do. I was told to go away and come back the following day. It was in fact a week before anyone saw me. The delay was annoying in one way but it had one advantage. It enabled me to witness the arrival of the American President (*Woodrow Wilson - American President from 1913 to 1921*) as he drove with the King to Buckingham Palace. According to Mrs. Wilson, who wrote an account of this visit in her memoirs, it took place on Boxing Day because she and her husband had been visiting American soldiers in a French hospital and had nothing else to do. That was rather the impression I got as I saw the King's face as he passed down Pall Mall. The President, who by this time was used to European acclamations, was smiling and raising his hat but the King did not seem to be enjoying the occasion. He must have cheered up later for the picture in Mrs. Wilson's book makes him look as if he didn't very much mind Presidents arriving at Christmas and wasn't going to take it too seriously.

On the last day of the year I finally got away and returned to France. I crossed the channel and arrived in Calais, which was now crammed with English soldiers on their home for demobilisation. It was exactly four years since I had set foot in England on my return from South America and volunteered to sign up. How completely my life had changed in that relatively short time!

I was sent to a camp on the outskirts of the town, where some bell tents had been pitched in a field. I did not expect to live in a tent now the war was over and, after spending so long in hospital, did not relish the prospect very much. It was also raining hard and the field in which the tents had been set up had become more like a swamp. I tried to make my new home as watertight as possible, covered myself with coats and blankets and attempted to rest. 1918 was about to end and, when it did, I wanted to be asleep.

As 1919 approached I surveyed my tent arrangements with some pride. I thought I had done well to keep out most of the rain. I burrowed under my blankets and coats and was approaching the stage when dozing would soon merge into sleep. It was then that I heard someone outside my tent. Hands fumbled with the opening, which I had carefully closed and a voice from outside give me unwelcome news.

It seemed that men from a Scottish regiment, who were fed up with waiting for demobilisation, were expected to raid the wet canteen and all officers were expected to turn out with their revolvers. It was no doubt their idea of celebrating New Year's Day. Well, I did not have a revolver. I had lost mine when I was wounded, and I did not fancy myself shooting at Scots after years of real warfare. So I stayed in my camp bed and listened to the rain, which sang like a lullaby until I fell asleep. Next morning I was glad to hear that there had been no riot and the camp appeared to be intact.

As there seemed to be nothing to do I decided to go into Calais, which was now more like an English town than a French one. Indeed we were told that the French people had begun to be anxious about ever getting rid of their allies. My only other activity during the days I remained at the camp was to be summoned to stores, where I was once again to be provided with a gas mask and a tin hat. It seemed like a joke at the time but evidently no chances were being taken. The makers of such things clearly still wanted to get rid of many as possible.

Eventually new orders arrived and I discovered that I was to Longpre, which was on the main railway line from Boulogne to Paris. I remembered Longpre as I had marched through it or passed by on a train. It was a small railway junction with nothing nearer than Amiens in the way of civilisation.

When I eventually arrived there I found the R.T.O. who was there at the time had no intention of departing, so all I could do was potter about.

I found a billet in a house which belonged to of a very Old French Colonel, who lived in great poverty on a microscopic pension. He was a merry good-natured person who used to do business in London but it was clear that he did not want me, so I kept out of his way.

I soon got bored and complained about having nothing to do so one or two jobs were created for me. There was a great deal of pilfering from wagons in sidings at night and guards had been posted to keep watch. I was put in charge of them. Being used to infantry life it seemed best to make them fall in and march to the place where they would work. I did that once but soon gathered that they preferred to drop in at the time they thought they were to go on duty. After a time I acquiesced, as I thought t was likely that the guards themselves were not above pilfering.

Soon after that experience I was given another useless job. I was sent up the line to the next station, and told to await a hospital train, which was on its way to England. It was reported to be full of casualties, who had not been well enough to move up until then.

I climbed up on the engine of a French goods train, which was heading that way, and talked to the driver as we wobbled along the racks. The engine wobbled about so much I felt that at any moment it might fall off the rails, but it got me where I wanted to be. There was a small cafe near the station and there I found I could get a bed, so if the hospital train did not up all the night, I could get some rest. It wasn't much of a place and, when it began to fill up with French soldiers and civilians in the evening, I went for a walk. I returned when it had closed. There was no sign of any train and, after talking a girl who served the drinks, I went to lie' down leaving instructions to be called if any train came.

At 4 a.m. she hammered on my door. I got up immediately and I went out to the train. It was quite dark when I clambered sleepily aboard and found myself in a dimly lit corridor. A nurse then arrived and I told her I had been sent to meet the train. I had no idea why, and neither had she, so I got off and went back to bed again. And that was all I ever heard about that assignment.

A few days later I decided to go to Airaines, where I had been billeted in a house, which belonged to a little draper man, three years before. I hoped the trip would revive the pleasant memories I had of that time. Recapturing the past is always difficult and I found it hard reconcile the streets, which were now empty apart from the occasional villager, with the ones I had know when they had been packed with troops. I went to the Epicerie, where we had sometimes gone in the evenings and drunk liqueurs in a room behind the shop. That too had changed and when an old woman ambled in from the back of the premises she was a stranger. Even the cordial little draper man seemed to have decided to forget the past. He was a little detached when I reminded of my last visit early in 1916. Then I had slept in a room, which overlooked the square. I could still vividly remember the mountainous father bed and a room full of shell-like ornaments and knick-knacks but when I recalled those days he made no response.

It was while I was at Longpre that I enacted the closing scene of my long chase after a new revolver to replace the Smith and Wesson one which had fallen out of my hand at 11 p.m. on November 30th 1917, when I had been knocked on the head. In 1918 when I had been crawling back to life, I had put in for a replacement. Now, a year later, correspondence concerning that request was still following me around all over France. I no longer anticipated any success but was interested to find out how long such a correspondence could go on. My file on it was already two inches thick. One day I was surprised to be told by the quartermaster that at last the weapon was coming. I got ready to receive and sigh for it for it but before the day before it was due to arrive I was posted back to the devastated regions. So I never got my new revolver. Perhaps the Quartermaster did? I felt I had been beaten just when I was about reach the winning post, without reaping the fruits of victory, which seemed to be a common complaint at that time.

To get back to the devastated regions I first caught a train and then had to wait till I could find someone with a lorry or a car to help me complete my journey. As we left the inhabited regions behind and the villages became more dilapidated, I looked out for the old front line, which I thought would be easy to spot. Men were busy clearing up but there was still an immense sea of rusty barbed wire which had so far had defeated their efforts. The country all around was still desolate. There were no inhabitants and no buildings. Just crumpled ruins and mounds or broken rubble. The devastation went on for miles.

I moved on and eventually came to the shell of a building, of which as much remained as the stump of a tooth. This was apparently, the headquarters to which I had been instructed to report, but no one was interested in my arrival. I wandered about and eventually came to the remains of a house, which still had some walls standing. It was on the edge of the-railway line and letters "R.T.O." were painted on a board outside. There I found a man who told me that this was now to be my headquarters. I did not sleep there but found a portable hut nearby. It only measured about ten feet by five but it was certainly better a tent. My predecessor had lived there and I decided that I would too. It was rather lonely because the nearest camp was a mile away. It housed the men who were clearing up. About the same distance away, in another direction, there was a war cemetery. The weather, which had been cold when I arrived, got colder and then it froze day and night for three weeks. Everything in my little hut froze solid. Then we had snow.

One day I noticed someone moving rather painfully along the snowy road. When I got nearer I saw it was an old woman and I wondered how she had come all the way, because the nearest human habitation was miles away. A little later I found her prodding about in some rubble, hidden in the snow. When I spoke to her she seemed unwilling to reply but, after a while, she told me she was trying to find where her home had been.

As I still had nothing whatever to do I thought I would walk about a little and explore. I went up the road till I got to a bend and saw a notice, which was still hanging there. It said "Achtung", and it was covered with barbed wire. A little farther on I came to a cemetery and saw long rows of wooden crosses, with names written on aluminium strips. Under its pall of snow it seemed deathly silent and eerily still. Not far from the cemetery I came across a pile of boards, which might have been a building at some time. Ferreting at amongst the debris I found a paper book, partly spoiled by dampness and decay, but still legible in parts. I separated damaged pages and inside read a note which gave a name and alongside there was a note - "Temperature rising. Do not think he will last the night." Alongside that there was another brief note.

"*Unconscious since morning.*" Those and similar entries made it clear that the pile of boards had once been a hospital.

From time to time stray Chinamen could be seen wandering about in the snow. I wondered what they were doing and recalled that, when I had been in Calais, some German prisoners had offended a group of Chinese there people by calling them "Chinks". They had replied by lobbing a Mills bomb over the fence.

One night I was invited to a concert given by the men who were doing all the clearing up. It was quite an education to me as they were all north countrymen and their language was in some ways more foreign to me than French. They sang lots of songs. One I recall was called "Dem Golden Kippers". It was an interesting night but even that illuminating experience did little to relieve the monotony.

After three weeks of boredom, with the frost and snow showing no signs of abating, I decided to write to Railway Traffic H.Q. I told them I had been there for three weeks and had only seen one train and had one telephone call. I had also lived in the devastated regions for three years, while they were being devastated, and would now like a move. The latter produced results and in due course I got what I had asked for.

While I was waiting for a response, to while away the time, I decided to spend a day in Amiens. There was a light army railway, which ran most of the way there, when the trains manage to say on the lines, which was not always the case. I started off in good spirits and stood on the engine as we proceeded through the snow, past village sites with only mounds of rubble where houses had once been. Approaching one village site we disturbed a cat which been left behind. It had reverted to its wild state, living on birds and anything it could hunt. I saw it spring like a small tiger from one pile of snow covered debris to another as the puffing of our distant engine disturbed it. There was some game there too. I spotted a pheasant and, as the train sped past borrowed a rifle from the engine driver and had a shot but I missed!

In its Christmas card setting, the old town of Amiens looked quite romantic. As I walked round its streets, which were covered with snow, I felt there was a fairy tale air about the place. Near the cathedral, which was still protected with sandbags, red-nosed German prisoners were picking up stones broken in the bombardments of 1918 and stacking them in neat piles. They looked very angry and were no doubt annoyed at being kept so long after the Armistice.

Inside the cathedral an even more unusual impression was given. All the glass had been taken out of the windows, so wind and rain swept freely through the building making pillars seem in the trunks of trees in a glade in the winter twilight. The East End of the church was out of use and the high altar had been placed by the west door.

The war had brought many changes to Amiens.

As the town was very busy, I knew it would be difficult to find anywhere to stay. I decided to look in at the Hotel du Rhin, which I remembered well. There I ran into our old Brigadier, who, much to my surprise, recognised me and remembered my name after nearly two years. Perhaps he remembered me for the occasion when he had made a jest at the expense of one of my company officers. I knew that the officer concerned was standing just out of sight in the dugout, so I made no response as I thought he would hear. I would have liked to have spent more time in Amiens, but I had been told that being away for even one day was stretching a point as my transfer might come through at any time. Reluctantly I got ready to go back next day.

Soon after my return I received orders to go to a place called Heilly. It was near Corbie, on the way to Arras. It marked the extreme point in the German advance of 1918. Most of the village had been destroyed but just beyond the station I was told there was a "Halte Repas." I did not know what that meant but soon discovered that it was a spot on the line where trains full of soldiers on their way to be demobilised stopped for refreshments. There were a number of huts just beyond the station for the purpose of cooking meals and housing staff. The idea was that notice of an approaching train would be sent down in time for the meals to be prepared. All we would then have to do was greet the men and clean up afterwards. It sounded simple enough, but in practice it did not work out like that, because the trains hardly ever stopped. We were advised of their departure and probable time of arrival and a lot of food was cooked, but we could do nothing to stop the trains, which just went by. I never discovered what happened to the uneaten food. That was not my department, but I daresay someone knew. Perhaps that was why the trains didn't stop.

To get food ready for several hundred men, and wait at the side of a railway track for a very long time, was bad enough. To then watch the train speed past without stopping was just too much, so I made a report and we waited to see what would happen next.

We were eventually told when the next train would come, and got ready to welcome it. At the appointed time we heard it in the distance. Having got food ready once again, we advanced towards the track and watched as the train approached us round a bend.

It was slowing down and we felt confident it would stop - and it did, so my complaint had not been in vain. At last we would be able to feed the hungry with good things. It was a very long train, of closed cattle trucks. We expected the men to be hungry and ready for their food. Perhaps they would be standing at the sliding doors, open ready to open up. We were all prepared but not for what occurred. When staff approached the train, nothing happened so we moved in and opened one of doors. Inside, the men were lying down in various attitudes, and they were all completely drunk. We discovered that, after many hours of crawling along at a snail's pace, they had been shunted into a siding. In the siding there was a train loaded with barrels of wine. The men, most of whom were Australians, rolled out the barrels and drank as much as they could. By the time they reached us, it was obviously not going to be possible to get them off the train, so once again the food was not eaten. I was at Heilly for some time and that was the only train that ever stopped, so my efforts were not very productive.

When we were not waiting for trains, there was little else to keep us occupied. There was not much to do in the neighbourhood, and the remains of Corbie, which was a short walk away, looked particularly desolate on a cold winter's day when I paid it a visit. I found the square full of English horses about to be sold into captivity. It was a sad end to their war service and their large melancholy eyes seemed to say as much. Often in later years, when I spotted an English horse in a forge or on a farm in France or Belgium, I would say a few words in English to see if it would stir any distant memories.

The weather continued to be cheerless and my latent fever began to rear its head again. Having no quinine and no army doctor within reach, I approached a German doctor who was with some prisoners in the next village. I do not know if it was the dirt and cold of the hut I was living in, or something to do with the septic poisoning of my head, but I felt very dizzy and soon found myself in hospital again. The hospital was at Longeau, which was near Amiens, and I stayed there for a long and painful week. There were more nurses than usual but the place swarmed with the chaplains who were waiting to be sent home. When I saw one approaching I pretended I was asleep.

At last I was told I was well enough to move out. On the appointed day I got ready and waited transport to come, but it did not arrive until 2 a.m., when I was enjoying a cup of tea with the night nurse. It was good to breathe fresh air after the stuffy hospital. I had been ordered to go to Antwerp. Though I would have preferred to remain in France I thought it would be pleasant living in a town for the first time since I had left England in 1915.

I did not mean to hurry on my journey, as I expected pass through places I had known before the war and should be glad to see again. It was after midnight when I eventually got to Belgium. I was ready for a good night's sleep but was not sure exactly where I was. The Germans had destroyed many bridges before they left and so few trains were running. I eventually discovered I was near Bruges and at 2 a.m., when the train crawled snorting into Bruges station, I decided to get off. Why do trains always snort and pant at Bruges, as if they were short of breath? Perhaps it is because they may have come from as far away as Constantinople.

I thought it would be easy to find somewhere to sleep but I was mistaken. 2. a.m. is not the time to find hotel staff at their most welcoming. Perhaps they were full up, but I got tired of wandering about and finally settled for a rather a seedy place which was near the station. I remembered seeing it before, years ago when Bruges had been overflowing with people who were on holiday. I had looked at it then and found it seemed to be full of full of birdcages. It looked distinctly shoddy and I had given it a miss, but now I was just glad to find room.

It was a strange experience in a town I had known well in previous days, after many pleasant holiday visits. I remembered the shops and incidents connected with various places. I was surprised to note that there was a complete absence of the war-weary look I had seen in France and even in England.

I reached the Headquarters of the Railway Traffic Department in Antwerp just before it closed for the day. It had the peacetime air of an ordinary commercial of business. They greeted me civilly enough and told me that I could live at the Y.M.C.A., which did not fill me with enthusiasm until I found it was actually the Grand Hotel which had been taken over by the Y.M.C.A. earlier in the war. It proved to be excellent and cheap and made me feel like a tourist having a holiday at someone else's expense. It was only a few yards from the Gare Central, where I was to work, so it was convenient too.

The following day I set out to explore my new surroundings. On the main platform of the very impressive station building I found an office devoted to my labours.

I thought that someone must be pulling my leg. Surely I could not be going to work in such a prestigious place. But there was no catch. I really did belong to this terminus and my duties were not onerous. Indeed they were so light that I wondered what do to pass the time. I bought a book on Spanish Grammar, with the intention of trying to improve on the basic knowledge of the language I had manage to acquire when I was lived in South America. My chief job was to meet the trains. But no one ever seemed to get off them or need my assistance. The only enquiries I got were from people who came into my office thinking they were somewhere else. I did see a woman with a baby, who arrived one evening just as I was about to leave. She explained that she was English and had married a Belgian soldier when he was in England, but she had not seen him since. I sent her off to the British Consul. Such odd people turned up that I wondered why they had chosen to see me. I later discovered that there was an old enamelled notice above the door to my office, inviting people in four languages to step inside and make enquiries.

I thought I had found the ideal life, but knew it was too good to last for long. I was then told to report to the docks and help with the unloading of trains full of German guns. Docks can be pretty miserable places and these were particularly wretched. They were also very difficult to get to and from. I had to set off for work before the trams were running and as it took an hour of fast walking along cobbled streets, after getting up in the dark. On rare occasions a motorcar would sometimes overtake me. So I listened carefully as I walked along in case one passed by. One morning a General who was also staying at the Y.M.C.A drew up alongside and told me to hop in. He was well known for his love of athletics and other products of Army life and had a bright and breezy manner. Driving with him alongside was hard work, but I appreciated his stopping and hoped I showed that in my remarks without wishing to see him ever again.

Several days later, I when I was loading some trucks from a train at crack of dawn, I noticed him watching. If you have ever tried to unload heavy guns in the dark, from a train nearly a mile long, to a platform which extends for just 25 yards, you will realise the difficulty of doing it with despatch. The General evidently thought it could be done better.

"You're the R.T.O," he shouted angrily: "Can't you manage things better than that? Haven't you had any training?"

"None whatever," I replied, mentally yawning. "I never saw a train until a few weeks ago, except as a passenger. I was four years in the infantry."

The trains were old German rolling stock, and no one cared how much they were knocked about, so very heavy guns were dragged off anyhow, knocking them to pieces. Unfortunately a heavy gun damaged one of the men too, when it ran down the ramp, out of control.

My stay at the Y.M.C.A was coming to an end. I knew I was too good to last and I was duly despatched by the Major in charge of the office, to a bleak camp at the docks where I was to spend my nights as well days. There I had to live In a Nissan hut[1]. If the sun shone, the heat inside became unbearable. So I spent as much time as I could in the centre of Antwerp. After mid-day, when I generally finished work, I had meals at restaurants and wandered around until late at night, when I caught the last lorry back to the camp. There were always cafes to sit outside and, as often as I could, I went to Brussels, which I got to by train. Time passed pleasantly enough but we were never allowed to go away, even for week-end which made it impossible for me to visit places I had known in the war. The only thing to spoil the illusion of a Continental holiday was the Nissan hut. Next to me in another hut of the same kind, there lived a Scottish baronet, who we were told was "under training". We did not know what for. He did not stay long and had very definite views about his discomfort. When he left I decided to try to find a flat in Antwerp. When there seemed to be nothing available, I discovered a roomy wooden hut some distance from the main camp. There I put up my camp bed and covered the floor with army blankets, so that it was comparatively civilised.

Antwerp at that time was quite important because it was the base not only of the British army of occupation, but also for the Americans. At the Y.M.C.A there had been many American officers. I used to have meals with them at times, but did not get very far in my attempts at conversation. The magnificent arrangements made for entertaining

1   Prefabricated steel structure made from a half-cylindrical skin of corrugated steel.

the American troops made us feel rather paupers. It was hard for us to forget that we had endured so much before the Americans arrived. Another awkward moment I remember occurred at Antwerp zoo one Sunday afternoon. I was having tea in the pretty grounds with some American officers. It was then the custom for the band to play the national Anthems of the Allies. When "God save the King" was played the Americans politely stood up. Unfortunately I did not know what the American national anthem sounded like so I kept on standing up in terror in case I was found out.

The zoo was a pleasant place to sit in and, as it was next the Gare Central and the Y.M.C.A, it was handy for me while I was working at that end of the town. There were not many animals, due to the war when food was scarce, and the giraffe was knock-kneed. He had survived but his legs sagged a little.

Perhaps the most noticeable feature of post war Antwerp, and also Brussels, was the number of cabarets and parties where dancing took place. The floors were sometimes so crowded with dancers that couples could not move and bobbed up and down where they were, marking time. Most of the customers were English or American and there seemed to be a lot of very good American dancers. Staff officers were also to be seen amongst the crowds. To sit and watch them was as good a way as any to pass the time, but things did not really warm up until after midnight, when I was usually back in bed. They warmed up so much that some places were put out of bounds. We were told that early one morning, when military police were on their rounds, they went into an area which had been declared out of bounds and found the General who had issued the order sitting there, with a girl who has not over-dressed sitting on his knee.

Most of the places were harmless enough for anyone not looking for trouble, but I remember a burly N.C.O. telling me one day how he and some others had been charged high prices for some drinks. They had refused to pay. When the proprietors had insisted, they had wrecked the place and left all the mirrors, which covered the walls in smithereens. Another N.C.O. - a rather quiet type - told me to me that on his last night out he had been relieved of £24, which he had saved up. On another evening I came across an unconscious soldier who was covered with blood and surrounded by Belgian civilians. He must have had a row with someone when he was drunk. I told another soldier to search his pockets, find out where he lived and get him home. He still had his money on him. I was curious enough to call at the place where he belonged and found out that it had been duly handed over.

English was hardly a foreign language in Belgium at that time, because of the large numbers of returning refugees. Amongst them were many children who had gone away when they were very young and were now returning to their native land after four years away. They spoke English fluently but did not know any French or Flemish. I stopped to talk to some of them when they were playing in a street. I thought they were English but they explained that they had learnt perfect English in England while the war was going on. Another refugee I met - a Belgian lady- overheard me asking for a stamp to put on a postcard I had bought. She insisted on giving me one and, when I offered her some cash, she refused and said that people had been so kind to her in England she felt it was a pleasure to do something for me.

Unfortunately not all the reminders of war were pleasant. One day I saw a long procession of British gun carriages carrying coffins covered with the Belgian flag. They contained the bodies of Belgians who had been shot as spies during the German occupation of Antwerp. They had been dug up in order to give them the ceremonial burial due to national heroes.

While I was at Antwerp the body of Captain Fryatt was brought there from Bruges. He had been shot for resisting the Germans when he was in command of a ship in the channel. It was an important event and I got involved in it because I was it back, for the day, at the Grand Gare, in my capacity as Transport Officer. For some time before the train arrived one of the imposing halls of the station began to fill up with Belgian dignitaries and representatives of the British Army of Occupation. The British Ambassador, whose name was Villiers, was also there. My job was to stand on the platform and await the arrival of the train. The guard's van, in which the body lay, was draped in purple and when the side door was opened it looked dignified and simple. The chief R.T.O. had arrived by this time and he and I both appeared in a newsreel, which was made to record the event. As I had been told I was responsible for the reception of the body, I went to report its arrival to the illustrious assembly. They took no notice at all when I gave them the news, but it did give be a chance to get a close up view of all the VIPs. A procession was then formed on the platform. It moved off, down some steps to the central hall and then into the street. The body was then carried through the town to the river, where a British destroyer was waiting to take it to England.

As Antwerp was the main base for the army of occupation, supply trains were despatched ever day to a wide range of destinations. We had to check them and see them off. They included insulated meat wagons and, from time to time, they would become detached on the way and be found later in a siding with their contents decomposed. To prevent that happening an R.T.O was detailed to escort every train travelling from Antwerp to Cologne and, on several occasions, I was given that task.

It was a dreary job especially after the German frontier was crossed. There the Belgian guard was exchanged for a German one and I had to leave my ordinary passenger compartment and complete the journey in the guard's van, to see that he behaved. He, of course, did not relish having me there and usually sat in sulky silence. The only official stop, other than at the frontier, was at a Halte-Repas, where troops on the train could alight and get a meal. I was interested to see a Halte Repas where trains really did stop!

I was always glad to leave the train at the end of the journey. At that time Cologne was rather dreary. It did not have the carefree atmosphere of Belgium and France and things were not at their best after four years of war. The food shops had nothing in their windows. There were just rows of empty shelves and the people looked pale, ill and under nourished. The whole atmosphere was forbidding. I stayed at a comfortable hotel for next to nothing on account of the low value of the mark, and experienced the chill being regarded as an enemy.

When I returned to Belgium it was clear that a date for my demobilisation would soon be fixed. A London newspaper was getting indignant about the cost of maintaining the army of occupation and the authorities were looking for ways to reduce numbers and keep costs in check. With that in mind, I thought it would be a good time to put in for some leave. My request was granted almost immediately and I set off for Brussels.

My journey by train was slow but not without incident. Just outside Brussels, the train went off the line. I was sitting in a first class compartment with only two other passengers, both of whom were French. In the farther corner there was a French officer and opposite me French nurse, in uniform. The first thing I noticed was a violent bumping. It seemed to go on for a long time but it was really only a few seconds. The bumping became so bad that I had to hold on to me to steady myself. I knew then that we were in for something unusual. The carriage swayed violently from side to side and finally it toppled over on its side and down a bank, where it stopped altogether. The next thing I realised was that I was looking through the side window of the carriage, which somehow had become the roof and that I was treading on something soft. That turned out to be the French nurse, who had been sitting opposite me. I was vaguely aware that trains can catch fire in such circumstances and decided that that the sooner we were out of it the better. The French officer managed to make a hole in the glass window that had become a roof, and quite soon were hauled through it one by one. Miraculously we no one was hurt. To me the most remarkable thing about the whole affair was that not a word had been spoken from start to finish.

When I got back to Antwerp I was greeted with the news that I was next on the list of names to be 'axed'. The other R.T.O.s gave me the usual farewell dinner and I felt sad that the end had come. When I had to reply to a toast at the end I found myself tongue-tied. It was not emotion but the result of not having had to put two words together for five years.

Cross channel steamers sailed from Antwerp to England but that would have been too easy for the army and I found myself being transported via Cologne to Dover. The last part of my journey took three days to complete, much of which was spent in a cattle truck. As dawn broke on my last day I slid the door open and looked out. We were passing Armentieres. I thought back to my first visit there in 1915, when I had stopped for a night as a new second Lieutenant on my way to join my battalion. So much had changed since then. The train rattled on and swayed so much that I had to hold on tight. At last, after thirty-six hours, the sand dunes of a sea coast came in sight. We had finally reached Calais.

The town was packed with English soldiers on their way home for demobilisation. I found as small room in a hotel and waited for my final orders to depart. They came a few days later and I sailed out on a Saturday night. It was cold and the sea was rough. As we moved from the quay towards for the harbour entrance I looked back at the receding shores of France where so much had happened during the past five years. Most of it had been a time of hardship and danger but it had also had its lighter moments. And now I was embarking on the sea of an uncertain post-war world. It seemed more of a full stop that I had reached and I was doubtful about starting again.

When I got back to England I was told to report to the Crystal Palace for demobilisation. I approached that museum of faded splendour in the gloom of a late October afternoon. The main door was locked but I crept in by a side entrance and eventually found an officer who was just about to leave.

"You should have been here yesterday", he said but I made no reply. And that was how I left the army, which I had joined five years before in a basement off the Euston road. I was sad to be leaving. It felt very lonely being a civilian. But London was lighting up and the stars were out already.

POSTSCRIPT
By JOHN BURDER

When the war ended my father, like many servicemen before and since, found it difficult to adjust to normal life. He had excellent qualifications. A degree from Cambridge University, one of the highest military honours it is possible to get and a wealth of experience of working in different parts of the world but, when he returned to England in 1918, he found he had come back to a different world. Four years earlier he had set aside his clerical career and volunteered to serve as a private solider, earning two shillings a day. He then spent five years risking his life in the service of king and country, which he graphically described in the text of this book.

In 1918, when the war was over, he found himself without a job in a country which had changed dramatically during the years, while he had been fighting at the front. By then those who has chosen an easier way of life had taken most of the available jobs and servicemen returning to civilian life were often regarded with suspicion. Writing these words, in the autumn of 2010, ninety years as after my father first put his ideas for this book on paper; the situation is in some ways much the same. In today's newspapers we still read of war casualties. Young men who have done what my father did and chosen a military career are still dying in the service of their country. Many more still experience problems when they have to switch from military to civilian life. I know what that means, because the difficulties my father encountered affected our family life for three generations and they still affect my life today, seventy years after he died.

In 1918 my father needed a job. As an ordained priest in the Church of England he felt his best course would probably be to become a parish priest somewhere in England. He had been ordained in 1905 and had been a curate in churches in Bristol and Swindon. He then started his travels and became Delta Chaplain at Bassein in Burma and then chaplain in St Servain in Brittany in 1913. It was there that he started a lifelong love of all things French. From Brittany he moved to South America and he was there when war was declared, as he has described in the first chapter of this book. All those appointments equipped him well for his later life. As you will have discovered reading his words, he knew what life was about and made the best of it wherever he was. He also had a quiet faith in God, which kept him on course when the going got tough.

When he approached the church authorities after demobilisation one might have thought they would have welcomed him with open arms. After reading the accounts of his experiences in this book, you will not be surprised to know that they did not. He soon discovered that all the clerical posts worth having had been given to those who had not volunteered to join the forces but had stayed behind. With no job in prospect, he decided to get married and in 1921 he married another parson's very beautiful daughter – Gabrielle Mary Fielding Ould. My father always had an eye for a pretty girl, as you will probably have noticed reading this book. The girl he chose to marry was stunning in every way but, when their engagement was announced, they ran into plenty of opposition. The bride's father was Rector of a fashionable parish in one of the smartest parts of London (Regent's Park). When his daughter fell in love with a penniless curate, who had been severely wounded in the recent war, the news must have come as quite a shock. The fact that she was 21 years old and he was 40 cannot have helped much either, but the marriage eventually went ahead and it proved to be a perfect match.

Though there were the inevitable differences of opinion all families experience from time to time, Claud and Gabrielle clearly loved each other from day one. When he died, forty-seven years after they were married, the bond was as close as it had been when they met. My mother lived on for 26 more years. When she died in 1994, at the age of 92, the photograph of my father in his military uniform, which is on the cover of this book, was still at her bedside.

After the wedding, in 1921 my father returned to Cambridge University to complete his Masters degree. He was then offered a job as Rector of St Mary's Church in Huntingdon – an East Anglian county town which was then more important that it is today. Their first son – George Christopher Burder - was born in 1924. At that time the future must have looked brighter than it had done for some time, but it was not to be.

A second child – Mary Claudine Burder (to whom my father dedicated this book) was also born when he was living in Huntingdon. The family was photographed several times that year and some of the pictures have been reproduced in this book. At the age of six, Mary caught whooping cough. In those days doctors did not have the range of drugs they can use today. What should have been a relatively simple childhood illness developed complications. She was admitted to the local county hospital, of which at the time my father happened to be Honorary Chaplain. A simple operation was performed but she died the following day. I don't think my father ever recovered from the shock of that event. Mary's bedroom was shut off from the rest of the house. It was not opened again until he retired and the family moved out thirty years later.

I think very few people could have put up with the experiences my father had to cope with during the war, and the blow of his beloved daughter's death. His war wounds had affected his sight and hearing and eventually the strain of it all became too much. In 1935 he moved to Wyton, which was a smaller country parish, where he continued to work as a parish priest. He also became Officiating Chaplain for RAF Wyton – a major RAF base which was in located in the parish. He held that post from 1936 to 1941.

When the second war started, my father was 59 years old. His first son - George - was about to leave Canford school to join the army. A second son (me!) – John Henry Burder was born on the second of August 1940. My father was then 61 and my mother 40. While all that was going on, without telling anyone, dad must have found time to write this book. His original notes, penned in 1918, were transcribed in 1942 to five typescript volumes, which I found in 2009, and have subsequently edited to form the basis of this book. As my father would never talk about his war experiences it was entirely in character that he did not mention his literary work to anyone while he was alive. It was only by chance that the results of his efforts were ever discovered.

When he finished working on his texts, he must have hoped for a quieter life and better luck in the years ahead but again, that was not to be. When he left school, my older brother joined the Rifle Brigade. He trained with them and became a Lieutenant just as the second war was starting. He served with them until the 13th March 1945 when he was killed while serving with his regiment in Germany. George was 21 years old. He was posthumously awarded the Military Cross.

I am sure you can imagine how my parents must have felt when, after George's death; the King presented his Military Cross to them at Buckingham Palace. They battled on, courageously trying to make the world a better place, but it must have seemed an impossible task. My father eventually retired in 1968. We then moved to Brighton and for the first time in our lives acquired a car and a fridge. My mother, who had learned to drive during the war, drove my father round Sussex in a twenty year old car for endless picnics in local beauty spots. I left school and went to work for the BBC, where I spent three years learning film and television production skills at Ealing studios. I have since spent fifty years putting into practice what learned then. My mother died in 1994. As far as I am aware, I am still alive as I write these words.

John Burder ©
Bournemouth – England March 2010

Above: The town of Armentiers during the war.

Below: Armentiers after the war.

Left:
The inside of the Church in Foncquevillers.

Below:
The Church from the outside.

Above: Ypres. Below: Reinforcements.

Above: World War I tanks

Above: Antwerp 1914. Below: The author (right) Antwerp.

Left:
The author's first formal portrait as an officer. The only surviving copy of this picture was found in the wallet of his son when he was killed in action in 1945.

Below:
Early aircraft dog-fight.

Above: The author outside the RTO in 1916.

Above: Gabrielle and Claud Burder on their wedding day in 1921.

Above right: Their first son George ,who was killed in action in the second world war. He was posthumously awarded the Military Cross.

Below right: Their daughter Mary.

Index